Parapsychology

Psychic and other 'exceptional' experiences are surprisingly common but opinions as to their cause vary widely. Can tricks of the mind such as hallucinations, mistaken perception and errors of judgement explain such phenomena or does some yet to be understood non-sensory means of communication come into play?

In *Parapsychology*, leading researchers from both the UK and the USA combine their expertise to offer a lucid account of research into the science of psychic experience. Beginning with an introduction to the methodology employed, *Parapsychology* addresses topics such as coincidence, telepathy, precognition, psychokinesis, healing, apparitions, reincarnation and out-of-body experiences. Each chapter describes the phenomenon, outlines the main lines of research and discusses the merits of various possible explanations for such anomalous experiences. Extensive suggestions for relevant further reading on each individual subject are provided, along with a detailed glossary of terms.

Parapsychology provides an accessible and succinct overview of the research and current thinking on the subject of psychic and allied experiences. This balanced account of work in this fascinating area will be of great interest to students and researchers in psychology as well as anyone with an interest in the field.

Jane Henry is a psychologist and senior lecturer at the Open University where she chairs the Experiential Research Group. She was founding Chair of the British Psychological Society's Consciousness and Experiential Psychology Section.

Contributors: John Beloff, Daniel J. Benor, Susan Blackmore, Shari A. Cohn-Simmen, Deborah L. Delanoy, Christopher C. French, Alan Gauld, Keith Hearne, Jane Henry, Stanley Krippner, Andrew MacKenzie, Julie Milton, Canon Michael Perry, Wyllys Poynton, Rupert Sheldrake, Ian Stevenson, Robin Taylor and Caroline Watt.

Parapsychology

Research on Exceptional Experiences

Edited by Jane Henry

LONDON AND NEW YORK

First published 2005 by Routledge
27 Church Road, Hove, East Sussex, BN3 2FA

Simultaneously published in the USA and Canada
by Routledge
270 Madison Avenue, New York, NY 10016

Routledge is an imprint of the Taylor & Francis Group

Typeset in Times by Garfield Morgan, Rhayader, Powys, UK
Printed and bound in Great Britain by TJ International Ltd, Padstow, Cornwall
Paperback cover design by Sandra Heath

This publication has been produced with paper manufactured to strict environmental standards and with pulp derived from sustainable forests.

British Library Cataloguing in Publication Data
A catalogue record for this book is available from the British Library

Library of Congress Cataloging in Publication Data
Parapsychology : research on exceptional experiences / [edited by] Jane Henry.— 1st ed.
p. cm.
Includes bibliographical references and index.
ISBN 0-415-21359-2 (hardcover)
1. Parapsychology—Research. I. Henry, Jane.
BF1040.5.P37 2004
130—dc22

2004003837

ISBN 0-415-21359-2 (hbk)
ISBN 0-415-21360-6 (pbk)

Contents

List of illustrations

Tables

Figures

About the authors

John Beloff, former senior lecturer at the Department of Psychology, University of Edinburgh, has been President both of the international Parapsychological Association and of the Society for Psychical Research (of London). His books include *Parapsychology: A Concise History* (1993).

Daniel J. Benor is a psychiatrist who combines spiritual healing with his practice of psychotherapy in Philadelphia and New Jersey. His twenty years of studies on the efficacy of spiritual healing are summarised in *Healing Research, Volumes I–III* (2001), *IV* (in press).

Susan Blackmore is a writer and lecturer based in Bristol. She is author of *Beyond the Body*, *In Search of the Light*, *Dying to Live*, *Test your Psychic Powers* and the controversial bestseller *The Meme Machine*.

Shari A. Cohn-Simmen is a Research Fellow in the Department of Celtic and Scottish Studies at the University of Edinburgh, and has undertaken research on second sight and other psychic experiences.

Deborah L. Delanoy is Professor of Psychology at University College Northampton. She was previously a Research Fellow at the Koestler Parapsychology Unit, University of Edinburgh.

Christopher C. French is Professor of Psychology and head of the Anomalistic Psychology Research Unit at Goldsmiths College, University of London. He is co-editor of *The Skeptic* and has published many articles on psychological factors associated with paranormal belief and is a frequent broadcaster.

Alan Gauld was formerly a Reader in Psychology at the University of Nottingham. His publications include *The Founders of Psychical Research* (1968), *Poltergeists* (1979, with A.D. Cornell), *Mediumship and Survival* (1982) and *A History of Hypnotism* (1992).

Keith Hearne conducted the first sleep-laboratory research into lucid dreams. He has researched several areas of parapsychology, in particular premonitions.

Jane Henry directs the Open University Experiential Research Group and chairs the BPS Consciousness and Experiential Psychology Section. She was editor of the *Psi Researcher* for many years and is currently editor of *Consciousness and Experiential Psychology*. She has published a number of books and many articles on applied psychology.

Stanley Krippner is Alan W. Watts Professor of Psychology at Saybrook Graduate School and Research Center, San Francisco, California. A former president of the Parapsychological Association, he is editor of eight volumes of *Advances in Parapsychological Research* and co-author of *Dream Telepathy*, *The Mythic Path* and *Extraordinary Dreams and How to Use Them.*

Andrew MacKenzie, journalist and author, was an SPR Vice-President. He wrote eight books on spontaneous cases in psychical research including *Adventures in Time: A Study of Retrocognition* 1997.

Julie Milton is a Senior Research Fellow at the Institute of Child Health, University College London. She was previously a Research Fellow with the Koestler Parapsychology Unit, University of Edinburgh, and has written many articles on parapsychology.

Canon Michael Perry, a former Archdeacon of Durham and Sub-Dean of Durham Cathedral, is President of the Churches' Fellowship for Psychical and Spiritual Studies, and editor of *The Christian Parapsychologist*.

Wyllys Poynton was a teacher in South Africa and is now the Librarian for the Society for Psychical Research.

Rupert Sheldrake was a Fellow of Clare College, Cambridge and a Research Fellow of the Royal Society. He is a Fellow of the Institute of Noetic Sciences in California, and lives in London. He is the author of five books and over fifty papers in scientific journals.

Ian Stevenson is Research Professor of Psychiatry in the Division of Personality Studies, Department of Psychiatric Medicine, University of Virginia Health System, Charlottesville, USA.

Robin Taylor is a consultant psychologist. He was previously a lecturer at the University of the South Pacific, Fiji and a researcher with the Koestler Parapsychology Unit at the University of Edinburgh.

Caroline Watt is a Senior Research Fellow with the Koestler Parapsychology Unit at the University of Edinburgh. Her research interests include experimenter effects in parapsychology, and the psychology of anomalous experiences.

Acknowledgements

The publisher is grateful to the following for the illustrative material: Caroline Watt for Figure 4.1 Example of a threatening stimulus; Rupert Sheldrake for Figure 9.1 Pam Smart with Jaytee; Stanley Krippner for Figure 12.1 Maria Sabina conducting a shamanistic ritual and Robin Taylor for Figures 17.1 and 17.2.

Introduction

Since time immemorial people from all over the world have reported extraordinary experiences such as apparitions, visions, telepathy, hauntings, divination, healing, out-of-body, near-death and abduction experiences. In addition miraculous and supernatural phenomena are central to most traditions of religious belief. Traditionally many apparently paranormal experiences were assumed to involve communication with an unseen spirit world. The modern interpretation tends to assume that tricks of the mind such as hallucinations, mistaken perception, errors of judgement, deception and fraud often offer the more obvious explanation. However, interest in phenomena such as telepathy, clairvoyance, and contact with the dead, collectively known as psychic or paranormal experiences, remains high among the lay public. About three-quarters of the general public believe in psychic phenomena and somewhere between a half and two-thirds claim to have had a psychic experience such as telepathy or communication with the dead.

This book documents scientists' attempts to investigate and understand these paranormal experiences. Paranormal is the term ascribed to experiences that suggest an interaction, information transfer or communication between a being and the environment or another being that cannot yet be explained by normal means. Many of those studying these phenomena are termed parapsychologists. Currently this is a select profession with perhaps fifty professionals world-wide (largely because the area has not been especially well-funded to date rather than for want of interest). Many are psychologists but, since this is an interdisciplinary field, physicists, engineers, statisticians, social anthropologists and psychiatrists are also involved. In addition some psychologists with an interest in anomalous experience study the part played by anomalies of attention, imagery, perception, recall, recognition, identity, judgement, belief and consciousness. There is also a long-standing tradition of lay psychical research. Psychical researchers have traditionally concentrated more on phenomena that occur spontaneously such as apparitions, haunting and poltergeists, as well as mediumship.

Parapsychology is an area where views often polarise, with believers taking for granted that paranormal phenomena are a reality and sceptics ruling the possibility out of hand. Some scientists take a third position, which is to accept the reality of psi experiences and to study their nature without taking a position on their origin. Parapsychology conferences provide a rare chance to meet with such agnostics. The authors in this text are no exception and incline to varying a priori attitudes to the phenomenon under question – Christopher French, Julie Milton and Susan Blackmore are now known for their more sceptical orientation, whereas Ian Stevenson, Rupert Sheldrake, John Beloff and Daniel Benor find the data more persuasive, and others are genuinely agnostic. However, all the authors represented here share a commitment to the scientific study of parapsychological phenomena, an awareness of work in the field and an openness to data.

Sceptics have asserted that parapsychology has made no progress in the last hundred years; however, some of the parapsychological meta-analyses available in the last decade appear to offer the promise of significant repeatable results, not presently explicable by normal means. So this is an exciting time for the field.

Chapter overview

Much of the literature on exceptional experience falls into three camps: popular and generally unreliable accounts, sceptical and partial accounts, or thorough expositions aimed at a specialist academic audience. This book is designed to provide an accessible introduction to research on, and responsible sources of information about, 'psychic' phenomena. It is written by practising researchers who are experts in their field, (pp. ix–xi provide author details). Each chapter describes the phenomena, outlines the main lines of research, discusses possible explanations for the results and recommends further introductory and advanced reading. Most chapters include substantial references so that readers will be able to follow up areas that particularly interest them. (Note that articles and books cited as recommended reading appear in the section of that name and are not repeated in the references section.) Each chapter is designed to be free-standing, which has led to some overlap of content.

Traditionally parapsychology has focused on extrasensory perception (ESP), psychokinesis (PK) and apparitional phenomena. But there are researchers interested in animal psi, coincidence, healing, reincarnation, shamanism, near-death experiences (NDEs) and survival, and work on these areas has been included here.

The chapters have been grouped in five sections: parapsychology, paranormal cognition, paranormal action, anomalous experiences and after-life phenomena.

The first section offers an overview of work in parapsychology, the science of psychic experience. In Chapter 1 Jane Henry provides a brief history of work in parapsychology. In Chapter 2 Julie Milton introduces typical parapsychological protocols and explains why the positive meta-analyses of groups of experiments need to be treated with caution. In Chapter 3 Deborah Delanoy presents some of the striking results obtained from meta-analyses of parapsychology experiments. In Chapter 4, Caroline Watt outlines some of the psychological factors that might make us think that spontaneous paranormal experiences are significant when they are not and describes psychologists' attempts to screen out extraneous factors so that they can identify correlates of apparently paranormal events. In Chapter 5 Christopher French elaborates on the sceptical approach to parapsychology. Ironically there are many more sceptics trying to show the world why seemingly extraordinary feats such as telepathy and psychokinesis are explicable by normal means, than there are parapsychologists investigating such experiences!

The second section on 'Paranormal cognition' explores several lines of work related to extrasensory perception – the transfer of information by some yet to be understood paranormal means. In Chapter 6 Shari Cohn-Simmen discusses the folk tradition of second sight, a psychic ability believed to be passed on in certain families. In Chapter 7 John Beloff and Jane Henry outline some of the parapsychological work on extrasensory perception. In Chapter 8 on precognition and premonitions Keith Hearne and Jane Henry outline some work on foretelling the future. In Chapter 9 Rupert Sheldrake reviews some of the evidence on human to animal, animal to animal and animal to machine communication that appears to bypass the standard senses.

The third section on 'Paranormal action' explores cases where mental intention seems to have an effect on living and non-living systems. In Chapter 10 Jane Henry provides an overview of work on psychokinesis, and in Chapter 11 Daniel Benor reviews studies of healing which are beginning to show interesting results in well-controlled trials. Shamanistic rituals often feature ceremonies where apparently paranormal events are central. Stanley Krippner examines the evidence on shamanism and points out the pitfalls of research in this area in Chapter 12.

The fourth section introduces a variety of other anomalous experiences. Jane Henry outlines the varieties of coincidence experiences in Chapter 13. Andrew MacKenzie and Jane Henry outline some of the phenomena associated with ghostly apparitions and alien encounters in Chapter 14. Many occult traditions have long held that it is possible for human consciousness to travel across space. In Chapter 15 Susan Blackmore discusses out-of-body experiences, an interest stemming from her own spontaneous experience of this kind. Recently, near-death experiences have become much talked about. Quite a high proportion of people in life-threatening situations experience a sense of peace, a tunnel, bright light and/or a life review, commonly termed a near-death experience. In Chapter 16 Susan Blackmore offers various explanations as to why this might be. It is a question of debate whether such experiences are hallucinations or something more. In Chapter 17 Robin Taylor discusses the role of imagery in parapsychological experiences.

While many parapsychologists are happy to investigate ESP and psychokinesis the idea that some part of us might survive death and be capable of communicating from an after-life is beyond the boggle factor of many scientists. The fifth section includes three chapters dealing with phenomena that can be interpreted as being suggestive of an after-life. Alan Gauld presents a critical appraisal of the evidence on survival in Chapter 18. Many cultures believe in reincarnation. In Chapter 19 Ian Stevenson presents the evidence for this phenomenon and discusses the merits of different interpretations. All religious traditions report seemingly miraculous phenomena which fit clearly within a paranormal remit. In Chapter 20 on religion, Canon Michael Perry elaborates on the sometimes uneasy relationship between parapsychology and religion.

Appendix 1 offers a glossary of parapsychological terms. The definitions in the glossary follow those given in the relevant chapter in this book. For those of you inspired to pursue an interest in parapsychology, in Appendix 2 Wyllys Poynton provides a list of some relevant parapsychological and related organisations, journals and websites.

My interest in exceptional experiences is long-standing, as the Open University undergraduates, Oxford extra-mural students and others who have participated in my lectures on this subject can attest. A decade ago a number of the contributors to this volume wrote brief pieces for a collection of Fact Sheets on Psychical Research which I compiled and edited for the SPR (Society for Psychical Research), an earlier attempt to provide brief accounts of some of the topics covered here. Since then the field has progressed and this volume documents some of the developments. A number of the chapters here build on these earlier efforts. I am grateful to all the contributors for sharing their expertise and to the SPR, and also for suggestions for improvement provided by the book's reviewers.

Jane Henry
Open University

Parapsychology

Chapter 1

Parapsychology

Jane Henry

Parapsychology is the study of psychic phenomena, i.e. the exchange of information or some other interaction between an organism and its environment, without the mediation of the senses. This includes mind to mind communication (paranormal cognition) such as telepathy and movement of (or influence on) matter by mind (paranormal action) which is referred to by parapsychologists as psychokinesis.

Psi phenomena

Psi phenomena have been reported since the earliest times, from biblical miracles and the Delphic oracle, through medieval witches, to nineteenth-century spiritualism and twentieth-century spoonbending. Psychic powers are claimed in every culture whether by shaman, rain maker, voodoo practitioner or faith healer. Along with religious belief and drug taking, psychic experiences seem to be universal.

The field of parapsychology takes four main groups of phenomena as its subject matter: extrasensory perception, psychokinesis, anomalous experience and apparitional phenomena. Examples of each follow:

Extrasensory perception (ESP)	Telepathy Clairvoyance Precognition Retrocognition
Psychokinesis (PK)	Macro-PK (visible effects), e.g. metal bending, apports Micro-PK (statistically measurable non-visible effects), e.g. random number generator (RNG) effects Direct mental interaction with living systems (DMILS), e.g. on electrodermal activity

	Recurrent spontaneous PK (RSPK), e.g. poltergeists
Anomalous experience	Out-of-body experiences
	Near-death experiences
	Past-life experiences
	Coincidence experiences
Apparitional phenomena	Ghosts
	Aliens
	Spirits
	Visions

The two classes of psi phenomena which get most attention from parapsychologists are extrasensory perception and psychokinesis. Extrasensory perception (ESP) covers both telepathy, where someone perceives information directly from another mind, and clairvoyance, where information is sensed directly from the environment. ESP appears to occur in real time or apparently precognitively, as in the premonition of a future disaster. There are also cases of retrocognition where unknown information from the past is apparently picked up psychically.

Psychokinesis (PK) may be split into macro-PK, where solid objects are affected and the result can be seen by the naked eye, such as bending a spoon or moving an object purely via intention, and micro-PK, where ultra-sensitive instruments such as strain gauges and random number generators are apparently affected by intention and the significance of the results is assessed statistically. Naturally occurring psychokinesis, known as recurrent spontaneous PK (RSPK) in the field, is associated with phenomena such as poltergeists. Direct mental interaction with a living system (DMILS) refers to PK on a live organism where physiology, such as electrodermal (skin conductance) activity or blood pressure, is altered purely by intention. Distant and non-contact healing offers another example.

Apparitions are experienced as outside the person and perceived as external to the self, the classic example being a ghost. Sometimes the 'apparition' appears pretty solid and at other times it is less obviously person-like. In previous centuries reports of demon visitations were quite common. In the latter half of the twentieth century, in keeping with the technological age, similar experiences appear to have been interpreted as visits by aliens. In non-western cultures experiences of spirits of one kind or another are often accepted as part of life. In the west reports of exceptional visions are now rare, though there are some well-known cases featuring visions of the Virgin Mary.

In contrast to apparitions, the anomalous experiences listed above – out-of-body, near-death, past-life and synchronicity experiences – are felt as happening to the individual him- or herself. There are other anomalous phenomena, such as UFOs, and other exceptional experiences, such as altered states of consciousness, mystical experience and Kundalini experiences, that are traditionally studied by groups other than parapsychologists. There is a case for bringing together work on the different types of anomalous phenomena and exceptional experience, and several recent texts have done this (e.g. Cardena *et al.* 2000).

Exceptional experience

Anticipating the trend, White (1993) offered a classification of exceptional experiences which aims to embrace phenomena traditionally studied by parapsychologists and others interested in anomalous and exceptional experiences. These are:

- mystical experiences (including peak experience, stigmata, transformational experience)
- psychic experiences (including apports, synchronicity, telepathy, PK and out-of-body experiences)
- encounter-type experiences (including apparitions, angels, ufo encounters, sense of presence)
- death-related experiences (e.g. near-death and past-life)
- exceptional normal experiences (e.g. *déjà vu*, hynagogia)

Inglis (1986) and Cardena *et al.* (2000) offer extended discussions of ostensibly paranormal anomalous phenomena and exceptional experiences.

Despite their name, anomalous psi experiences appear to be quite common. Around six in ten people in Europe and the USA claim to have had a psychic experience (Haraldsson 1985). At least a third claim to have experienced telepathy and about a fifth clairvoyance, but under a tenth psychokinesis (Haraldsson and Houtkooper 1991). Something like three-quarters of the population in Europe and the USA believe psi exists, which is more than double the number who claim to believe in God or 'some power or presence beyond themselves', found in similar surveys (Hay and Morisy 1977), though this figure may be an underestimate as qualitative interviews produce a considerably higher percentage of believers (Hay 1987).[1] In addition one-quarter of Americans believe in ghosts and a tenth claim to have seen or sensed one (Gallup and Newport 1991). Psi experiences also often have a profound effect on people. The frequency and impact of psi experiences is reason enough for psychologists to study such experiences. Some people have taken this further and have tried to apply psi in police work, war, business, mining and archaeology.

Different sorts of scientists are engaged in investigating psi experiences. Parapsychology is an interdisciplinary field and has attracted physicists and engineers as well as psychologists. Those interested in the psychology of anomalous experience often have as their primary focus possible normal explanations for ostensibly paranormal experiences. Those describing themselves as parapsychologists are more likely to be involved in investigations that try to rule out normal explanations for ESP and PK experiments, find correlates of positive psi performance and test theoretical models of psi experimentally as well as surveying the beliefs of those experiencing such phenomena spontaneously. Psychical researchers are more likely to be engaged in fieldwork investigating spontaneous psi events such as apparitions, hauntings and poltergeists. It was to these areas that early researchers turned their attention.

Early research

Mediumship

Spiritualism was a widespread and a popular movement in the nineteenth century and serious scientific study of paranormal phenomena began in the latter part of the century. The eminent psychologists W. Myers, William James, Jung and Freud were all early members of the Society for Psychical Research (SPR) in London.

The SPR investigated both physical mediums who appeared to cause the movement of objects, materialisations, levitation and so on and mental mediums who, in trance, seemed to have access to information that they would not normally know. The controls used to stop mediums cheating included physical restraint – for instance, holding the medium's hands and feet throughout the experiment – and insisting the experiment take place in a room supplied by the researchers. Many of the mediums proved to be nothing more than frauds but a few stand out. Daniel Dunglas Home apparently produced a range of phenomena including table raps, levitation, elongating his neck and handling burning coals over a period of twenty years, sometimes in well-lit conditions. Other physical mediums include Eusapia Palladino and the Austrian Rudi Schneider (see Braude 1986 for a discussion). Among the mental mediums some of the most impressive are Mrs Leonard and Leonora Piper, both of whom submitted to numerous tests over a sixty-year period (see Chapter 18 and Gauld 1982 for more on mental mediums).

Spontaneous cases

A parallel series of investigations concerned the collection and scrutiny of spontaneously occurring psychic phenomena, such as dreams coinciding with events elsewhere or apparitions of the dead. A mammoth collection of such experiences can be found in Gurney *et al.*'s *Phantasms of the Living*

(1886). To be accepted each anecdote had to be witnessed and satisfy certain other criteria.

The trouble with field investigations of this kind is that the nature of the phenomena is so extraordinary that many people will not believe it unless they have seen it with their own eyes. Others dismiss mediumistic claims as fraud and anecdotal evidence as misperceived, misremembered or just coincidence. Modern parapsychologists have devoted their efforts to experimental research in the hope that their findings cannot be dismissed so readily.

Forced-choice experiments

By the 1930s parapsychologists had turned their attention to the laboratory and the control offered by experiments. J.B. Rhine and his wife Louisa followed McDougall from Harvard to Duke University to set up the first parapsychological laboratory. McDougall saw psychical research as an ally in his campaign against the behaviourism and materialism that dominated psychology at the time. Ironically Rhine carried out numerous standardised experiments which are behaviourist in character! The subject had to guess which one of a limited number of targets had been chosen for that trial.

The card-guessing deck he used for many experiments was a pack of twenty-five Zener cards. This consists of five symbols: a star, square, wavy lines, plus sign and circle. The mean chance expectation for twenty-five guesses in a trial using a pack of twenty-five Zener cards is five. Rhine was looking for people who could score significantly better than that. He conducted many tests with students. Initially the experimenter took the shuffled deck of cards and looked at each card in turn in an attempt to 'send' the appropriate image to the subject telepathically.

Other experiments required the sender or agent to merely turn over each card in turn without looking at it. This was used to test the possibility of clairvoyance, that the subject's mind was taking information directly from the cards, but, as the experimenter subsequently learned the card order, precognitive telepathy is an alternative explanation. Later on, experimenters got subjects to guess at targets selected randomly by machine and input their guesses. The machine then matched the guesses against the target and calculated the results, but never printed out what the targets were. This procedure appears to rule out a precognitive telepathy explanation and confirm the possibility of clairvoyance. Devising procedures which rule out clairvoyance in favour of telepathy is harder and many researchers refer to the more general term, extrasensory perception, or ESP, acknowledging the difficulty of distinguishing between the two.

Rhine and others found above-chance scores in telepathy and clairvoyant experiments. One interpretation of the results is that, despite the precautions Rhine took to control for sensory cueing and for artefacts – for example by using randomised target selection and mechanical dice – the methods were in some way deficient. Modern experiments of this type are better controlled; for instance the number of trials is preset so that experimenters cannot stop when things are going well, the randomising procedures tend to be superior, and the target order is determined by machine so that neither the person recording the subject's response nor the experimenter, or anyone else in contact with the subject, knows the target order, and they cannot give inadvertent clues.

Psi-stars

Most of the positive results obtained with unselected subjects show a small positive effect, but a few individuals, the so-called psi-stars, seem to have a particular facility for this kind of work and have scored well above chance in a number of well-controlled experiments. Pavel Stepanek, a Czech bank clerk, was one such star. His speciality was guessing the colour of an upturned card, typically whether it was either black or white or green or white. The card was initially covered in an envelope, which in later experiments was in turn placed in a cover which was placed in a padded jacket, thus weight, possible card or envelope warping and other visual cues were controlled. He conducted a large number of these experiments over a period of ten years in the 1960s with scientists from various parts of the world. In one series he got 1,140 right out of 2,000 guesses or about 57 per cent. This is statistically highly significant but the effect itself is quite weak and typical of success in forced-choice experiments of this kind.

Milan Ryzl, the Czech experimenter who worked with Stepanek, had the idea of what has subsequently come to be known as the *majority vote* technique. Essentially this involves representing the same targets to the subject on a number of occasions, in this case presenting 100 targets ten times each, and counting the majority as the call – for instance seven blacks and three whites would count as black. In this particular experiment Stepanek achieved a remarkable 71 per cent success rate (Pratt 1973).

Another psi-star, Bill Delmore, took part in some well-controlled experiments where he had to guess which card had been drawn from 10 packs of 52 ordinary playing cards. In 42 runs of 52 trials Delmore got the suit and number correct in 6 per cent of cases, compared to the 2 per cent you would expect by chance. Delmore was particularly accurate on the rare occasions when he stated in advance of his call that he thought he was right. He made twenty such confidence calls in one run of 364 guesses and in fourteen he was right about both suit and number; he got the number right in five others and the suit in the one remaining, a truly remarkable feat (Kelly and Kanthamani 1972). However, some commentators have criticised the experiments with Delmore (e.g. Hansen 1992). Individuals who can score well above chance consistently in parapsychology experiments seem to be rare.

The mood and state in which the stars produce their best work seems to be as variable as they are. Stepanek was comfortable with routine, and happy to make a thousand calls a day, whereas Delmore was lively, worked fast but with a low number of trials per day and rest periods. Ted Serios, whose speciality was producing images on film, liked to drink large quantities of beer! Ingo Swann was relaxed, still, preferred quick feedback on his success or failure and varied tasks (Schmeidler 1982).

Like many a standard psychology experiment there is a tendency for subjects doing forced-choice tasks to exhibit a decline effect over time or within sessions. Some argue that the trivial and tedious nature of the task in this kind of experiment is not likely to bring out the best in potential psychics and that the use of free-response images, where the target might be any kind of image, is likely to be more interesting and therefore more psi conducive. This does indeed appear to be the case and nowadays most ESP experiments employ free-response targets.

The English psychic Malcolm Bessent performed successfully in the precognitive dreaming experiments described below. Fourteen out of the sixteen targets he attempted were considered hits by judges. In another experiment he was the receiver for pictures sent by 2,000 odd senders at a series of Grateful Dead concerts miles away! He got four out of six correct (Ullman *et al.* 1989). He also performed successfully on other precognitive and telepathic experiments elsewhere, notably at PRL in Princeton (Honorton 1970). More commonly parapsychology experiments are often carried out with subjects who do not claim special psychic ability.

Free-response experiments

Early experiments of this type used an entirely free choice of image, for example the telepathic drawings carried out by Upton Sinclair (1930) and his wife in the 1930s. Upton drew a sketch and his wife attempted to replicate that sketch; her guesses show some failures but many striking similarities. This type of experiment often produces dramatic results with certain receivers drawing an image which seems very close to the original.

However, there can be problems in interpreting the results. Asked to sketch an image, the probability of it being a house, face or tree is much higher than less obvious images like a garden swing or cooker. It can be argued that people who know each other well may be able to use unconscious inference to anticipate what image the other party is likely to draw. Nowadays parapsychologists get round this problem by randomly selecting the images that people need to guess from a target pool.

Dreams

In a series of experiments in the 1960s at the Maimonides Medical Centre in New York, the targets were prints of famous paintings. The experimenters asked their subjects to attempt to dream the target and subsequently describe their dreams. Typically the subject was woken after each REM dream phase and asked to describe their dream. This description was recorded and transcribed. The subject and usually several independent judges subsequently selected which one of a number of targets best matched the dream description (Ullman *et al.* 1973). Child's (1985) meta-analysis of the dream-ESP studies showed that the probability that the results could be obtained by chance was $p < .000002$. Of the 450 sessions conducted between 1966 and 1973 the success rate was 63 per cent compared to the expected 50 per cent. The chance against that is 75 million to one, which is highly significant. The main drawback with this form of dream telepathy is that it is very time-consuming.

Remote viewing

In the 1970s Targ and Puthoff, two physicists from the Stanford Research Institute, conducted a series of remote viewing experiments. Here the experimenter selects a target site randomly, the agent or sender travels to it and attempts to 'send' back images of the place chosen through mental intention. For practical reasons the site was generally within thirty minutes of the laboratory but replications have taken place over thousands of miles (Schlitz and Gruber 1980, 1981). Some of Targ and Puthoff's well-known experiments were with ex-police commissioner Pat Price. An independent judge was asked to visit each of the nine target locations in this series and rank each of Price's target drawings and descriptions from one to nine according to how well they matched. Seven of the nine were ranked first, matching the correct site (Targ and Puthoff 1978). Price, like many of the psi-stars, was very down to earth and successful in his normal life; this is about as far removed as you can get from the more ethereal image traditionally associated with those who claim telepathic powers.

It would be very useful indeed if people could describe unseen targets thousands of miles away accurately, and the military have not been slow to see the potential. Indeed the US government and no doubt others have funded programs to investigate its potential for warfare. For example Ed May conducted a number of remote viewing experiments funded by the American military at SAIC (the Science Applications International Corporation). A review of the remote viewing experiments funded by the American military may be found in Mumford *et al.* (1995). These experiments produced interesting results but perhaps not at the level of reliability needed for regular application. Utts (1991) reports an effect size of about

0.2 for the hundreds of remote viewing trials conducted at SRI and SAIC. Experienced successful remote reviewers achieved better results. See p. 46 for more on meta-analyses of the remote viewing experiments and p. 102 for a summary of the conclusions drawn by the government report evaluating these SRI and SAIC remote viewing experiments.

Ganzfeld

Charles Honorton, who was one of the researchers at the Maimonides laboratory, went on to do a series of experiments which aimed to put subjects into a mental state that is receptive to psi. Based on a survey, ranging from ancient Indian literature describing the psychic experiences of yoga adepts to more recent writings of psychics themselves, Honorton concluded that a psi conducive state required a relaxed mind, a quieting of the normal senses and an inward mental focus. He attempted to induce this experimentally by using welcoming staff, pleasant surroundings, seating subjects in a reclining comfortable chair, playing white noise into the subject's ears to block out external sound and red light on to half a ping-pong ball covering the eyes which produces a diffuse glow. The subject then listens to a twenty-minute relaxation tape. Meanwhile a target is randomly selected from a target pool of 1,024 still photographs, pictures and clips of moving film. Once relaxed the subject describes out loud the images that come to them over a period of perhaps twenty minutes. These data are recorded and a verbatim transcript made (Honorton 1985).

In practice, in this and other free-response experiments the image the subject draws or describes is rarely identical to the target, but it often has many striking correspondences, for instance the shape or colour may be right but the scale or function wrong, a cone rather than a pyramid, or the sun rather than an orange beach ball for instance.

Judging is done independently and by the subject. Typically the subject is asked to rank which of four images they think the target is. (The four images are randomly selected by computer.) Independently a third party unconnected with the experiment may be presented with a transcript of the subject's mentation about the target and a copy of the same four images presented to the subject, and asked to rank which of the four pictures the transcript most closely matches and which second and so on. Computer ratings of success have also been used. Each of Honorton's 1,024 targets differs from all the others as regards the presence or absence of at least one of ten characteristics such as colour, humans, animals, architecture, activity versus a static quality, etc. The subject can be asked to answer these ten questions about his image of the target. Other researchers ask more extensive questions, for example the English researcher James Spottiswoode used 100 questions in his remote viewing experiments (Spottiswoode 1985).

By 1997 a total of over 2,500 Ganzfeld sessions had been conducted around the world with an average success rate of 33 per cent compared to the 25 per cent expected by chance (Radin 1997, p. 88.) This appeared to provide impressive evidence for a psi effect. However Milton and Wiseman's (1999b) meta-analysis of thirty subsequent ganzfeld studies found an effect near chance; Milton (1999) found a significant but lower effect size. Bem *et al.*'s (2001) reanalysis of forty subsequent studies, including Milton and Wiseman's thirty, suggested that those studies that followed the classic ganzfeld procedure closely, for example using similar visual targets, did come very close to replicating the original effect size whereas those trying something different, for example using musical targets, did not. (Chapter 2 on methodology and Chapter 3 on meta-analyses elaborate on the debate about the significance of the ganzfeld studies.)

Staring

More recently, Rupert Sheldrake (2003) has advocated and Schlitz and others have conducted a series of remote staring experiments. These are experimental versions of the old idea that if you stare at the back of someone's head they will 'feel' it and turn round. An observer and a participant are placed in separate rooms. In some experiments the observer views the participant on a camera monitor and attempts to alter their physiology as directed at particular times. Typically the participant's electrodermal activity (EDA) is monitored during a number of short – for example, thirty-second – sampling periods. Half of these periods are controls; in the other half the observer is asked to attempt to raise or lower the participant's electrodermal activity or blood pressure, for example. A number of successful experiments of this kind have been conducted (Schlitz and LaBerge 1994). In other experiments changes in EDA are tracked in periods when participants are stared at and compared with control periods when they are not being stared at. Schlitz and Braude's (1997) meta-analyses showed a highly significant effect in both types of experiment and Schmidt *et al.* (2004) a significant but less marked effect, see p. 52. This work suggests that psi can operate below the threshold of consciousness as participants are generally unaware of the changes in their physiology that take place in such experiments.

Psychokinesis

In the 1980s there was considerable interest in macro-PK effects like metal bending, but this ability seems to be relatively rare, and this difficulty, coupled with some well-publicised frauds, meant interest turned to micro-PK experiments, where any effect is measured statistically. The late 1980s and 1990s were dominated by experiments centring around the use of computer-mediated random number generators. Recently there has been renewed interest in attempts to influence human physiology.

Random number generators

On the assumption that it might be easier to move very small things and affect labile systems various investigators have conducted experiments using random number generators of one sort or another. Typically the participant is asked to affect a computer display purely by intention, for example to move a horizontal line upwards, then downwards. The computer display is linked to a random output of some sort, for example radioactive decay or electronic noise, which produces output which should vary randomly about a mean over a large number of trials. The random event generator (REG) machines used are sophisticated and are tested extensively to ensure the output is random. Literally millions of trials have been conducted by various researchers, notably Schmidt, Radin, Jahn and Nelson. Meta-analyses of this sort of experiment show a small effect, in the sense that overall participants only manage to shift the output just above chance, but because so many trials have been conducted the results are very significant indeed (Radin and Nelson 1989). (See Chapter 3, p. 54).

The random source and machine used do not seem to be critical as performance seems unaffected when these are varied during experiments. However, psychological factors do appear to affect performance, as certain patterns of output are associated with particular subjects regardless of the type of machine involved (Nelson *et al.* 1986). (See Chapter 10 for a fuller account of parapsychological work on psychokinesis.)

Psi correlates

Quite a lot of the research, especially in the 1950s, 1960s and 1970s, was aimed at finding a psi-conducive state in which to undertake experiments or entailed searching for the personality correlates of psi ability (see Palmer 1977).

Belief

Research suggests that some populations appear to be more gifted at psychic tasks than others. One interesting finding is that those who believe in ESP (sheep) tend to score higher than those who do not believe (goats). Gertrude Schmeidler of City University New York found this effect over a period of ten years studying over a thousand subjects (Schmeidler and McConnell 1958). The effect is small, with believers tending to score just above chance, and non-believers tending to score just below chance (Palmer 1971). For example, in a Zener card task, one would expect a subject to get one in five guesses right purely by chance, so someone who gets only two or three right out of 100 guesses is scoring improbably below chance or psi-missing. Psi-missers may wish to avoid getting the right answer and the consequent threat to their belief system that psi may exist!

There is some evidence that extraversion is correlated with success in psi experiments in the laboratory (Palmer and Carpenter 1998). However, this relationship is not necessarily found in experiments where subjects work alone at home (Schmidt and Schlitz 1989). See p. 55 for a fuller discussion of extraversion meta-analyses. MBTI personality type F (feeling) and P (perception) were predictors of success for novices in ganzfeld experiments (Honorton 1992). Dalton (1997) and Schlitz have independently had considerable success in parapsychology experiments with creative arts students as participants, obtaining some of the best ganzfeld results ever, with a hit rate of near one in two where one in four would be expected by chance (Schlitz and Honorton 1992).

Experimenter effect

Parapsychological data also suggest a marked experimenter effect, in that some experimenters seem to get consistently better results than others (a phenomenon familiar in psychology (Rosenthal 1976)). One theory is that this effect may have a psychological component, that is, that the successful experimenters may be better at making their participants feel more comfortable. However, in parapsychology the experimenter effect has also appeared with subjects ignorant of the experimenter they were working with. For instance, Fisk asked subjects to guess what time two hands showed on a clock face covered in an envelope. Unknown to the subjects Fisk set half the hands and West set the other half. Professor West had the reputation of being a psi-inhibitor and indeed the subjects guessing his clock faces got chance scores whereas Fisk's were significantly above chance (West 1954). MacFarland found an experimenter effect within subjects. He compared an experimenter who had only got positive results with one who had only got chance results, by getting five subjects to make 15,300 calls for two different packs of cards simultaneously. True to form and with the same subjects the psi-inhibitor experimenter got chance results again and the other experimenter was successful once more (White 1977). Relling *et al.* (1962) attempted a replication of work showing a relationship between a teacher's belief in psi and his class's success at a clairvoyant task. Of the four professors used, one did believe in ESP and his class got the highest result (5.2), another was more agnostic and his class came second with 5, the remaining two were sceptical and their classes scored 4.9 and 4.6 respectively. More recently, Wiseman, a sceptic, and Schlitz, a psi-conducive experimenter, have attempted several staring experiments where the experimenter aims to affect the participant's electrodermal activity during randomly chosen trials. Each experimenter performed the same experiment in the same location with subjects drawn from the same subject pool. Sure enough, Wiseman got chance results and Schlitz positive ones (Wiseman and Schlitz 1997). If the experimenter psi effect is real, one wonders what effect the experimenter's belief has on the outcome of psychology and medical experiments more generally.

Geomagnetic effect

In addition to investigating the characteristics of the individuals involved in experiments, some attention has been given to the impact of environmental factors on experimental outcome. A growing body of data suggests there may be a small relationship between geomagnetic fields and parapsychological outcomes, with some studies suggesting that certain parapsychology results are better and ESP activity is greater when geomagnetic disturbance is low (e.g. Persinger 1985). For example, Zilberman (1995) found that French and Russian lottery payouts were higher when geomagnetic activity decreased (the odds of this happening by chance were 400 to 1). In some experiments Radin (1998) found a relationship between gambling and the lunar cycle suggesting gamblers might be able to increase the payout by about 2 per cent if they gambled near the full moon and avoided gambling around the new moon.

Explanations

Given that the nature of psychic phenomena is so extraordinary it is understandable that the validity of parapsychological findings is questioned. Explanations for parapsychological phenomena range from writing off anomalous experiences as mistaken attribution to accepting that parapsychological experiments appear to present an anomaly that science has yet to explain. Explanations that attempt to explain away anomalous phenomena include questioning the reliability of the testimony, the honesty of the participants and the validity of the methodology. Attempts to understand how apparently paranormal phenomena might come about range from neurophysiological artefact, through psychological predisposition for such experiences, to the role of various paraphysical theories or some kind of psi field. Some of the main explanations voiced for parapsychological phenomena are outlined below. (For explanations of specific parapsychological phenomena see those given in the relevant chapters elsewhere in this book.)

Misperception

Attempts to explain away everyday psi experiences often focus around misperception, faulty memory or coincidence. The idea is that people misattribute significance to an event due to a tendency to fantasise, see meaning and magic where none exist, inaccurately estimate probability or misremember. There seems no doubt that psychological factors probably do account for many experiences of this kind; however there remain a small number of accounts that cannot readily be explained by psychological factors. (Chapter 4 amplifies on the possible role of psychological factors in parapsychological experiences.)

Neurophysiology may also play a part in some instances. Recently Persinger (1999) has been able to replicate a number of phenomena associated with a sense of presence and out-of-body experiences in certain participants by stimulating the temporal lobe with a complex magnetic field. Tandy (2000) has shown that standing waves can induce a sense of presence. Blanke *et al.* (2002) have shown that out-of-body experiences can be triggered by stimulating the angular gyrus in the right cortex. This work suggests that at least some psychic experiences appear to be caused by the effect of electromagnetic anomalies on the brain.

Artefact

Well-controlled experiments with significant results require an alternative explanation. The main doubts over experimental data have concerned sensory leakage, fraud, possible artefacts, the representiveness of published studies and non-replicability. (Chapter 2 offers an account of some of the methodological problems facing parapsychology.)

Some of the early experimental work may have failed to eliminate all *sensory cues* or been methodologically unsound in some other way. Sender and receiver clearly need to be in separate rooms and far enough away so that there could be no sensory leakage. Targets need to be randomly selected so that *inferring* which target the experimenter is likely to pick can be ruled out. The modern-day parapsychologist uses double-blind procedures, random target selection, automatic presentation and independent third-party judging and sometimes electromagnetic screening. Indeed parapsychological experiments appear to be among the best controlled in the social and hard sciences (Sheldrake 1998). In addition, significance levels do not appear to have declined noticeably as methodology has got more sophisticated. Questions about study quality do not seem to provide sufficient explanation for the positive outcomes in parapsychology as several meta-analyses have shown that outcome has not been correlated with study quality.

In databases such as the micro-PK studies the parapsychological effect itself is very small indeed. This leads a number of those familiar with the data to feel that it presents an anomaly in need of explanation. However, the parapsychology methodology used is very sophisticated, a large number of people have been involved and the databases cover millions of trials. The same level of significance as that achieved in these experiments would be accepted as a positive effect in other fields.

Fraud

Another charge against parapsychology and psychical research is fraud, in particular subject fraud. Because certain psi effects, such as metal bending, can be replicated by magicians and certain ESP effects by mentalists, it is sometimes argued that subjects in psi experiments may have used similar tricks to achieve positive results. Some fakirs and stage psychics use tricks, some mediums are fraudulent, and parapsychology, like most other disciplines, has had a few cases of experimenter and subject fraud (e.g. Marwick 1978). This is one of the reasons that the modern parapsychological experiment is designed to control procedures so that fraud is effectively ruled out as an explanation. The controls include random automated target selection, automated result recording, predetermining the number of trials, screening and independent judging.

There remains the question of the number of researchers achieving positive results, as science is full of promising studies that were not replicated. Many of the most significant parapsychological experimental results seem to have been published by a relatively small number of experimenters who appeared adept at getting positive results. These experimenters include Braud, Dalton, Honorton, Radin, Schmidt, Schlitz and Jahn *et al.* As in any other discipline, fraud seems a less plausible explanation if positive results are replicated under well-controlled conditions by many different investigators in different locations. Meta-analysis offers a tool to assess the significance of work by many different researchers involved in well-controlled parapsychological studies. Using this methodology various parapsychological databases have produced effects of billions to one against chance where a number of different investigators and participants were involved. It remains to be seen if these effects will continue to be replicated. (Chapter 3 on meta-analysis describes the results of various parapsychological meta-analyses.)

File drawer

The file drawer is a term used to describe unpublished unsuccessful studies. One charge is that parapsychologists may only publish the successful studies and that if all the unpublished, unsuccessful studies were examined too, they would balance out any positive effect. There have been surveys (e.g. Blackmore 1980) that have attempted to try to find out how many unreported studies there are, along with statistical attempts (e.g. Radin *et al.* 1985) to estimate how many there would need to be to cancel out the significant positive effect found in respect of various series of experiments in parapsychology. For example, both Rosenthal, an expert in meta-analysis, and Honorton, a parapsychologist, calculated that there would need to be 423 unreported negative studies to cancel out the positive effect of their 1985 ganzfeld meta-analysis (Utts 1995). They agreed there were just not enough experimenters to do this. It is accepted by most informed sceptics that the non-reporting of negative studies cannot account for the positive effects in parapsychology. In addition, reputable parapsychological laboratories declare in advance their intention to do an experiment and outline the design, and parapsychology journals will publish all experiments regardless of whether the findings are positive or negative.

Replicability

Another charge is that the findings are not replicable. As regards spontaneous phenomena it is certainly true that certain parapsychological effects, like physical mediumship, are now reported less commonly and this understandably casts doubt on their existence (see Braude 1986 for an opposing view). However, other phenomena, such as crisis telepathy (e.g. seeing or sensing an apparition of a relative at the time of death), have continued to be reported in studies across widely different time periods and cultures.

As regards the experimental data, it is true that some subjects and some experimenters seem to be more successful than others and that there is debate over whether one set of significant meta-analyses of parapsychological data has been replicated subsequently or not (e.g. Milton and Wiseman 1999a, Milton 1999, Bem *et al.* 2001). However, the majority of meta-analyses of parapsychological experiments suggest a small but highly significant effect in ESP, precognitive, RNG PK and DMILS experiments (e.g. Utts 1995). Further there is some evidence of replicability of effect size across different types of experiments, with RNG PK experiments producing a very small effect size only just above chance and ESP free-response studies and DMILS studies typically producing a markedly larger effect size. (Chapter 3 provides a detailed account of the relevant figures.)

Belief

Personal belief tends to play a big part in our interpretation of events, so some people find even good evidence for psi hard to accept due to an a priori belief that psi is simply not possible (Kurtz 1986).

Belief and intention also seem to affect psi performance. Belief in psi, for example, tends to be associated with a slightly better performance and lack of belief in psi a slightly worse one (Lawrence 1993). Whether psi ability or lack of it reinforces the belief or belief improves psi ability and disbelief inhibits it is an open question. The amount of time spent focusing on the desired outcome may also be a factor as effect sizes seem to be greater in experiments requiring a longer period per trial.

Psi field

Assuming the psi effect is real, we have little idea as to what causes it. A popular lay theory to explain psi postulates the existence of some kind of psi field or collective unconscious where we can tap into information. Sheldrake's notion of morphic resonance offers an alternative (see Chapter 9). Notions of a psi field may sound far-fetched but there is some evidence for a mass consciousness psi effect on physical systems. Radin (1997) reports that when a large group of people concentrate on a single thing, for example the Olympics, random number generators around the world seem to show more order. (See p. 125 in Chapter 10 on psychokinesis.)

Physical

Some people have wondered if a psi signal is transmitted electromagnetically via extremely low frequency ELF waves which can go through solid walls. However psi effects do not seem to attenuate over distance or time, and no shielding process has been shown to inhibit them (including a Faraday cage), hence electromagnetic theories of psi seem to be ruled out.

There are various speculative theories of psi based on aspects of paraphysics. These include those drawing on extra dimensions of space to offer an account of precognition and retrocognition and observational theories invoking the non-local nature of sub-atomic particles. For example, Schmidt suggested psi intention might modify the probability of different outcomes and Walker has argued that conscious observation was the critical factor, assuming that consciousness was involved in the collapse of the wave-function which was related to particular outcomes (Schmidt 1984). (Stokes 1987 presents an extended account of the many theories that aim to account for psi.)

There remains the problem of how the brain might translate a psi signal into recognisable information. At present none of the theories and speculations attempting to explain a real psi effect do so adequately. Nevertheless most parapsychologists assume that a mechanism to explain psi will eventually be discovered.

Conclusion

People often have strongly held *a priori* beliefs about parapsychological phenomena, one or more of which may overstep a given individual's 'boggle factor'. Thus some scientists accept telepathy but not precognition, reincarnation and survival of death. Surveys suggest that as regards paranormal beliefs, as in other areas, personal experience plays a large part in determining whether people find such phenomena credible or not.

Psychic experiences have been reported by a substantial proportion of the population for centuries, up to and including the present day. Experimental work in parapsychology is now methodologically very sophisticated. Meta-analyses of hundreds of parapsychological experiments show a small but, on the whole, consistent effect that cannot be explained away by the non-reporting of failed studies. If positive replications continue, parapsychological results appear to present an extraordinary anomaly that needs explaining.

Note

1 It can be argued that the figure of around a third of the population reporting religious experience under-reports the true incidence and that a third to a half or even two-thirds is a safer estimate; for instance Hay found an incidence of 65 per cent among his Nottinghamshire students (Hay 1987).

Recommended reading

Introductory

Blackmore, S. and Hart-Davis, A. (1995) *Test your Psychic Powers*, London: Thorsons. Accessible introduction to parapsychology experiments readers can try at home.

Radin, D. (1997) *The Conscious Universe*, San Francisco: Harper San Francisco. Clear review of parapsychological findings, particularly good on psychokinesis and experimental data.

Advanced

Cardena, E., Lynn, S.J. and Krippner, S. (eds) (2000) *Varieties of Anomalous Experience*, Washington, DC: American Psychological Association. Extensive review of anomalous phenomena, particularly good on experiential and clinical aspects.

Irwin, H.J. (2004) *Introduction to Parapsychology*, 4th edn, Jefferson, NC: McFarland. A parapsychology textbook aimed at undergraduates and others with a serious interest in the area.

References

Bem, D.J. and Honorton, C. (1991) Does psi exist? Replicable evidence for an anomalous process of information transfer, *Psychological Bulletin*, 115, 4–18.

Bem, D.J., Palmer, J. and Broughton, R.S. (2001) Updating the Ganzfeld database: is it a victim of its own success? *Journal of Parapsychology*, 65, 207–18.

Blackmore, S. (1980) The extent of selective reporting in ESP Ganzfeld studies, *European Journal of Parapsychology*, 3, 213–19.

Blanke, O., Ortigue, S., Landis, T. and Seeck, M. (2002) Stimulating illusory own-body perceptions, *Nature*, 419, 269–70

Braude, S. (1986) *The Limits of Influence*, London: Routledge and Kegan Paul.

Carrington, W. (1940) Experiments on the paranormal cognition of drawings, *Proceedings of the Society of Psychical Research*, 46, 34–151.

Child, I.L. (1985) Psychology and anomalous observations: the question of ESP in dreams, *American Psychologist*, 40, 1219–30.

Dalton, K. (1997) Exploring the links: Creativity and psi in the Ganzfeld. *The*

Parapsychological Association 40th Annual Convention Proceedings, Durham, NC: Parapsychological Association, 119–34.

Edge, H., Morris, R., Palmer, J. and Rush, J. (1986) *Foundations of Parapsychology*, London: Routledge and Kegan Paul.

Gauld, A. (1982) *Mediumship and Survival*, Oxford: Heinemann.

Gallup, G.H. and Newport, F. (1991) Belief in paranormal phenomena among Americans, *Skeptical Enquirer*, 15, 137–46.

Gratton-Guiness, I. (1982) *Psychical Research: A Guide to its Principles and Practices*, Northampton: Aquarian.

Gurney, E., Myers, F. and Podmore, F. (1886) *Phantasms of the Living*, 2 vols, London: Trubner.

Hansen, G. (1992) The research with B.D. and the legacy of magical ignorance, *Journal of Parapsychology*, 56, 4, 307–33.

Haraldsson, E. (1985) Representative national surveys of psychic phenomena, *Journal of the Society for Psychical Research*, 53, 138–44.

Haraldsson, E. and Houtkooper, J.M. (1991) Psychic experience in the multinational human values study: who reports them? *Journal of the American Society for Psychical Research*, 85, 145–65.

Hay, D. (1987) *Explaining Inner Space*, rev. edn, London: Mowbray.

Hay, D. and Morisy, A. (1977) *Reports of Ecstatic, Paranormal or Religious Experience in Great Britain and the United States*, Oxford: Alistair Hardy Research Centre.

Honorton, C. (1970) Psi and internal attention states. In D. Shapin and L. Coly (eds) *Psi and States of Awareness*, New York: Parapsychology Foundation, 79–90.

Honorton, C. (1985) Meta-analysis of psi Ganzfeld research, *Journal of Parapsychology*, 49, 51–91.

Honorton, C. (1992) The ganzfeld novice: four predictors of ESP performance. Paper presented to the 35th Annual Convention of the Parapsychological Association, Las Vegas.

Hyman, R. (1985) The Ganzfeld psi experiment: a critical appraisal, *Journal of Parapsychology*, 49, 3–49.

Inglis, B. (1986) *The Paranormal: An Encyclopedia of Psychic Phenomena*, London: Paladin.

Kanthamani, K. and Kelly, E. (1974) Awareness of success in an exceptional subject, *Journal of Parapsychology*, 38, 355–82.

Kelly, E. and Kanthamani, K. (1972) A subject's efforts towards voluntary control, *Journal of Parapsychology*, 36, 185–97.

Kurtz, P. (1986) *A Skeptic's Handbook of Parapsychology*, Buffalo, NY: Prometheus.

Lawrence, T. (1993) Bringing in the sheep, a meta-analysis of sheep/goat experiments. In M.J. Schlitz (ed.) *Papers from the 36th Annual Parapsychological Association Convention*, Fairhaven, MA: Parapsychological Association.

Marwick, B. (1978) The Soal–Goldney experiments with Basil Shakleton: new evidence of data manipulation, *Proceedings of the Society for Psychical Research*, 56, 250–81.

Milton, J. (1999) Should Ganzfeld research continue to be critical in the search for a replicable psi effect? Part 1, *Journal of Parapsychology*, 63, 4, 309–34.

Milton, J. and Wiseman, R. (1999a) Does psi exist? Lack of replication of an anomalous information transfer, *Psychological Bulletin*, 1125, 387–91.

Milton, J. and Wiseman, R. (1999b) A meta-analysis of mass media tests of extrasensory perception, *British Journal of Psychology*, 90, 235–40.

Mumford, M.D., Rose, A.M. and Goslin, D.A. (1995) *An Evaluation of Remote Viewing: Research and Applications*, Washington, DC: American Institutes for Research.

Myers, F. (1903) *Human Personality and its Survival of Bodily Death*, London: Longmans and Green.

Nelson, R.D., Jahn, R.G. and Dunne, B.J. (1986) Operator-related anomalies in physical systems and information processes, *Journal of the Society for Psychical Research*, 53, 261–85.

Palmer, J. (1971) Scoring in ESP as a function of belief in ESP. Part 1: The sheep–goat effect, *Journal of the American Society of Psychical Research*, 65, 373–408.

Palmer, J. (1977) Attitudes and personality traits in experimental ESP research. In B. Wolman (ed.) (1986) *Handbook of Parapsychology*, Jefferson, NJ: McFarland, 175–201.

Palmer, J. and Carpenter, J.C. (1998) Comments on the extraversion–ESP meta-analysis by Honorton, Ferrari and Bem, *Journal of Parapsychology*, 62, 277–82.

Persinger, M.A. (1985) Geophysical variables and behaviour: intense paranormal experiences occur during days of quiet, global, geomagnetic activity, *Perceptual and Motor Skills*, 61, 320–22.

Persinger, M. (1999) Near-death experiences and ecstasy: a product of the organization of the human brain. In S. Della Sala (ed.) *Mind Myths*, London: Wiley.

Pratt, J. (1973) A decade of research with a selected ESP subject: an overview and reappraisal of the work with Pavel Stepanek. In J. Beloff (ed.) (1974) *New Directions in Parapsychology*, London: Paul Elek.

Radin, D. (1998) Seeking psi in the casino, *Journal of the Society for Psychical Research*, 62, 850, 193–219.

Radin, D. and Nelson, R. (1989) Evidence of consciousness related anomalies in random physical systems, *Foundations of Physics*, 19, 1499–514.

Radin, D., May, E. and Thompson, M. (1985) Psi experiments with random number generators: meta-analysis part 1, *Proceedings of the Parapsychological Association*, 28th Annual Convention.

Rilling, M., Pettijohn, C. and Adams, J.Q. (1962) A summary of some clairvoyance experiments conducted in classroom situations, *Journal of the American Society for Psychical Research*, 56, 125–30.

Rosenthal, R. (1976) *Experimenter Effects in Behavioural Research*, Irvington.

Schlitz, M. and Gruber, E. (1980) Transcontinental remote viewing, *Journal of Parapsychology*, 44, 305–17.

Schlitz, M. and Gruber, E. (1981) Transcontinental remote viewing: a rejudging, *Journal of Parapsychology*, 45, 233–7.

Schlitz, M. and Honorton, C. (1992) Ganzfeld psi performance within an artistically gifted population, *Journal of the American Society for Psychical Research*, 86, 83–98.

Schlitz, M. and LaBerge, S. (1994) *Autonomic Detection of Remote Observation: Two Conceptual Replications*, Petaluma, CA: Institute of Noetics.

Schlitz, M. and Braude, S. (1997) Distant intentionality and healing: Assessing the evidence, *Alternative Therapies*, 3, 6, 62–73.

Schmeidler, G. (1982) *Some Guidelines from Research Findings in Psychical Research*. In I. Grattan-guiness, *Psychical Research*, Wellingborough: Acquarian, 265–283.

Schmeidler, G. and McConnell, R. (1958) *ESP and Personality Patterns*, Haven, CT: Yale University Press.

Schmidt, H. (1984) Comparison of a teleological model with a quantum collapse model of psi, *Journal of Parapsychology*, 48, 4, 261–76.

Schmidt, H. and Schlitz, M. (1989) A large scale PK pilot experiment with prerecorded random events. In L.A. Henkel and R.E. Berger (eds) *Research in Parapsychology 1988*, Metuchen, NJ: Scarecrow Press, 6–10.

Schmidt, S., Schneider, R., Utts, J. and Walach, H. (2004) Distant intentionality and the feeling of being stared at: Two meta analyses, *British Journal of Psychology*, 95, 1235–47.

Sheldrake, R. (1998) Experimenter effects in scientific research: how widely are they neglected, *Journal of Scientific Exploration*, 12, 1.

Sheldrake, R. (2003) *The Sense of being Stared at*, London: Hutchinson.

Sinclair, U. (1930) *Mental Radio*, Springfield, IL: Thomas. 2nd edn 1962.

Spottiswoode, J. (1985) Displacement in Associative Remote Viewing: Analytic Scoring and Other Possible Solutions. In N.L. Zingrone and M.J. Schlitz (eds) (1998) *Research in Parapsychology, 1993: Abstracts and papers from the 36th Annual Convention of the Parapsychological Association, 1993*, (pp. 47–50) Lanham, MD: Scarecrow Press, Inc.

Stokes, D. (1987) Theoretical parapsychology. In S. Krippner (ed.) *Advances in Parapsychology V*, Jefferson, NJ: McFarland.

Tandy, V. (2000) Something in the cellar, *Journal for the Society for Psychical Research*, 64, 3, 129–140.

Targ, R. and Puthoff, H. (1978) *Mind-Reach*, London: Granada.

Ullman, M., Krippner, S. and Vaughan, A. (1973) *Dream Telepathy*, New York: Macmillan.

Ullman, M., Krippner, S. and Vaughan, A. (1989) *Dream Telepathy: Experiments in Nocturnal ESP*, Jefferson, NJ: McFarland.

Utts, J. (1991) Replication and meta-analysis in parapsychology, *Statistical Science*, 6, 363–403.

Utts, J. (1995) An assessment of the evidence for psychic functioning, *Journal of Parapsychology*, 59, 289–320.

West, D. (1954) *Psychical Research Today*, London: Duckworth.

White, R. (1977) The influence of experimenter motivation, attitudes and methods of handling subjects on psi test results. In B. Wolman (ed.) (1986) *Handbook of Parapsychology*, Jefferson, NJ: McFarland, 273–301.

White, R.A. (1993) Working classification of EHEs, *Exceptional Human Experience*, 11, 2, 149–50.

Wiseman, R. and Schlitz, M. (1997) Experimenter effects and the remote detection of staring, *Journal of Parapsychology*, 61, 3, 197–208.

Wolman, B. (ed.) (1986) *Handbook of Parapsychology*, Jefferson, NJ: McFarland. First published 1977, Van Nostrand Reinhold.

Zilberman, M.S. (1995) Public numerical lotteries, an international parapsychological experiment covering a decade: a data analysis of French and Soviet numerical lotteries, *Journal of the Society for Psychical Research*, 60, 149–60.

Chapter 2

Methodology

Julie Milton

In everyday life, many people report experiences that they believe might have been paranormal. These experiences often have to do with apparent extrasensory perception (ESP) – the acquisition of information without any apparent physical means. For example, someone might think of an old friend that they have lost touch with and not thought about in years, only to receive a telephone call the same day to tell them that their friend has just died. The coincidence may seem so unlikely that the event is taken as evidence of ESP. Other experiences may relate to apparent psychokinesis (PK) – the influence of someone's thoughts upon the physical world. For example, someone might be having a particularly stressful time at work and shout at their computer, which immediately breaks down. They might wonder whether this was evidence of psychokinesis.

Interpretation

Everyday life, however, is messy. There are three main difficulties in taking events such as these as strong evidence that paranormal phenomena exist.

Intervening variable

The first problem is that it is *difficult to rule out the possibility that normal, physical channels were involved.* In the first example given above, a mutual acquaintance might have mentioned that the friend was ill some time before. The person who experienced the coincidence might have forgotten being told this but the unconscious memory might have prompted the idea of the friend's death some time later. This would make the coincidence much less remarkable. In the second example, the person shouting at the computer might have made a sudden movement when they did so. Vibration from this movement might have been enough to trigger a mechanical fault that had been on the verge of happening for some time.

Likelihood

The second problem with everyday life events is that in order to tell *how surprising* a coincidence is, it is necessary to know how often the observed event would be expected to happen by chance alone. In order to calculate this, we need to know how often the two events that make up the coincidence happen. For example, if people very often shout at their computers and computers very often break down at random times then by chance alone the two events will occur together relatively often in a large enough group of people. For everyday life events such as these, there is almost never any data on which to estimate how often they happen. For example, no one measures how often people shout at their computers or how often computers break down. However, some researchers have attempted to estimate such likelihoods for events that contribute to experiences commonly claimed as paranormal, such as the example of thinking of a friend or relative and then hearing soon afterwards that that person has died. Zusne and Jones (1989), for example, calculated that the probability of thinking about any of the people we knew of by chance alone within five minutes of learning of their death would be about one in 30,000 per year. Although this would be a rare event for an individual, in a country the size of the USA, about 3,000 adults would have such an experience by chance alone in any given year and so it should not be surprising to hear of such instances. This shows clearly how even what appear to be remarkable coincidences may not be the strong evidence for ESP that they may at first appear.

Report accuracy

The third major problem with taking events from everyday life as evidence of paranormal phenomena is that it is *difficult to be sure that people are giving accurate accounts* of their experiences. As research on eyewitness testimony shows, human memory and observation are far from perfect (Loftus 1996) and people might exaggerate or even fabricate stories or evidence in order to impress or hoax others (e.g. Keene 1976).

Experimental parapsychology

These problems present considerable difficulties to scientists who are interested in finding out whether paranormal phenomena exist and, if so, how they work. As a result, most parapsychology studies are conducted in laboratories where researchers can attempt to rule out any known physical channels of influence, can make precise calculations of the probabilities of events, and do not have to rely on possibly unreliable testimony to know what actually happened. Almost all experiments involve ordinary people, based on the assumption that if ESP and PK are genuine abilities or faculties, then, as with most other human abilities or faculties, a small proportion of people will be very bad at the task, most people somewhere near the middle and a small proportion will be star performers. People who make special claims of having strong psychic abilities are relatively rarely tested, not only because few of them make credible claims that appear worth testing but also because of the possibility that they might be fraudulent (Hansen 1990) requires extensive, time-consuming and potentially expensive experimental controls to rule out the possibility of cheating.

ESP studies

The two major types of paranormal phenomena investigated in the laboratory – *ESP and PK* – are investigated in slightly different ways, although the tests rely upon the same basic principles. In an ESP test, the experimenter chooses some sort of hidden stimulus or 'target' material for a participant (usually called the 'receiver') to guess. In a *forced-choice study*, the experimenter will tell the receiver what choices to guess from on each trial. In a study using the traditional ESP card symbols, there would be five choices on each trial – a circle, a cross, wavy lines, a square, or a star. In a different study, the receiver might have two choices, between guessing a zero or a one.

In *free-response studies*, the receiver attempts to describe something without being presented with a fixed choice. For example, the receiver might be asked to describe a picture, with no limits placed on what the picture might be. Objects, music, people and geographical locations have been used as target material in free-response studies (Milton 1997, Willin 1996). In forced-choice studies, each receiver usually does many trials, but in free-response studies, receivers usually contribute only one trial each to the study because each trial takes much longer to complete. Free-response studies often involve having participants in an altered state of consciousness such as dreaming, hypnosis and so on.

In any type of ESP experiment the experimenter has the target material placed in random order for guessing. The experimenter must remain unaware of the target sequence in order to avoid unconsciously helping the receiver to guess correctly. This randomisation process is therefore either automated or done by someone who does not meet the receiver. Published tables of random numbers or random number generators (electronic devices sampling random electrical processes) are some of the better methods used to place the targets in order, to make sure that the sequence cannot be at least partly guessed by normal means.

In telepathy or clairvoyance studies, the target material is placed out of sight of the receiver (and, depending on the type of target and whether someone else is with the target, out of earshot also). In a telepathy study, another person (the 'sender') looks at each target and may try to mentally convey its contents to the receiver, perhaps by concentrating hard on the target or imagining the receiver looking at the target. In a clairvoyance study, the target material is left alone with no one looking at it. In a precognition study, the target material is, in effect, hidden in the future. After the receiver has recorded his or her guesses, someone blind to those guesses randomly selects the targets.

At the end of the study, the experimenter compares the number of correct guesses obtained with the number expected by chance, using the appropriate statistical test. The statistical test gives the probability of obtaining by chance alone a result as good as the one observed. For example, the probability of making as many as 51 correct guesses in 100 trials where there are two target choices is 0.46. In other words, by chance alone someone would make as many as 51 out of 100 guesses on average 46 times in every 100 times they tried the task. However, if the same percentage of correct guesses is maintained over a large number of trials, the result is much more unlikely. For example, the probability of making as many as 5,100 guesses correctly in 10,000 trials by chance alone is 0.02, that is, only 2 in 100.

In psychology and most of its subdisciplines such as parapsychology, a somewhat arbitrary general rule of thumb is to consider it reasonably likely that a result was not due to chance if the probability of obtaining an effect at least as large as the one observed was less than 0.05 (one in twenty). An outcome that exceeds those odds is referred to as 'statistically significant'.

PK studies

As with ESP studies, there are different types of psychokinesis studies. Macro-PK studies involve the investigation of effects visible to the naked eye such as claims of paranormal metal-bending of the type that Uri Geller made famous (Palmer and Rush 1986). Micro-PK studies, on the other hand, investigate effects that require instrumentation or statistical analysis to detect them, such as examining the effects of someone's intention upon the rate of radioactive decay or the output of a noise diode in an electrical system (Palmer and Rush 1986). Bio-PK or DMILS (distant influence upon living systems) studies examine the effects of people's intentions upon other organisms' biologies or physiologies. For example, a DMILS study might examine whether someone's physiological activity decreases or increases in response to a distant person's intention that they become calm or excited (Braud and Schlitz 1983).

In a typical PK study, a computer might be connected to a micro-electronic random event generator that by chance alone would produce two different outcomes equally often. The equipment is arranged so that each of the two outcomes is associated with a different event that the participant sees. For example, one outcome might lead to a light bulb getting brighter, the other to it becoming dimmer. The participant's task might be to try mentally to influence the light bulb to become brighter and his or her performance would be measured in terms of how often this happened above the 50 per cent chance baseline. In order to make sure that the random event generators used are unbiased, they are also run at times when no one is there to influence them to check their output is random. As in ESP studies, the results are assessed statistically.

Process-oriented research

Almost all ESP and PK studies report statistics on whether their participants outperformed chance on whatever task they were given. However, most researchers assume as a working hypothesis that the phenomena are genuine and conduct their experiments in order to attempt to identify what variables might affect performance. This involves using the same methodology as is used in any area of experimental psychology. For some questions, groups of participants can be treated in different ways and their performance compared to see if they were affected by the difference in test conditions. For example, one group of participants might go through a relaxation exercise prior to an ESP test and be compared with another group that did not. For other questions, all participants might be treated the same way in the study but their performance might be examined in relation to some aspect of their personality or background. For example, an experimenter might examine whether people who believe that psychokinesis is a genuine phenomenon perform better on the task than those who think otherwise.

Combining the results

So far, I have described how individual studies are carried out in parapsychology. However, scientists almost never reach strong conclusions about any question on the basis of a single study. This is because any individual experiment might have methodological flaws, or a random combination of circumstances might have overcome methodological safeguards designed to rule out problems, or the experimenter or participants in the study might have been fraudulent. Also, individual studies are often too small on which to base a firm conclusion. For example, if ESP exists and in the average person leads to just getting 51 per cent of guesses correct when 50 per cent would be expected by chance, a study carrying out only 100 trials will not be likely to obtain statistically significant results and might lead to an incorrect conclusion that ESP is not a genuine effect. It is therefore necessary to look at all of the experiments that have been carried out on a particular topic in order to draw any strong conclusions. The task of examining a body of experiments has special methodologies of its own.

Meta-analysis

Particularly in the social sciences and medicine, meta-analysis – the use of statistical methods to synthesise and describe experiments and their outcomes – has become the leading methodology for combining the results of studies to provide an overall picture of a research area. Meta-analysis has many advantages in most cases over traditional narrative reviews in which studies are described individually and the reviewer uses his or her (often subjective) judgement to draw an overall conclusion. These advantages have led to an explosive increase in the use of meta-analysis in recent years (Hunt 1997). In medicine, for example, meta-analyses of randomised controlled trials have become the 'gold standard' by which to judge the effectiveness of treatments (Guyatt *et al.* 1995) and a vast and highly prestigious, international network of meta-analysts – the Cochrane Collaboration – synthesises the results of studies of a range of therapies for all major diseases and feeds the information back to the medical community (Chalmers and Haynes 1995).

Cumulative probability

The first valuable feature that a meta-analysis offers that a narrative review does not, is a precise estimate of how unlikely it is that the results of the entire group of studies that are being examined arose by chance alone. In order to make this calculation, the probability associated with each study's outcome is calculated and the probabilities are combined to reflect the overall outcome. In most parapsychological meta-analyses, the results obtained have been statistically significantly above chance. In large groups of studies, the results go well beyond mere statistical significance and have astronomical odds against having arisen by chance. For example, a meta-analysis of 309 forced-choice precognition studies obtained a result that would occur by chance only once in 1,000,000,000,000,000,000,000,000 times (Honorton and Ferrari 1989).

File-drawer estimate

There is a great concern in many areas of science that successful studies tend to be published, while studies that find no effect or an effect in the opposite direction from the one predicted are more often left in researchers' file drawers, because the editors of academic journals, or even the researchers themselves, think negative results not worth disseminating. If this is the case, then even a non-existent effect will appear to have been successfully demonstrated since, even with a null effect, a few statistically significant studies will arise by chance. With the criterion for statistical significance set at one in twenty, this means that, on average, one in twenty studies will be apparently successful by chance alone and so it is necessary to know how many studies have been conducted all together. Meta-analysis allows the calculation of the number of studies with an average zero effect that would have to be in the research 'file drawer' to bring the observed overall result in a meta-analysis down to the point at which it became statistically non-significant. If the calculation indicates a relatively small number of studies in the file drawer then selective publication becomes a plausible alternative explanation for the observed results. In most parapsychology meta-analyses conducted so far, however, the file drawer estimates are so large that this does not appear to be a reasonable counter-explanation for the observed results. For example, in the precognition meta-analysis, forty-six zero-effect file-drawer studies would be needed for each published study to reduce the observed odds to below one in twenty (Honorton and Ferrari 1989).

Effect size

One of the most valuable aspects of meta-analysis is a focus on looking at studies not just in terms of their statistical significance levels (the traditional approach) but also in terms of their effect sizes, all measured on the same scale. This is important because most parapsychological research questions involve wanting to know about levels of performance in some task under different conditions, not just how unlikely the levels of performance were (Rosenthal and Rubin, 1992–3).

Study quality

Another advantage of meta-analysis is its quantitative approach to describing study quality, which gives much more information about how well controlled a group of studies is compared to narrative review methods. In a parapsychological meta-analysis, each study is typically assessed on a number of quality criteria, such as whether an adequately tested source of randomness was used in a PK experiment, whether there was adequate sensory shielding between the receiver and the target in an ESP study, and so on. Each study either does or does not receive a point for each criterion it passes and the points are added to reflect its overall quality.

If psi experiment results were due to poor methodological controls rather than to genuine phenomena, each study's quality might be expected to be negatively related to its effect size; that is, the better controlled a study, the smaller its outcome. However, in almost all parapsychology meta-analyses, no statistically significant relationships have been demonstrated between overall study quality and effect size (Milton 1995).

Replicability

In parapsychology, the quantitative approach of meta-analysis also involves examining whether only a few experimenters obtain statistically significant results. In the cases where this has been examined, a much higher proportion appear to do so than the 5 per cent expected by chance. Honorton and Ferrari (1989), for example, report that 30 per cent of studies and 37 per cent of experimenters obtained statistically significant results. Replication across investigators is important because it makes it less likely that any overall success is due to the carelessness or dishonesty of a few experimenters.

Problems with meta-analysis

The results of most parapsychology meta-analyses so far – their highly statistically significant cumulated outcomes, their apparent resistance to explanations in terms of selective reporting, their general lack of statistically significant relationships between individual studies' overall quality and effect size and the apparent replicability of successful studies within them across experimenters – have led to their being presented both within and outside parapsychology as providing strong evidence that psi is a genuine anomaly that replicates across experimenters (e.g. Honorton and Ferrari 1989, Radin and Nelson 1989, Utts 1991).

However, although meta-analysis has considerable advantages as a way of synthesising research findings, it is not all-powerful in answering all of the questions about a body of research that we would like to ask. In particular, there are many potentially serious problems in interpreting the results of any meta-analysis of studies that are of low or uncertain quality. Unfortunately, it is far from clear how well conducted the studies in the parapsychology meta-analyses were. In half of the meta-analyses conducted so far, each study obtained on average fewer than half of the quality points available and two meta-analyses did not report the average study quality at all (Milton 1999). This does not necessarily mean that the studies were not well-conducted. Many experimenters may not have mentioned in their published reports all of the methodological safeguards that they used and so the number of quality points that they obtained will have under-represented the quality of the studies. However, the fact that study quality is not demonstrably high in the meta-analyses makes it difficult to conclude that their positive results were due to psi and not to methodological problems.

This is the case even when overall study quality does not appear to relate statistically significantly to effect size, as is the case in most of the parapsychology meta-analyses. In a group of studies of low or uncertain quality, many factors can obscure a genuine relationship between the two. For example, if, as is likely, many studies do not report all of the safeguards that they used, the estimate of their methodological quality will be inaccurate, making it difficult to detect a relationship between quality and effect size. Some methodological problems might have bigger effects than others, such that simply adding quality points to give an overall estimate of quality will be misleading and again might obscure a genuine impact of methodological quality upon effect size. Some experimenters whose studies were unsuccessful may have thought it pointless to describe the methodological precautions that they took (as Pratt (1966) states that he did). As a group, these studies would make it falsely appear that low quality was associated with low effect size and would make it hard to detect that, in other studies, low quality was associated with higher effect sizes. In parapsychology, the researchers who have carried out the task of assessing the studies have almost always done so without being blind to the studies' results. This introduces the possibility that they might be influenced in how to award each study's quality points according to their beliefs about the existence of paranormal phenomena. A believer might be inclined to give a high quality rating to a successful study and a non-believer to withhold quality points from it. Conversely, they might try to remain uninfluenced by their expectations but overcompensate in the other direction. Either way, their ratings would be inaccurate and make insensitive any analysis to detect a relationship between overall quality and effect size.

These problems are just a selection of those that affect the interpretation of meta-analyses of groups of studies whose quality is unclear (Milton 1999). Clearly, if studies' outcomes have been inflated by methodological problems, then their combined statistical significance, file-drawer estimates and replicability levels cannot be taken as strong evidence for genuine psi phenomena. It is by no means certain that methodological problems have inflated study outcomes in parapsychology; there is very little positive evidence that this is the case. However, although the results of the meta-analyses conducted so far appear promising for the psi hypothesis, the uncertain quality of the studies they contain means that strong conclusions cannot be drawn from their results.

Ganzfeld research

Disagreement over how to interpret a meta-analysis of a particularly promising group of ESP studies of uncertain quality has led to a systematic effort to produce high-quality studies in that area and to attempt to use these studies to resolve the question of whether they show strong evidence of a genuine effect. The studies in question are free-response studies in which the receiver is placed in the ganzfeld (German for 'whole field'), a special sensory environment, described in Chapter 1, p. 15. The ganzfeld helps to produce a mildly altered state of consciousness in which people experience a flow of random, disconnected and often bizarre images, similar to those that some people experience naturally just as they are falling asleep. ESP is believed by some researchers to work better if receivers pay attention to material arising from their unconscious, and the ganzfeld, by blocking out the outside world and producing a flow of imagery, was thought likely to lead to particularly successful experiments.

The first ganzfeld meta-analyses

The first published ganzfeld study, by Charles Honorton and Sharon Harper, appeared in 1974 and by the end of the decade it was being claimed that the technique did indeed produce successful results that could be replicated reasonably often by other experimenters and under conditions that were well controlled. This claim attracted the attention of Ray Hyman, a psychologist who thought ESP unlikely to exist and who was looking at the time for a body of research to assess in parapsychology to represent the field's strongest case. Ganzfeld research was the obvious choice and Honorton, who had become a strong proponent of the ganzfeld technique in parapsychology, provided him with copies of all of the relevant experimental reports.

Hyman (1985) conducted a meta-analysis of the forty-two studies that had been conducted up to the time of his assessment in 1981. Although the combined outcome of the studies was highly statistically significant, Hyman identified a number of methodological problems in the studies that he considered to be potentially serious enough to account for the observed results. In response, Honorton (1985) conducted his own meta-analysis of the studies. He also obtained a statistically significant overall outcome but, despite conceding that the studies contained potential methodological problems, did not agree that the problems were sufficient to account for the overall outcome.

Methodological guidelines and the autoganzfeld

Rather than continue to dispute the matter, Hyman and Honorton (1986) instead jointly drew up a set of methodological guidelines for the stringent conduct of future ganzfeld studies, agreeing that the case for psi in the ganzfeld would rely on a broad range of experimenters obtaining positive results under such conditions. Meanwhile, Honorton and his research team at Princeton Research Laboratories had begun in 1982 a series of partially automated ganzfeld studies – 'autoganzfeld studies' – designed to meet Hyman's methodological concerns (Bem and Honorton 1994). Eleven series were completed before PRL closed in 1989, obtaining a statistically significant overall outcome and a mean effect size nearly identical to that obtained in Honorton's (1985) meta-analysis of the earlier ganzfeld database. Replication of the early ganzfeld results under stringent conditions appeared to suggest that methodological problems were unlikely to have accounted entirely for the effects obtained in the earlier studies. However, Bem and Honorton pointed out that it still remained for their results to be replicated by other experimenters under similarly stringent conditions.

Recent studies

In early 1997, a new meta-analysis was carried out to attempt to determine whether other experimenters had indeed succeeded in replicating these results under well-controlled conditions, by meta-analysing the thirty published ganzfeld studies conducted since the publication of Hyman and Honorton's methodological guidelines (Milton and Wiseman 1999). The studies' combined outcome was not statistically significant and the mean effect size was near zero. Updating the studies to include nine studies published by March 1999 renders the meta-analysis overall statistically significant, but only due to the inclusion of one extremely successful study (Milton 1999), indicating that the effect size found in the autoganzfeld studies does not replicate across experimenters.*

The reasons for the Milton and Wiseman 1999 replication failure are not clear. Although a few potential methodological problems have been identified in the autoganzfeld studies, they do not appear sufficiently serious to have accounted for the results. If the new studies have been unsuccessful as a group because they used different procedures from the autoganzfeld studies, which were themselves quite varied, it is unclear which procedures made the difference. For example, if receivers who believe ESP to be possible perform better in ESP tasks, as some evidence may suggest (Lawrence 1993), then if the autoganzfeld studies used a higher proportion of believers as receivers than did the new studies, this might partially account for the new studies' lack of combined success. However, most of the new studies do not report measures of their participants' belief in ESP and so it is difficult to determine whether this or other potentially important variables were exploited less effectively in the new studies than in the autoganzfeld studies. In addition, any one of a number of procedures used in the autoganzfeld studies may have been crucial for their replication but research has not progressed to the point at which any variables have been reliably identified that might affect success in ESP ganzfeld studies, if psi is a genuine effect. Because there appears to be no clearly convincing explanation for the 1999 replication failure either in normal or paranormal terms, more research will be needed to resolve the issue.

This being the case, it seems that the next step in the search for strong evidence for psi will involve more systematic research to identify what, if any, variables affect ESP performance in ganzfeld ESP studies, if ESP is indeed a genuine effect. The next meta-analysis might restrict itself to studies that replicate the autoganzfeld studies in their essentials. For parapsychologists' views on the ganzfeld meta-analyses see Schmeidler and Edge (1999).

Conclusion

It is clear that methodology in parapsychology is a crucial issue. As in any field of science, if the methodology of an experiment or of a meta-analysis cannot be trusted, neither can its results.

Recommended reading

Introductory

Broughton, R.S. (1991) *Parapsychology: The Controversial Science*, New York: Ballantine. An interesting, non-technical account of parapsychology research, strong on what it is like to take part in an experiment. Excellent, readable chapter – 'Adding it all up' – on meta-analysis in parapsychology suitable for people with no specialist knowledge of statistics. Also interesting, non-technical account of ganzfeld research (pp. 99–114) and the ganzfeld debate up to 1991 (pp. 285–8).

Hunt, M. (1997) *How Science Takes Stock: The Story of Meta-Analysis*, New York: Russell Sage Foundation. An entertaining account of meta-analysis as applied to many interesting topics in the medical and social sciences, aimed at the general reader.

Koestler Chair of Parapsychology Research Unit Website: http://moebius.psy.ed.ac.uk Offers its own web experiments and links to other major parapsychology institutions. A number of parapsychology laboratories carry out experiments using the worldwide web or use their homepages to recruit participants locally for studies in the laboratory.

Advanced

Experimental methodology

Milton, J. and Wiseman, R. (1997) *Guidelines for Extrasensory Perception Research*, Hatfield: University of Hertfordshire Press. A detailed set of guidelines for the conduct of extrasensory perception experiments.

Palmer, J. (1986) Experimental methods in ESP research. In H. Edge, R.L. Morris, J. Palmer and J.H. Rush (eds) *Foundations of Parapsychology*, London: Routledge, 111–37.

Palmer, J. and Rush, J.H. (1986) Experimental methods in PK research. In H. Edge, R.L. Morris, J. Palmer and J.H. Rush (eds) *Foundations of Parapsychology*, London: Routledge, 223–36. Technical discussion of experimental methodology in parapsychology.

Meta-analysis

Milton, J. (1999) Should ganzfeld research continue to be crucial in the search for a replicable psi effect? Part 1: Discussion paper and introduction to an electronic mail discussion, *Journal of Parapsychology*, Special Issue, 63, 4, 302–34. A critical assessment of the evidence for paranormal effects in meta-analyses to 1998, including arguments for treating the results with caution. See also ensuing debate (Schmeidler and Edge 1999).

Radin, D. (1997) *The Conscious Universe: The Scientific Truth of Psychic Phenomena*, San Francisco, CA: HarperEdge. An extended popular account of meta-analysis in parapsychology.

Utts, J. (1991) Replication and meta-analysis in parapsychology, *Statistical Science*, 6, 363–78. A technical summary of the evidence for paranormal phenomena from meta-analysis.

Ganzfeld research

Bem, D.J. and Honorton, C. (1994) Does psi exist? Replicable evidence for an anomalous process of information transfer, *Psychological Bulletin*, 115, 4–18. Describes the important autoganzfeld research and its findings.

Milton, J. and Wiseman, R. (1999) Does psi exist? Lack of replication of an anomalous process of information transfer, *Psychological Bulletin*, 125, 387–91. Describes the replication failure of the meta-analysis of studies and the implications for future ganzfeld research.

References

Bem, D.J. and Honorton, C. (1994) Does psi exist? Replicable evidence for an anomalous process of information transfer, *Psychological Bulletin*, 115, 4–18.

Braud, W.G. and Schlitz, M. (1983) Psychokinetic influence on electrodermal activity, *Journal of Parapsychology*, 47, 95–119.

Chalmers, I. and Haynes, B. (1995) Reporting, updating, and correcting systematic reviews of the effects of health care. In I. Chalmers and D.G. Altman (eds) *Systematic Reviews*, London: BMJ, 86–95.

Guyatt, G.H., Sackett, D.L., Sinclair, J.C. *et al.* (1995) Users' guides to the medical literature IX. A method for grading health care recommendations, *Journal of the American Medical Association*, 274, 1800–4.

Hansen, G.P. (1990) Deception by subjects in psi research, *Journal of the American Society for Psychical Research*, 84, 25–80.

Honorton, C. (1985) Meta-analysis of psi ganzfeld research: a response to Hyman, *Journal of Parapsychology*, 49, 51–91.

Honorton, C. and Ferrari, D.C. (1989) Meta-analysis of forced-choice precognition experiments, *Journal of Parapsychology*, 53, 281–308.

Honorton, C. and Harper, S. (1974) Psi-mediated imagery and ideation in an experimental procedure for regulating perceptual input, *Journal of the American Society for Psychical Research*, 68, 156–68.

Hyman, R. (1985) The ganzfeld psi experiment: a critical appraisal, *Journal of Parapsychology*, 49, 3–49.

Hyman, R. and Honorton, C. (1986) A joint communiqué: the psi ganzfeld controversy, *Journal of Parapsychology*, 50, 350–64.

Keene, M.L. (1976) *The Psychic Mafia*, New York, NY: Dell.

Lawrence, T. (1993) Gathering in the sheep and goats: A meta-analysis of forced-choice sheep-goat ESP studies, 1947–1993, *The Parapsychological Association 36th Annual Convention Proceedings*, Fairhaven, MA: Parapsychological Association, 75–86.

Loftus, E. (1996) *Eyewitness Testimony*, Cambridge, MA: Harvard University Press.

Milton, J. (1995) Issues in the adoption of methodological safeguards in parapsychology experiments, *The Parapsychological Association 38th Annual Convention Proceedings*, Fairhaven, MA: Parapsychological Association, 226–43.

Milton, J. (1997) Meta-analysis of free-response studies without altered states of consciousness, *Journal of Parapsychology*, 61, 279–319.

Pratt, J.G. (1966) New ESP tests with Mrs. Gloria Stewart, *Journal of the American Society for Psychical Research*, 60, 321–39.

Radin, D.I. and Nelson, R.D. (1989) Evidence for consciousness-related anomalies in random physical systems, *Foundations of Physics*, 19, 1499–514.

Rosenthal, R. and Rubin, D.B. (1992–3) An effect size estimator for parapsychological research, *European Journal of Parapsychology*, 9, 1–11.

Schmeidler, G. and Edge, H. (1999) Should ganzfeld research continue to be crucial in the search for a replicable psi effect? Part II: Edited Ganzfeld debate, *Journal of Parapsychology*, Special Issue, 63, 4, 335–88.

Willin, M.J. (1996) A ganzfeld experiment using musical targets, *Journal of the Society for Psychical Research*, 61, 1–17.

Zusne, L. and Jones, W.H. (1989) *Anomalistic Psychology: A Study of Magical Thinking*, Hillsdale, NJ: Lawrence Erlbaum.

Editor's note

* See p. 46 for reference to recent ganzfeld meta-analyses and the ensuing debate on experimental results in this area.

Chapter 3

Meta-analyses

Deborah L. Delanoy

A vast array of parapsychological work has been conducted over the past century. Summarising and describing parts of this work have been greatly aided by recent meta-analyses of some areas of parapsychological research. Meta-analysis of some groups of experimental studies has provided a way of assessing the overall significance of a large number of studies (i.e. examining the likelihood that the outcomes are due to chance), arriving at an estimate of the magnitude of the effect being examined (i.e. determining the effect size of an experimental outcome), and has aided in uncovering trends and patterns contained within the databases. (See Chapter 2 for a discussion of meta-analytic procedures, including the procedure's strengths and weaknesses.)

Below, the findings of meta-analyses of nine parapsychological databases are discussed. All of the key meta-analyses have been fully published in refereed journals. They represent a variety of different experimental procedures. The databases include extrasensory perception (ESP) and psychokinesis (PK) studies, as well as some of the research relating psi performance to personality. Collectively these studies represent a sizeable proportion of the parapsychological experimental literature conducted over the last sixty years.

Ganzfeld studies

The ganzfeld technique aims to help percipients obtain ESP impressions. The ganzfeld may be psi-conducive by helping a participant to better direct their attention to their internal processes and thereby become more aware of subtle ESP impressions which might otherwise be drowned-out by our normal, more noticeable, sensory input (Honorton 1977). Ganzfeld stimulation can bring on a mildly altered state of consciousness, often thought to be similar in experience to the hypnagogic state. While receiving this stimulus, the percipient says out loud all their mental experiences (these are referred to as 'mentations'), with the goal of receiving impressions of a sensorially isolated and remotely located target picture or short video clip.

The target is frequently being watched by another (a 'sender') who attempts to mentally convey impressions of the target to the percipient (or receiver).

These studies utilise a 'free-response' methodology. Having no information about the target content, percipients are free to respond to any and all impressions they experience. The most common method of analysis used in ganzfeld studies is for the percipient or an independent judge(s) to compare the impressions obtained during the stimulus period to four different target pictures/video clips. Of these four potential targets, one is a duplicate of the actual target, and the other three are decoys. Having no information about the identity of the actual target, the percipient or independent judge looks for similarities between the mentation and the four pictures. The pictures are then ranked or rated according to the degree of observed correspondence. A 'hit' is scored if the actual target is chosen as showing the most similarity to the mentation. There is a one in four chance of correctly identifying the actual target by chance alone (i.e. chance = 25 per cent 'hit rate'). The outcome of a ganzfeld study is then based upon whether similarities between the percipient's impressions and the actual target enable the target to be correctly identified significantly more often than chance would allow. For further information regarding this experimental technique, procedural details and methods of analysis, see Honorton (1985) and Honorton *et al.* (1990).

Debate

The ESP ganzfeld studies are probably the most controversial and frequently analysed group of parapsychological studies. This 'debate' started with an initial exchange about the quality and true replication rate of the ganzfeld studies between a leading ganzfeld researcher, Honorton, and a critic of this work, Hyman. Honorton and Hyman each made meta-analyses of these studies and arrived at different conclusions. Subsequently many other 'pro' and 'con' evaluations and commentaries have been published.

Hyman (1985) found a significant psi outcome in his meta-analysis of the ganzfeld studies but he also found a significant correlation between study outcomes and flaws. Given this, he concluded that the apparent success of the ganzfeld technique was an artefact due to flaws contained in the ganzfeld studies and thus it did not represent an ESP effect. Honorton's (1985) meta-analysis of twenty-eight ganzfeld studies also obtained a highly significant overall ESP effect, but did not find any significant relationship between study quality and outcome. These differing interpretations of the database show the importance of the flaw analysis procedure, and illustrate how different coding procedures and/or categories can lead to different outcomes. In these meta-analyses neither author was blind to study outcome when they performed the flaw coding, and thus it is possible that their personal biases may have influenced their coding to some degree. Indeed, Honorton did criticise Hyman's flaw categorisations, and additionally a psychometrician, Saunders (1985), notes faults in Hyman's statistical analyses. Honorton's analysis found a large, highly significant overall combined z-score for the twenty-eight ganzfeld studies included in his meta-analysis (Stouffer $z = 6.6$, $p < 10^{-9}$); that is, the odds against this being a chance, random finding are over one thousand million to one. The effect sizes from these twenty-eight studies were homogeneous overall (across the studies) and they were consistent across the different experimenters who had conducted the studies.

In an attempt to resolve the disagreement, Rosenthal, an independent observer of the debate who wished to promote the use of meta-analysis in the social sciences and was neither a proponent nor a sceptic of psi phenomena, conducted his own meta-analysis of the database. Rosenthal (1986) found an overall, combined z-score of 6.6 for the twenty-eight ganzfeld studies. His file-drawer estimate concurred with Honorton's, requiring 423 unreported studies, with no effect (i.e. $z = 0$), to reduce the significance of the database to chance. After considering the possible influence of methodological flaws on study outcome, Rosenthal estimated the overall hit rate of the studies to be 33 per cent (where chance expectancy was 25 per cent), with an estimated effect size of 0.18. These findings led Rosenthal to conclude that 'it would be implausible to entertain the null hypothesis' (p. 333), that is, there is a genuine effect in these studies.

To explore the possible impact of a file-drawer effect, a sceptic, Blackmore (1980), conducted a survey to discover the number of unreported ganzfeld studies (i.e. the size of the file-drawer problem), prior to the Honorton/Hyman debate. Blackmore found thirty-two unreported studies, with twelve being uncompleted, and one which could not be analysed. Of the nineteen remaining studies, fourteen were judged to have adequate methodology, and of these five (i.e. 36 per cent) obtained significant results. Blackmore concluded that 'the bias introduced by selective reporting of ESP ganzfeld studies is not a major contributor to the overall proportion of significant results' (Blackmore 1980, p. 217).

Subsequently, Hyman and Honorton (1986) agreed that there was an overall effect in the database, but they 'agreed to disagree' about whether this effect may have been influenced by methodological flaws. They concluded that more studies, using a set of controls they documented, needed to be conducted before making any final verdict about the database.

Autoganzfeld studies

The subsequent autoganzfeld studies were designed to meet the controls agreed upon by Hyman and Honorton (1986), and placed much of the experimental procedure under computer-automated control. Honorton's

Psychophysical Research Laboratory (PRL) conducted 355 autoganzfeld sessions using eight different experimenters. These sessions obtained similar findings to the earlier studies (Honorton *et al.* 1990; see also the meta-analysis by Bem and Honorton 1994). Overall, the autoganzfeld sessions obtained a hit rate of 34.4 per cent, with a per trial effect size of 0.20 (the overall, combined studies $z = 3.89$, $p = 0.00005$). The effect sizes by series and by experimenter were both homogeneous, and performance was consistent across the 241 participants who contributed to the database. Indeed, the autoganzfeld studies, with improved methodology, obtained slightly better ESP scoring than the earlier studies. Combining the autoganzfeld and the earlier ganzfeld studies resulted in a highly significant overall effect across the thirty-nine studies (Stouffer $z = 7.39$, $p = 9 \times 10^{-14}$).

In both the earlier and autoganzfeld studies, various procedural factors were analysed to assess their potential impact on study outcome. These analyses helped to identify two procedures that may contribute to a successful ganzfeld outcome. As the autoganzfeld findings are consistent with those of the initial meta-analysis, the combined results from both these databases are presented here. First, sessions using dynamic targets (i.e. a video clip or a series of thematically related slides) obtained significantly better ESP scoring than sessions using still target pictures (dynamic targets: 37 per cent hit rate; static targets: 27 per cent hit rate). Another analysis examining the impact of sender/receiver pairing found slightly better ESP performance when the sender and receiver were friends than when the sender was a laboratory-assigned staff member (35 per cent hit rate vs. 29 per cent).

Thus there was consistency between the outcomes from the earlier ganzfeld studies and those of the autoganzfeld, both in terms of significant overall ESP performance, and with regard to the two moderating variables. In commenting upon the apparent continuing replication of the ESP ganzfeld effect, Hyman (1994, p. 19) stated 'we have to wait for independent replication of these experiments before we can conclude that a replicable anomaly or psi has been demonstrated'.

Accordingly, Milton and Wiseman (1999) conducted a meta-analysis of thirty studies that were produced after those included in the Honorton *et al.* (1990) analysis. No significant overall effect was found and the previously observed effect size was not replicated. In considering reasons why the ganzfeld effect was not replicated in the later studies, Milton (1999) noted as a possible contributing factor the lack of a well-defined set of procedures necessary to produce the ganzfeld effect. Indeed, in a published e-mail discussion about the ganzfeld debate initiated by Milton (1999), it was observed (Schmeidler and Edge 1999) that some of these thirty studies had marked procedural differences from the 'standard' ganzfeld study, using the ganzfeld procedure definition found in Bem and Honorton (1994). Criticism of the Milton and Wiseman meta-analysis has led to further pro and con discussions (e.g. Milton 1999, Schmeidler and Edge 1999, Storm 2000, Storm and Ertel 2001, Milton and Wiseman 2001, Storm and Ertel 2002).

The most recent addition to this debate is a meta-analysis by Bem *et al.* (2001) examining ten studies produced after those included in the Milton and Wiseman database. Bem *et al.* (2001) found a significant combined outcome from these ten studies (Stouffer $z = 3.97$, $p = 3.5 \times 10^{-5}$), with a hit rate of 37 per cent. Adding these to the studies of Milton and Wiseman's meta-analysis, the forty ganzfeld experiments' combined outcome remained significant (Stouffer $z = 2.59$, $p = 0.0048$), with a hit rate of 30 per cent. However, the mean effect size (0.05) was so small that it fell outside of the confidence intervals of the previous effect (Bem and Honorton 1994), representing another failure to replicate. Bem *et al.* (2001) conducted a further analysis of these forty studies to see whether procedural variations may have contributed to replication difficulties. They found a subset of twenty-nine studies that, following the standard autoganzfeld procedure most closely (as described in Bem and Honorton 1994), had a mean effect size of 0.10, which did fall within the confidence intervals of the original database. In contrast, the nine non-standard replications obtained a mean effect size of –0.10, with there being a significant difference between the two effect sizes ($U = 90.5$, $p = 0.02$, one-tailed).

This debate helps illustrate how variations can exist between different meta-analyses of the same database by different researchers, and how subsequent meta-analyses of new studies may not necessarily agree with the findings of previous meta-analyses. Also, it highlights how meta-analysis can assist in better understanding apparent failures to replicate, for example the Bem *et al.* 2001 finding regarding the impact of procedural differences upon the ganzfeld replication findings. Further experimentation will undoubtedly shed more light upon the overall outcome of the ganzfeld studies.

Free-response ESP studies without altered states of consciousness

Remote viewing studies

Utts (1995) noted the conceptual similarities between ganzfeld studies and remote viewing studies. Both are types of free-response ESP studies in which a receiver attempts to gain information about a remote target. The primary differences between remote viewing and ganzfeld studies are that in remote viewing studies the receiver is in an ordinary waking state of consciousness (no ganzfeld stimulation is received), most commonly there is no sender (whereas most ganzfeld studies have a sender) and session outcome is usually determined by an independent judge (in most ganzfeld studies, the receiver does their own judging). Utts (1995) conducted an overview of the US government-sponsored remote viewing research conducted at Stanford Research Institute (now referred to as SRI International) and Science Applications International Corporation (SAIC). Using effect size as the most reliable measure of replication (see Utts 1988, 1991), an overall effect size of 0.21 was found for the 770 remote viewing trials conducted at SRI, with the 445 trials conducted at SAIC producing an effect size of 0.23. A detailed examination of various possible methodological flaws led Utts to state that they did not influence the overall effect sizes. In reporting back to the American Institutes for Research who had commissioned Utts's analysis (at the request of the US Congress and Central Intelligence Agency) she concluded 'Using the standards applied to any other area of science, it is concluded that psychic functioning has been well established. The statistical results of the studies examined are far beyond what is expected by chance' (Utts 1995, p. 289).

In discussing the similarities between the outcomes from the remote viewing studies and the ganzfeld studies, Utts (1995) noted that the two methods of testing provided conceptual replication for each other, beyond the overall outcomes of the respective databases. For example, the effect size for all inexperienced autoganzfeld receivers (from Honorton's PRL data) and novice SRI remote viewers was 0.17 and 0.16 respectively. Similarly, for experienced, previously successful PRL ganzfeld receivers and experienced, successful SRI remote viewers it was 0.35 and 0.38 respectively.

The critic Hyman (1995) was commissioned to review the remote viewing database along with Utts. While his overall interpretation of the outcomes is that he does not believe the existence of ESP has yet been proven, he states that the remote viewing data provide the best data yet in support of a psi hypothesis. Considering the remote viewing data along with other 'contemporary findings', such as the ganzfeld, Hyman concedes that 'something beyond odd statistical hiccups is taking place. I also have to admit that I do not have a ready explanation for these observed effects' (Hyman 1995, p. 334). Additionally, Hyman thinks that it would be worthwhile to see if the remote viewing effects could be replicated at other laboratories, using other independent judges. While Hyman was generally impressed with the methodology of the remote viewing studies, the methodology of one of these studies was criticised by Wiseman and Milton (1998). These criticisms have been refuted and further discussed by May (1998) and Wiseman and Milton (1999).

Free-response waking state studies

Milton (1997) conducted a meta-analysis of free-response ESP studies where the receiver was in a waking, non-altered state of consciousness (non-ASC). This database included some of the remote viewing studies included in Utts's (1995) review, as well as the much larger database of which they were a subset. In total, seventy-eight studies were included in the meta-analysis. A highly significant overall effect was found with a combined Stouffer $z = 5.72$ ($p < 5.4 \times 10^{-9}$). The mean study effect size was 0.16, and it was concluded that methodological flaws had no notable effect on producing the positive outcome. Furthermore the studies were homogenous across investigators and, after the removal of three outlying studies, the mean study effect size was homogenous. A file-drawer estimate required an additional 866 null studies to reduce the overall significance level to chance. Milton thought it most unlikely that there would be this number of unreported studies.

Comparing these outcomes to those of the ganzfeld database, the twenty-eight ganzfeld studies included in Honorton's (1985) original meta-analysis produced a non-significantly higher effect size (0.26) than did the non-ASC database (effect size = 0.16). Yet the non-ASC effect size is somewhat (non-significantly) larger than the effect size of 0.10 found for the standard procedure ganzfeld studies of the Bem *et al.* (2001) meta-analysis.

Milton did note a possible confounding artefact in this database as 96 per cent of the studies failed to report whether their analyses were pre-planned. This may simply represent the authors failing to report data desired by the meta-analyst, in which case it would not impact upon the reported outcomes. However, an alternative explanation would be that analyses for these studies were not pre-planned which could result in the reported outcomes being inflated due to multiple analysis. No decision regarding the correct interpretation of this possibility can be made at this stage, although, if the effect sizes found in conceptually similar databases, such as the remote viewing studies, are taken into consideration, the relative consistency of effect sizes across databases could be seen as lending support to the validity of the obtained 0.16 effect size for the non-ASC database.

Precognition ESP studies

Throughout history individuals have claimed to be able to 'foretell' the future. Others have reported experiencing premonitions of events before they actually occur. While many of these claims and experiences are likely to be due to misinterpretation, misrepresentation or other flaws of human reasoning and perception, there are experimental findings which suggest that precognition may occur. (See Morris 1986 and Wiseman and Morris 1995 for a summary of ways we can be deceived or deceive ourselves into interpreting normal events as being paranormal.)

Honorton and Ferrari (1989) conducted a meta-analysis of 309 precognition studies, published between 1935 and 1987. These studies all used a 'forced-choice' methodology, where the percipient is aware of the possible target choices and identifies one of them as their answer. Precognition studies require the percipient to give their answer before any target has been randomly chosen. Thus the percipients' answers are to targets which do not exist when they make their response. These studies are thought by some to be methodologically superior to other ESP studies as there is no possibility of the subject 'cheating', or receiving any subtle cues about a target which has not yet been chosen when responses are made.

The 309 studies included in this meta-analysis were conducted by 62 different senior experimenters, involved over 50,000 percipients and included nearly two million individual trials. The mean effect size per trial was small (es = 0.02), but positive. The overall, combined effect from these studies was highly significant (Stouffer $z = 11.41$, $p = 6.3 \times 10^{-25}$). No significant relationship was found between study outcome and study quality, although there was a slight trend for better quality studies to obtain higher effect sizes, contrary to the usual claims of critics. A 'fail-safe N' file-drawer estimate required 14,268 unreported, null studies to reduce the significance of these studies to chance levels. This ratio of forty-six unreported, null studies for each reported study, far exceeds the five to one 'safe' ratio recommended by Rosenthal.

Moderating variables

The precognition meta-analysis found four 'moderating' variables that related systematically to study outcome. The first variable involved the participant population. Studies using percipients selected on the basis of *good ESP performance* in previous experimental sessions obtained significantly better ESP effects than those studies using unselected participants. There was no significant difference in quality between studies using selected and unselected percipients, a finding contrary to some claims by critics who suggest that selected, skilled participants might be producing their psi effects by fraudulent means. Another variable was whether the participants were tested individually or in groups. Studies using *individual testing* procedures obtained significantly higher study quality than those utilising group testing procedures.

A further moderating variable addressed when participants receive *feedback* about the accuracy of their responses. There were four feedback categories used in this meta-analysis: no feedback; delayed feedback (usually via the post); feedback given after a sequence of responses (often after twenty-five responses); and feedback given after each response. Of the 104 studies which supplied the necessary information, there was a linear and clearly significant correlation between the precognition effect and immediacy of feedback, with stronger ESP being associated with more rapidly received feedback. A related finding involved the *time interval* between the subject's responses and the target selection. This finding is confounded by when feedback was given, as time duration between the response and target generation may co-vary with when feedback is given (i.e. when feedback was given after every response, the time interval between response and target selection would have to be shorter than was necessarily the case when feedback was given after a sequence of calls, or a month after the responses had been made). There are seven different interval categories (intervals between response and target generation), varying from a millisecond to months. A significant decline in precognition effect sizes occurred as the time interval between response and target selection increased.

In summarising the precognition meta-analyses findings, Honorton and Ferrari (1989) conclude that the 'forced-choice precognition experiments confirms the existence of a small but highly significant precognition effect' (p. 300). Furthermore, they concluded that the most important outcome of the meta-analysis was the identification of moderating variables. These provide guidelines for future research, and also serve to expand our understanding of the phenomenon.

Comparing precognition and clairvoyance studies

Meta-analysis has been used to explore questions about potential psi functioning mechanisms as well as to evaluate overall outcomes and find patterns in the data. Steinkamp *et al.* (1998) conducted a meta-analysis comparing the outcomes of forced-choice precognition studies and clairvoyant studies. Clairvoyant studies have no sender, and thus the receiver is thought to obtain the information about the target in 'real-time' directly from the target, as opposed to obtaining information from another mind as in ganzfeld studies that use a sender, or from the future as in precognition trials. Thus in clairvoyant trials the target information already exists at the time the response is generated. Nonetheless, it is an open question whether there is any difference between the underlying processes of clairvoyant and precognition studies. For example, all seemingly 'real-time' clairvoyant studies could be explained by individuals using their precognition to look ahead into the future and learn what they are told about the target identity in the future, at the time of feedback. If this were the case, one would not expect to find any differences in effect size between clairvoyant and precognition studies. (See Steinkamp *et al.* 1998 for information about other models of and predictions about clairvoyance and precognition.)

In this meta-analysis the relationship between forced-choice precognition and clairvoyance studies was explored by examining experiments that included both types of ESP. Looking at the most comparable data from twenty-two study pairs of clairvoyant and precognitive trials, both types of ESP obtained significant, cumulative effects (precognition: Stouffer $z = 4.15$, $p = 2 \times 10^{-5}$; clairvoyance: Stouffer $z = 2.86$, $p = 0.004$). Additionally, the effect sizes of the two were nearly identical, with an effect size of 0.010 for precognition and 0.009 for clairvoyance. No significant evidence was found that methodological flaws had helped produce the overall effects. In interpreting these outcomes, the authors note that it would be premature to draw a firm conclusion from such a relatively small database and that different coding methods could lead to different findings. Nonetheless, they state that the burden of proof lies with those who would suggest that there is a difference between the effect sizes produced by clairvoyant and precognition studies.

Direct mental interactions with living systems (DMILS)

Direct mental interactions with living systems (DMILS) research involves testing procedures where a person (an 'agent') tries to interact with a biological target system, for example, another person's physiological responses or a behavioural response. In DMILS studies the biological target organism is located in an environment that prevents any physical contact with the agent from occurring. The target's activity is monitored continuously while the agent, during randomly interspersed interaction and non-interaction (i.e. control) periods, tries to mentally influence the target's activity in a pre-specified manner. The target system has no contact with the agent, and thus no information about the timing or goal orientation (e.g. interaction or non-interaction) of the agent's mental intentions. When human physiological responses are the target system, the responder's only goal during the experimental session is to remain passively alert and to mentally wish that their physiology will unconsciously respond appropriately to the agent's distant intentions. The mental strategies used by the agent to interact with the remote, shielded target can include wishing and willing the desired changes to manifest in the target, mentally imagining the desired outcome, and in some instances simply paying attention to the target system. The randomised order of the interaction or non-interaction periods is usually conveyed to the agent by a message on a computer monitor; the monitor may also convey to the agent the actual recordings of the target's activity, thereby providing on-going feedback about the effects of their mental intentions upon the remote target system. The experimental design eliminates possible confounding factors such as recording errors, placebo effects, confounding internal rhythms and chance correspondences (Braud and Schlitz 1991).

Recent DMILS research has been procedurally based on the work conducted by Braud and his colleagues, as described in a meta-analytic summary of thirty-seven of their experiments, conducted between the late 1970s and early 1990s (Braud and Schlitz 1991). These studies involved thirteen different experimenters, 655 sessions, and utilised seven different target systems, including various human physiological responses (e.g. electrodermal activity and blood pressure), fish orientation, mammal locomotion, and the rate of hemolysis of *in vitro* human red blood cells. The most frequently used response system was human electrodermal activity (EDA), which reflects arousal levels. In these studies, the agent tries to increase or decrease the responder's EDA by attempting to remotely 'calm' or 'activate' the responder during the randomly scheduled interaction periods. These thirty-seven experiments were very successful, with a highly significant overall, combined outcome (Stouffer $z = 7.72$, $p = 2.58 \times 10^{-14}$). The mean per session effect size is 0.33. Although these thirty-seven studies were conducted by thirteen different experimenters, they were all performed at the same laboratory. The success of these studies prompted similar work at other laboratories.

These replication attempts have largely used EDA as the response system. A more recent review of the EDA DMILS literature (Schlitz and Braud 1997) found nineteen EDA 'calm/activate' studies that had achieved a significant combined Stouffer $z = 4.82$ ($p = 0.0000007$). Eleven studies were found that had used EDA to assess whether individuals could detect when they were being remotely stared at via a closed circuit camera system. These remote staring studies also obtained a significant, cumulative effect (Stouffer $z = 3.87$, $p = 0.00005$). The mean study effect sizes from the two groups of EDA studies were identical (effect size = 0.25).

The methodology of some of these studies has been criticised from a psychophysiological perspective (Schmidt and Walach 2000), with most of these criticisms relating to shortcomings in the EDA measurement procedure or the reporting thereof. These criticisms have been useful in promoting better methodological practices in EDA DMILS studies. Nonetheless, as most of the identified flaws would have impacted equally on both the interaction and non-interaction periods within a session, they are unlikely to account for the significance of the database. The most recent meta-analyses took a highly conservative approach to the database, stating that their goal was to conduct a 'critical evaluation from a sceptical perspective' (Schmidt *et al.* 2004, p. 236). Nevertheless they reported significant effects in both the remote staring and calm/activate data sets, albeit with reduced mean effect sizes of 0.13 ($p = 0.1$, 15 staring studies) and 0.11 ($p = 0.001$, 36 calm/activate studies).

The DMILS studies appear to demonstrate psi functioning on an unconscious, autonomic level. Until now this chapter has only presented data that required conscious processing of information to make a response. The DMILS data demonstrate that conscious processing of psi information does not appear to be a necessary component to obtain significant psi effects. This interpretation is supported by the few studies that have made a systematic comparison between conscious and unconscious (e.g. psychophysiological) psi responses. All of these studies obtained significant psi effects from the unconscious, physiological responses, but no significant effect was found in the conscious response measure (Tart 1974, Targ and Puthoff 1974, Delanoy and Sah 1994).

'Mind over matter' meta-analyses

Meta-analyses of two types of studies dealing with psychokinetic (PK) effects follow. Both these databases involve participants attempting to make a random system behave in a non-random manner.

Dice

The first group of studies involves people trying to influence the outcome of falling dice. For example, participants may try to make a rolled die land so that a six face is uppermost. This work was first suggested to one of the founders of experimental parapsychology, J.B. Rhine, by gamblers who claimed to be able to influence the outcome in dice-throwing situations in gaming casinos.

Radin and Ferrari (1991) conducted a meta-analysis of 148 dice studies conducted between 1935 and 1987. This database also included thirty-one control studies in which no conscious influence on outcome was attempted. The results found a highly significant overall effect for the combined experimental influence studies (Stouffer $z = 18.2$), with a small, mean study effect size of 0.012 (quality weighted). The combined results of the control studies did not differ from chance (Stouffer $z = 0.18$). Looking at eleven different study quality measures, there was a tendency for effect sizes to decrease as study quality increased, although the relationship was not significant.

Another methodological problem affecting this database is that the probability of obtaining a specific outcome is not equally distributed across all the die faces, as the six typically has the least mass and is thus most likely to come up (i.e. the six is often marked by six pips cut into the die, making the six face lighter than the other die faces that have fewer pips). To assess the possible influence of this 'non-random' aspect of dice throwing, a subset of sixty-nine studies, where the targets were balanced equally across the six die faces, was examined. A significant overall effect was still obtained (Stouffer $z = 7.617$, $p < 10^{-11}$) in this subset of studies. The effect sizes of these sixty-nine studies were generally consistent across different study quality measures. A file-drawer analysis reveals that a twenty to one ratio of unreported, non-significant studies for each reported study was required to reduce the database to chance expectations. The authors conclude 'that the aggregate evidence suggests the presence of a weak, genuine mental effect' (Radin and Ferrari 1991, p. 80).

RNG

The second 'mind over matter' meta-analysis involves influencing a random number generator (RNG) to behave in a non-random manner. To accomplish this, a participant attempts to mentally influence, in accordance with pre-specified instructions, an RNG which drives a visual display. Participants are often instructed to try to influence the visual display using mental strategies similar to those used in DMILS studies (described above), without necessarily thinking about the random source that is driving the display. For example, the display could consist of a circle of sequentially flashing lights and the participant's goal is to keep the lights flashing in a clockwise order by visualising and wishing this to occur. In the absence of any PK effect, the random source should result in a roughly equal number of clockwise and anticlockwise light flashes. The randomness of the RNG is usually provided by radioactive decay, electronic noise or pseudo-random number sequence seeded with true random sources, and the RNGs are monitored frequently to ensure true random output. The participant may start a 'trial' by means of a button push, which initiates the collection of a fixed-length sequence of data. For each data sequence a z-score may then be computed.

This meta-analysis, by Radin and Nelson (1989, see also Utts 1991), involved the largest of the parapsychological databases, encompassing 832 studies. Of these, 597 were experimental studies, where the participant attempts to influence the outcome, and 235 were control studies, where there was no influence attempt. The mean effect size for the experimental studies was very small (0.0003), but it was significantly higher than the mean effect size for the control studies ($z = 4.1$). The mean effect size for the control studies did not significantly differ from chance (control study = 0.00004). Using sixteen study quality measures, effect size did not significantly co-vary with study quality. Using a common procedure in meta-analysis, 17 per cent of these studies were identified as outliers and deleted in order to obtain homogeneity of effect sizes. Of these deleted studies, 77 per cent deviated from the overall mean in the positive (i.e. desired outcome or PK) direction. The file-drawer estimate for this database is enormous, requiring 54,000 null, unreported studies to reduce the observed effect to chance levels. Given these findings, Radin and Nelson concluded that 'it is difficult to avoid the conclusion that under certain circumstances, consciousness interacts with random physical systems' (p. 1512).

In contrast to the Radin and Nelson findings, the most recent meta-analysis of RNG studies (Steinkamp *et al.* 2002) found no differences between the effect sizes of 357 experimental studies and 142 control studies. Also, the experimental studies were extremely heterogeneous (i.e. the studies' outcomes differed from each other to a very significant degree). A significant correlation was found between effect size and study size, suggesting that any experimental effect stemmed mainly from the smaller studies. Various moderating variables were examined, and the authors concluded that their interpretation required further, more detailed analyses. However, information about this recent meta-analysis is based upon a conference presentation, and the findings should be treated with caution pending refereed journal publication.

ESP and personality

Parapsychologists have long been interested in exploring why some people report having more psi experiences in their everyday life than do others. Also, while most experimental work is done with volunteer participants who have not been chosen on the basis of their supposed psi ability, findings such as those from the precognition meta-analysis (described above) indicate that some people appear to do better in experimental psi tests than others. One approach to examining possible reasons for these differences involves exploring the relationship between personality and psi ability. In looking for a relationship with psi-scoring, one of the most commonly researched personality traits is extraversion. (For reviews relating other personality factors to psi-scoring, see Palmer 1977 and 1978, and Broughton 1991.)

Extraversion

Extraversion is a personality trait that has been much studied in relation to psi performance. Honorton *et al.* (1998) published a meta-analysis of sixty studies examining this relationship. Prior to this meta-analysis, several descriptive reviews of this database had concluded that extraverts performed better than introverts on psi tasks, leading to a widespread belief among psi researchers that extraversion was a psi-conducive trait (see reviews by Eysenck (1967), Palmer (1977) and Sargent (1981)). However, the ability of meta-analysis to identify flaws and modifying variables led Honorton and his co-authors to arrive at a different conclusion.

Initially the meta-analysis did find a significant overall effect, but the effect sizes were heterogeneous (not consistent with each other). So, the investigators divided the studies into smaller groups according to various procedural variables to see if they could discover the source of the heterogeneity. Separating the forty-five studies using forced-choice procedures from the fourteen studies using free-response methods revealed significant effects in both groups of studies. But again, both groups had heterogeneous effect sizes. The next division of these two groups of studies was made to examine whether testing participants individually or in groups had any impact on the outcomes. This analysis revealed that, of the forced-choice studies, twenty-one studies had tested participants individually, and had heterogeneous effect sizes. In the twenty-four forced-choice studies where participants were tested in groups, there was homogeneity (the effect sizes were consistent with each other), but there was no significant extraversion/psi effect. In other words, the only studies showing consistent results were those that did not find a relationship between extraversion and psi.

A flaw analysis shed more light on these surprising findings. In the forced-choice database the significant, but inconsistent, effect was due to flawed studies in which the extraversion measure had been given after the ESP test. In other words, the participants knew how they had performed on their psi task before they completed the extraversion questionnaire. This is a flaw because knowledge of their psi results may have influenced how they completed the extraversion questionnaire. This finding raises the possibility that the apparent psi/extraversion relationship was due to psychological, as opposed to paranormal, factors.

The previous descriptive reviews which had found a significant, positive relationship between extraversion and psi-scoring had failed to uncover the inconsistency in the degree to which this effect was present in these studies and the relationship between study quality and study outcome. The findings from their meta-analysis led Honorton *et al.* to conclude that the extraversion/psi relationship in forced-choice studies was artefactual.

The investigators then turned their attention to the fourteen free-response extraversion studies, and again found a significant but heterogeneous extraversion/psi outcome. Dividing the studies according to individual or group testing procedures revealed that the two studies employing group testing were responsible for the heterogeneity. The results for the twelve studies that tested participants individually were homogeneous and significant. Eleven of these studies documented the presentation order of the psi test and extraversion questionnaire. In all of these studies, the extraversion questionnaire was given prior to the ESP test, thereby avoiding the flaw contained in the forced-choice studies. These eleven studies show a significant homogeneous extraversion/ESP relationship ($z = 4.57$, $p = 0.000005$). After completing the extraversion/ESP meta-analysis, Honorton *et al.* examined the autoganzfeld database to see if they could confirm the relationship. For the 221 autoganzfeld trials for which they had extraversion data, they found a significant ESP/extraversion relationship, which was consistent with the findings from the free-response extraversion meta-analysis.

However, these findings have not gone unquestioned. Palmer and Carpenter (1998) argued that the meta-analytic findings were confounded by the test situation, specifically whether the participants were tested in groups or individually. From their analyses they argue that the extraversion–ESP relationship in forced-choice studies is valid, and the forced-choice extraversion–ESP effect is of a similar size to that found in the free-response studies.

Discussion

These nine databases represent only some of the recent meta-analyses that have been performed on parapsychological research. These were selected not only because they represent a large part of the psi experimental work, but also because they reveal important patterns in the data and involve a variety of parapsychological effects.

The effect sizes in these studies vary from the very small (e.g. RNG-PK) to moderate (e.g. DMILS) in size. Yet even the smaller effect sizes appear to be reliably found in the databases in the majority of the reported analyses, as demonstrated by the homogeneity of the effect sizes. The robustness of the psi-scoring found in these databases is reflected by the size of the combined *z*-scores. It should be emphasised that the size of an effect is not a good indicator of its potential meaningfulness or applicability. An example that may be familiar to readers involves a medical study investigating whether aspirin could help prevent heart attacks. This study was prematurely ended because the effectiveness of the treatment was so clearly demonstrated after six months of trials that the investigators thought it would be unethical to withhold the treatment from the control group. Indeed, the findings from the study were heralded as a major medical breakthrough. Due to a very large sample size of over 22,000 participants the study was highly significant ($p < 0.0000015$). However, the effect size from this study is 0.068, considerably smaller than some of the effect sizes found in the psi literature (the aspirin study is discussed in Utts 1991).

In considering the magnitude of the effect sizes reported for these meta-analyses, it must be remembered that they are not directly comparable across the databases. This is due to each meta-analysis being based upon different measurements within each database. For example, a ganzfeld session will typically produce a large number of verbal impressions during a 30- to 35-minute mentation period, with these many responses then being 'condensed' into a single 'hit or miss' data point; whereas in a forced-choice procedure, such as Zener card guessing, each guess could be treated as a separate 'hit or miss' response, generating many data points during a comparable period of time. Similarly, while both the RNG-PK and DMILS meta-analyses report the 'mean per trial' effect sizes, a trial represents very different things in these two study groups. In the RNG-PK meta-analysis, the very small effect size is based on a unit of data collection which took far less than a second for the RNG to generate; whereas the much larger effect size found in the DMILS studies is based on all the data generated over a 20- to 30-minute period. Thus, it should not necessarily be concluded that the psi effect is greater in DMILS studies than in RNG-PK studies, because their units of measurements (the trials) are not directly comparable.

Implications

What do these findings tell us about psi? Taken as a whole, they indicate that while the experimental psi effects are generally small, they are nonetheless robust, in that they are found in many studies. In other words, these data can be interpreted as representing generally small, but genuine effects. Furthermore, there appear to be consistent trends and patterns in these databases. The modifying variables revealed in the precognition studies, the consistency of the free-response ESP findings, the variety of target systems showing DMILS effects, the relationships between personality and ESP scoring, and the largely robust PK findings all point to lawful relationships, and help us better understand the phenomenon.

This is not to say that these effects are consistently found in meta-analyses of different parts of a given database, for example meta-analysis of more recent studies may arrive at different findings than one based on earlier studies. Furthermore, the same meta-analysis may give rise to different interpretations, and different meta-analyses of the same database will not necessarily produce the same outcomes. All these points are demonstrated by the various analyses of the ganzfeld database. Nonetheless, the majority of the meta-analyses have shown positive psi-scoring outcomes, which tend not to be related to study quality. Thus, these meta-analyses generally support the perspective that the reported psi findings are not artefacts due to poor methodology.

The variations found in some of the reported outcomes within a single database may relate to the fact that the mechanisms involved in producing these apparent psi effects are still unknown. In fact the phenomenon itself cannot even be clearly defined. For example, the division of psi effects into the two broad categories of ESP and PK is done to help us conceptualise these effects, with these terms representing 'working hypotheses'. As of yet there are no widely accepted theoretical distinctions between ESP and PK. In fact, if the effects found in the precognition database represent a genuine ability to gain information about future events, then many of the results presented in this chapter could be viewed in terms of an ESP precognition effect.

For example, as the name suggests, the RNG-PK database has traditionally been conceptualised as representing a mind over matter, PK influencing effect. However, May *et al.* (1995) have proposed an alternative theory in which these effects represent precognition, not PK. This theory is called Decision Augmentation Theory and consists of the participant using their precognition to select the best time to start a trial to obtain a sequence of random events which will give them the desired outcome. In other words, via precognition, participants time their button pushes (which start a trial) to make use of the random fluctuations found in RNG systems to create a non-random outcome. Having analysed much of the RNG-PK database, May *et al.* (1995) have found support for this interpretation. The discussion introducing the clairvoyance and precognition meta-analysis should make it clear that precognition provides an alternative explanation for all research typically thought of as representing some form of ESP, including 'real-time' studies involving a sender. Although more research is needed before the role of senders in psi studies can be firmly established, it is evident that a sender is not a necessary component in ESP studies (see Palmer 1978 for information about successful ESP studies having no agent). On the other hand, models where real-time psi can present an alternative to precognition interpretations have been considered as well (see Morris 1982 for a discussion of these issues).

While there are many possible interpretations of these findings, our current knowledge is insufficient to support any one view over another. (Readers interested in theoretical parapsychology are referred to a review of this by Stokes (1987).) As the meta-analyses demonstrate, our knowledge and understanding of the phenomenon are growing, but still it would be very premature to conclude that they support a specific theory, philosophy or religious perspective. Of course, some believe that psi is a phenomenon which by its very nature will always defy explanation in terms of physics-based theories. But others, including most parapsychological researchers, would probably agree that, while psi is an exceedingly complex problem area, the mechanisms and processes that give rise to the significant psi experimental results will one day be understood.

Most of the parapsychological research conducted today is process-oriented, as opposed to proof-oriented. Process-oriented research is aimed at learning about how psi functions, as opposed to simply trying to demonstrate that psi has occurred in a study. This emphasis on process may be one reason why some more recent meta-analyses have shown smaller effects, as process-oriented research involves testing different variables to determine their impact upon the study outcome. Inevitably, some manipulations will prove less successful than others and this could lead to smaller effects when combining results across studies. Nonetheless, as the number of process-oriented studies accumulate, future meta-analyses should be able to help identify the key moderating variables. Eventually such process-oriented work should lead either to the clear identification of the variables that gave rise to the artefactual findings or to establishing that psi phenomena exist.

Conclusion

By normal scientific standards, these meta-analyses by and large establish that 'something' is happening in these studies. But is this 'something' psi, or, as critics have argued, merely currently unrecognised statistical problems and/or undetected methodological artefacts? If the latter, since parapsychology uses the same statistical and methodological principles as the other sciences, these 'problems' are likely affecting the findings of all scientific experiments, to an unknown degree. In this context it should be noted that parapsychological research is subjected to an unusual degree of scrutiny, and potential artefacts discovered in parapsychological research may go unrecognised in work that is subjected to a less rigorous examination. It could be argued that if parapsychological effects are artefactual, understanding these artefacts becomes increasingly important as the traditional sciences continue to examine smaller, more subtle and complex physical effects and systems. Alternatively, many think the general consistency of these findings and the emerging patterns they reveal argue forcibly for the conclusion that these studies represent a previously unrecognised, genuine ability of mind. If this interpretation is correct, these meta-analyses suggest that this ability could be subtly affecting our thoughts, actions, environment and even our physiology, to an unknown degree, without our conscious awareness.

Having reviewed well over a thousand experiments, some may feel disheartened to hear that more research is needed to understand the meaning and ramifications of these findings. But if viewed in terms of 'the larger picture' these many studies represent a very small amount of greatly under-funded work, conducted by very few researchers. Far more effort, work-hours, and money are devoted every year to cancer research, for example, than has been expended on the totality of over sixty years of research presented herein. Parapsychology is still a 'borderline' area of research, which has received remarkably little attention and funding from the mainstream scientific establishment. Each reader must judge for themselves whether these funding and research priorities are well placed. In the author's opinion, regardless of whether these findings are eventually found to represent currently unknown artefacts or psi, their potential significance to our everyday lives, as well as our understanding of ourselves and our universe, makes this work of utmost importance.

Recommended reading

Introductory

Broughton, R.S. (1991) *Parapsychology: The Controversial Science*, London: Rider. Well-written and highly recommended as a general introduction to experimental, and other, areas of parapsychological research.

Eysenck, H.J. and Sargent, C.L. (1993) *Explaining the Unexplained*, London: Prion. A more general overview.

Radin, D. (1997) *The Conscious Universe*, San Francisco: HarperEdge, Chs 4–9. Acccessible explanation of meta-analysis and evidence from meta-analyses of some parapsychological data sets.

Advanced

Krippner, S., Braud, W., Child, I.L., Palmer, J., Rao, K.R., Schlitz, M., White, R.A. and Utts, J. (1993) Demonstration research and meta-analysis in parapsychology, *Journal of Parapsychology*, 57, 275–86. A brief introduction to the role of meta-analysis in parapsychological research.

Milton, J., Schmeidler, G.E. and Edge, H. (1999) The ESP–Ganzfeld controversy, *Journal of Parapsychology*, 63, 308–88. Technical discussion illustrating technicalities of applying meta-analysis.

Utts, J. (1988) Successful replication versus statistical significance, *Journal of Parapsychology*, 52, 305–20. A clear consideration of key issues when considering experimental replication.

Utts, J. (1991) Replication and meta-analysis in parapsychology, *Statistical Science*, 6, 363–78. An excellent overview of meta-analysis and its use in parapsychology.

References

Bem, D.J. and Honorton, C. (1994) Does psi exist? Replicable evidence for an anomalous process of information transfer, *Psychological Bulletin*, 115, 4–18.

Bem, D.J., Palmer, J. and Broughton, R.S. (2001) Updating the ganzfeld database: is it a victim of its own success? *Journal of Parapsychology*, 65, 207–18.

Blackmore, S.J. (1980) The extent of selective reporting of ESP ganzfeld studies, *European Journal of Parapsychology*, 3, 213–20.

Braud, W.G. and Schlitz, M.J. (1991) Consciousness interactions with remote biological systems: anomalous intentionality effects, *Subtle Energies*, 2, 1, 1–46.

Broughton, R.S. (1991) *Parapsychology: The Controversial Science*, London: Rider.

Delanoy, D.L. and Sah, S. (1994) Cognitive and physiological psi responses to remote positive and neutral emotional states, *Proceedings of Presented Papers of the 37th Annual Parapsychological Association Convention*, 128–38.

Eysenck, H.J. (1967) Personality and extrasensory perception, *Journal of the Society for Psychical Research*, 44, 55–70.

Eysenck, H.J. and Sargent, C.L. (1993) *Explaining the Unexplained*, London: Prion.

Honorton, C. (1977) Psi and internal attention states. In B.B. Wolman (ed.) *Handbook of Parapsychology*, New York: Van Nostrand Reinhold, 435–72.

Honorton, C. (1985) Meta-analysis of psi ganzfeld research: a response to Hyman, *Journal of Parapsychology*, 49, 51–91.

Honorton, C. and Ferrari, D.C. (1989) Future telling: a meta-analysis of forced-choice precognition experiments, 1935–1987, *Journal of Parapsychology*, 35, 281–308.

Honorton, C., Berger, R.E., Varvoglis, M.P., Quant, M., Derr, P., Schechter, E.I. and Ferrari, D.C. (1990) Psi communication in the ganzfeld, *Journal of Parapsychology*, 54, 99–139.

Honorton, C., Ferrari, D.C. and Bem, D.J. (1992) Extraversion and ESP performance: a meta-analysis and new confirmation. In L.A. Henkel and G.R. Schmeidler (eds) *Research in Parapsychology 1990*, Metuchen, NJ: Scarecrow Press, 35–8.

Honorton, C., Ferrari, D.C. and Bem, D.J. (1998) Extraversion and ESP performance: a meta-analysis and new confirmation, *Journal of Parapsychology*, 62, 255–76.

Hyman, R. (1985) The ganzfeld psi experiment: a critical appraisal, *Journal of Parapsychology*, 49, 3–50.

Hyman, R. (1994) Anomaly or artefact? Comments on Bem and Honorton, *Psychological Bulletin*, 115, 19–24.

Hyman, R. (1995) Evaluation of the program on anomalous mental phenomena, *Journal of Parapsychology*, 59, 321–51.

Hyman, R., and Honorton, C. (1986) A joint communiqué: the psi ganzfeld controversy, *Journal of Parapsychology*, 50, 351–64.

May, E.C. (1998) Response to 'Experiment one of the SAIC remote viewing program': a critical re-evaluation, *Journal of Parapsychology*, 62, 309–18.

May, E.C., Utts, J.M. and Spottiswoode, S.J.P. (1995) Decision augmentation theory: applications to the random number generator database, *Journal of Scientific Exploration*, 9, 453–88.

Milton, J. (1997) Meta-analysis of free-response ESP studies without altered states of consciousness, *Journal of Parapsychology*, 61, 279–319.

Milton, J. (1999) Should ganzfeld research continue to be crucial in the search for a replicable psi effect? Part 1: Discussion paper and introduction to an electronic mail discussion, *Journal of Parapsychology*, 63, 302–34.

Milton, J. and Wiseman, R. (1998) Experiment one of the SAIC remote viewing program: a critical re-evaluation, *Journal of Parapsychology*, 62, 297–308.

Milton, J. and Wiseman, R. (1999) Does psi exist? Lack of replication of an anomalous process of information transfer, *Psychological Bulletin*, 125, 387–91.

Milton, J. and Wiseman, R. (2001) Does psi exist? Reply to Storm and Ertel (2001), *Psychological Bulletin*, 127, 434–8.

Morris, R.L. (1982) Assessing experimental support for true precognition, *Journal of Parapsychology*, 46, 321–36.

Morris, R.L. (1986) What psi is not: the necessity for experiments. In H.L. Edge, R.L. Morris, J. Palmer and J.H. Rush, *Foundations of Parapsychology*, Boston: Routlege & Kegan Paul, 70–110.

Morris, R.L., Dalton, K., Delanoy, D.L. and Watt, C. (1995) Comparison of sender/no sender condition in the ganzfeld, *Proceedings of the 38th Annual Convention of the Parapsychological Association*, Durham, NC, August, 244–59.

Palmer, J. (1977) Attitudes and personality traits in experimental ESP research. In B.B. Wolman (ed.) *Handbook of Parapsychology*, New York: Van Nostrand Reinhold, 175–201.

Palmer, J. (1978) Extrasensory perception: research findings. In S. Krippner (ed.) *Advances in Parapsychological Research, 2 Extrasensory Perception*, New York: Plenum Press, 59–244.

Palmer, J. and Carpenter, J.C. (1998) Comments on the extraversion-ESP meta-analysis by Honorton, Ferrari and Bem, *Journal of Parapsychology*, 62, 277–82.

Radin, D.I. and Ferrari, D.C. (1991) Effects of consciousness on the fall of dice: a meta-analysis, *Journal of Scientific Explorations*, 5, 61–83.

Radin, D.I. and Nelson, R.D. (1989) Evidence for consciousness-related anomalies in random physical systems, *Foundations of Physics*, 19, 1499–514.

Rosenthal, R. (1986) Meta-analytic procedures and the nature of replication: the ganzfeld debate, *Journal of Parapsychology*, 50, 315–36.

Rosenthal, R. (1991) *Meta-Analytic Procedures for Social Research*, rev. edn, London: Sage.

Sargent, C.L. (1981) Extraversion and performance in 'extra-sensory perception' tasks, *Journal of Personality and Individual Differences*, 3, 137–43.

Saunders, D.R. (1985) On Hyman's factor analysis, *Journal of Parapsychology*, 49, 86–8.

Schlitz, M. and Braud, W. (1997) Distant intentionality and healing: assessing the evidence, *Alternative Therapies*, 3, 62–73.

Schmeidler, G.R. and Edge, H. (1999) Should ganzfeld research continue to be crucial in the search for a replicable psi effect? Part II. Edited ganzfeld debate, *Journal of Parapsychology*, 63, 335–88.

Schmidt, S. and Walach, H. (2000) Electrodermal activity (EDA) – state of the art measurement and techniques for parapsychological purposes, *Journal of Parapsychology*, 64, 139–63.

Schmidt, S., Schneider, R., Utts, J. and Walach, H. (2004) Distant intentionality and the feeling of being stared at: Two meta-analyses, *British Journal of Psychology*, 95, 235–47.

Steinkamp, F., Milton, J. and Morris, R.L. (1998) A meta-analysis of forced-choice experiments comparing clairvoyance and precognition, *Journal of Parapsychology*, 62, 193–218.

Steinkamp, F., Boller, E. and Bosch, H. (2002) Experiments examining the possibility of human intentions interacting with random number generators: a preliminary meta-analysis, *Proceedings of Presented Papers of the Parapsychological Association 45th Annual Convention*, 256–72.

Stokes, D.M. (1987) Theoretical parapsychology. In S. Krippner (ed.) *Advances in Parapsychological Research 5*, Jefferson, NC: McFarland, 77–189.

Storm, L. (2000) Replicable evidence of psi: a revision of Milton's 1999 meta-analysis of the ganzfeld databases, *Journal of Parapsychology*, 64, 411–16.

Storm, L. and Ertel, S. (2001) Does psi exist? Comments on Milton and Wiseman's (1999) meta-analysis of ganzfeld research, *Psychological Bulletin*, 127, 424–33.

Storm, L. and Ertel, S. (2002) The ganzfeld debate continued: a response to Milton and Wiseman (2001), *Journal of Parapsychology*, 66, 73–82.

Targ, R. and Puthoff, H. (1974) Information transmission under conditions of sensory shielding, *Nature*, 252, 602–7.

Tart, C.T. (1974) Physiological correlates of psi cognition, *International Journal of Parapsychology*, 5, 357–86.

Utts, J. (1988) Successful replication vs. statistical significance, *Journal of Parapsychology*, 52, 305–20.

Utts, J. (1991) Replication and meta-analysis in parapsychology, *Statistical Science*, 6, 363–403.

Utts, J. (1995) An assessment of the evidence for psychic functioning, *Journal of Parapsychology*, 59, 4, 289–320.

Wiseman, R. and Morris, R.L. (1995) *Guidelines for Testing Psychic Claimants*, Hatfield: University of Hertfordshire Press.

Wiseman, R. and Milton, J. (1998) Experiment One of the SAIC remote viewing program: a critical re-evaluation, *Journal of Parapsychology*, 62, 4, 297–308.

Wiseman, R. and Milton, J. (1999) Experiment One of the SAIC remote viewing program: a critical evaluation, *Journal of Parapsychology*, 63, 3–14.

Chapter 4

Psychological factors

Caroline Watt

As the word 'para-psychology' suggests, psychology plays a significant role in paranormal experiences and research. Where psychology studies behaviour and mental processes, parapsychology studies the *apparent* ability to interact with one's environment through means other than the currently understood sensory channels. The umbrella term 'psi' is used to denote extrasensory perception (ESP, where the mind seems to receive information from the environment) and psychokinesis (PK, where the mind seems to exert an influence over the environment). The above definition of parapsychology encompasses both 'what's not psychic but looks like it' – that is, pseudo-psi – and 'genuine' psi.

This chapter has two parts. First, a discussion of psychological explanations for everyday 'spontaneous' paranormal experiences. Second, a review of laboratory parapsychological research identifying important psychological factors.

Elsewhere, I and others have argued for the potential value of spontaneous experiences (Alvarado 1996, Watt 1994) in illustrating the operation of psi in naturalistic settings, and in helping to generate ecologically valid methods and meaningful hypotheses for further exploration in laboratory settings. However, the complex circumstances surrounding spontaneous paranormal experiences provide fertile ground for the operation of psychological factors. By its very nature, this first category of paranormal experiences offers many illustrations of pseudo-psi. The emphasis in my discussion of spontaneous experiences is on how normal psychological factors may operate to lead us to mistakenly conclude that something paranormal is going on.

On the other hand, the simplified and controlled circumstances in laboratory testing are intended to rule out pseudo-psi so that researchers may be more confident that their results are relevant to genuine psi. When discussing laboratory research, then, I stress the link between genuine psi and psychological factors. This emphasis is not meant to imply that all spontaneous experiences are pseudo-psi, nor that all laboratory research is immune to pseudo-psi. Simply, it is easier to rule out pseudo-psi in the laboratory than it is in 'real life'.

Psychology and spontaneous paranormal experiences

Everyday paranormal experiences are termed 'spontaneous' because they usually occur unexpectedly and without the deliberate intention of the experient. They may include experiences of meaningful coincidences, past life experiences, ESP and PK experiences, and impressions of future events (precognition). Further information about these experiences may be found by perusing other chapters in this book.

Demographic factors

Numerous opinion polls and surveys have demonstrated that paranormal beliefs are widely held, across a variety of cultures, ages, educational achievements, and religious beliefs (e.g. Irwin 1993, 1997, McClenon 1994). For instance, a recent representative Gallup poll (Newport and Strausberg 2001) found that 54 per cent of those polled believed in psychic healing, 50 per cent believed in ESP, and 42 per cent believed that houses can be haunted. In general, a higher proportion of females than males tend to report paranormal beliefs and experiences. Does this mean females are more psychic than males? It is hard to tell from this kind of poll, but research elsewhere (Schouten 1982, 1983) suggests that there may be a 'reporting bias' in collections of spontaneous experiences – that females may be more willing than males to report having had paranormal experiences – resulting in an inflated number of cases involving female experients.

Coincidence experiences

A coincidence may be defined as 'a surprising concurrence of events, perceived as meaningfully related, with no apparent causal connection' (Diaconis and Mosteller 1989). Chapter 13 by Jane Henry deals with coincidences in more detail, and elsewhere I have discussed psychology and coincidences at length (Watt 1990–1). The definition above highlights psychological factors such as surprise and the perception of a meaningful relationship.

Surprise and meaningfulness

What is it about coincidences that may make them feel surprising? One important factor is a feeling that the coincidence was statistically unlikely – it is surprising because it is felt to be a rare and unpredictable event.

However, psychologists have shown that most people, statisticians included, tend to make inaccurate probability judgements in everyday situations, typically underestimating the frequency with which surprising events happen by chance alone (e.g. Kahneman *et al.* 1982, Nisbett and Ross 1980, Matthews and Blackmore 1995, Utts 1996).

The 'Law of Large Numbers' states that events that are rare per person occur in quantity when there are large numbers of people. Although the precise array of events surrounding any coincidence is unique and unpredictable, what is predictable is that something staggering is happening to someone somewhere at this moment. Diaconis and Mosteller (1989) relate a story from the *New York Times* of a woman who won the New Jersey State lottery jackpot twice in a short time period. The newspaper reported the odds of this happening as one in seventeen trillion. However, these are the odds of a specific individual who plays the lottery exactly twice winning both times. Actually, it has been calculated that there would be at least a one in thirty chance of a double winner in a four-month period somewhere in the United States. So, striking coincidences are bound to happen by chance alone; it is when you are personally involved in the coincidence that feelings of surprise and meaningfulness are evoked.

People are not ignorant of the fact that amazing coincidences can occur purely by chance. Research has shown that when asked to rate the surprisingness of coincidences that have happened to others, individuals are not very surprised by the accounts. However, when they compare coincidences that have happened to themselves with those that others have experienced, the self-coincidences are consistently described as more surprising, even though others do not find these coincidences particularly surprising (Falk 1981–2, 1989). This 'egocentric bias' suggests that personal involvement in a coincidence makes the coincidence seem subjectively less likely.

Past life experiences

A considerable amount of scholarly research has been conducted into accounts of reincarnation (e.g. Stevenson 1966, Matlock 1990) – the feeling that one has lived before under a different identity – particularly in eastern cultures. In western cultures, reincarnation experiences are more rare. However, an increasingly common practice is for individuals to seek hypnotic 'past life regression' as therapy for feelings of unresolved conflicts.

It is very difficult to establish whether individuals really are visiting past lives under hypnosis. However, there are certain psychological characteristics of the hypnotic state (Hilgard 1965) that suggest it would be wise to exercise a great deal of caution in interpreting 'memories' apparently retrieved under hypnosis. First, hypnotised individuals tend to be highly susceptible to suggestion. Therefore, if the therapist asks leading questions, the hypnotic subject will readily incorporate the implicit suggestions into their experiences. Second, hypnosis increases the ability to fantasise and the ability to role-play. Therefore, the hypnotic state is an extremely fertile ground for the development and elaboration of entirely imaginary scenarios. Third, the hypnotised subject has reduced reality testing, suggesting that they are likely to accept 'recovered' memories as their own, particularly if there is some subtle implication or expectation from the therapist that this is so.

Given the current debate in psychology over recovered memories and false memories (e.g. Conway 1997, Tsai *et al.* 2000), it would be wise not to take apparent past lives recovered under hypnotic regression at face value.

ESP experiences

The feeling that one has received information from another person or from the environment by mind alone is the most commonly reported paranormal experience (for reviews of the frequency and characteristics of such experiences, see Palmer 1979 and Rhine 1953a).

Some cases are of 'crisis telepathy', where one individual receives a strong feeling or mental impression that someone else is in danger (Rhine 1953b). The concurrence of a feeling of crisis and an actual crisis happening elsewhere will of course occur from time to time by chance alone and, in everyday life, one can never rule out the possibility that the experience is not genuine psi. Clearly, the more cause one person has to worry about another (e.g. the distant person is ill, or is involved in a dangerous situation such as war), the more frequently feelings of danger or foreboding are likely to occur, increasing the likelihood of chance coincidence resembling crisis telepathy. However, there are numerous instances where one person has received a clear impression of danger in situations where there was no prior reason for concern and such cases are less easily dismissed.

Another situation in which ESP is commonly reported is between people who are especially close – married couples and twins, for instance (Lyon Playfair 2002). Often it is claimed that the pair know what each other is thinking or experiencing, without the need for speech, and this may occur even when the pair are physically separated and unaware of each other's situation. The difficulty in evaluating whether or not genuine psi is operating here is that of ruling out common thought patterns and mutual anticipations that are bound to occur when two people know each other particularly well. Also, close pairs may develop a great sensitivity to one another's moods and body language that can provide additional cues as to what each other is thinking. Even when pairs informally test each other's ESP, if the 'sender' personally chooses the target (the information, such as a picture, that is to be communicated via ESP), this can give a false suggestion of ESP because the 'receiver' can inadvertently feel attracted to the picture most likely to be chosen by the sender. That is why random target selection is critical in both formal and informal tests of ESP.

PK experiences

Psychokinesis, the experience of moving or influencing matter by mind alone, is much rarer than ESP experiences in everyday life (Palmer 1979). Apparently dramatic PK is sometimes seen in the media – claims of the ability to bend metal by mind power alone, for example. However, conjurors can simulate many such feats through normal means, suggesting that caution should be exercised in judging whether genuine psi has occurred.

Perhaps the most common everyday situation in which people may feel they have some PK ability is in gambling, where one is trying to influence the outcome of an event whose outcome would normally be determined by chance alone – for example, the roll of dice, the fall of the ball on the roulette wheel. In these and similar situations, gamblers act as if their skill can influence the event – throwing the dice softly for a one, throwing hard for a six for instance.

Psychologists have shown that people often have an 'illusion of control' over ostensibly random events and that it is possible to increase the illusion of control, and hence the feeling that one's PK powers may be operating, by increasing people's perceptions that skill is involved in the random task (Ayeroff and Abelson 1976, Benassi *et al.* 1979, Langer 1975). For instance, allowing practice, active rather than passive involvement, and choice of target set to be used, all tend to enhance the feeling that skill is involved and consequently enhance the illusion of control over the chance task. This characteristic is similar to Falk's finding, in her study of psychological aspects of coincidences, that when coincidences were made more personally meaningful (through the use of personal birth-dates versus the use of randomly assigned birth-dates), the perceived surprisingness of the coincidences increased (Falk 1989). In both cases, it seems that the more personally involved we become in an event, the more inclined we are to seek to impute some kind of illusory meaning to the event.

Precognitive experiences

The feeling that one can predict the future can become exaggerated through the operation of various psychological factors. For example, many people feel they can predict who is about to call on the telephone. Once we have ruled out normal factors of anticipation (where someone is unconsciously expecting the call anyway, for example), the phenomena of 'multiple endpoints' and 'hindsight bias' may still contribute to the erroneous perception that the identity of the caller was predicted in advance.

Multiple endpoints

Often, a close coincidence is regarded as almost as impressive as an exact coincidence (Diaconis and Mosteller 1989). For instance, someone may get a hunch that the phone is about to ring, and it will be Uncle Bert, who hasn't been in touch for years, making the call. As predicted, the phone does ring, only it's Uncle Bert's neighbour. That's still quite an impressive coincidence (between the prediction and the call), but you might also be impressed if it had been Bert's wife Maude on the line, or another uncle, or Bert's daughter . . . and so on. The prediction was quite specific, but if the experient allows for near misses to count, then the prediction has multiple endpoints. That is, there could be many near misses that could also be subjectively impressive, although the chances of a near miss are so much higher than the chances of the specific prediction coming true.

Hindsight bias

In addition to predictions having multiple endpoints, it is quite possible that the experient will forget how specific the original prediction or hunch was. In this case, the experient feels 'I knew it would happen' – a well-established psychological phenomenon dubbed the hindsight effect by Fischhoff (1975). The hindsight bias describes the phenomenon whereby, once an event has actually occurred, it seems subjectively more likely than it did prior to its occurrence. This phenomenon can increase our feelings of confidence in our ability to predict the future.

Overlooking non-events

A final important psychological factor in precognitive experiences is that non-events – the failure of a prediction to be confirmed, for example – tend to be less memorable than instances of predictions coming true. In this case, we can develop an exaggerated opinion of our predictive powers, due to a small number of successful predictions being easily remembered and a large number of less notable failed predictions being less easily brought to mind. Psychologists term this phenomenon 'judgement by availability' (Tversky and Kahneman 1974), or salience (Taylor and Fiske 1978), and it may exert a pervasive influence over our everyday judgements of causality and probability, affecting our conclusions about many ostensibly paranormal events (Watt 1990–1).

Implications

The previous sections illustrate a variety of psychological factors that may affect everyday paranormal experiences. Most of the literature that I have cited is concerned with judgement under uncertainty, not specifically with judgements about paranormal experiences. See Marks and Kammann (1980) for a specific consideration of psychology and psychic experiences.

The ambiguity and incompleteness of information that often characterises spontaneous paranormal experiences suggests that these experiences are likely to provide a fertile ground for the operation of psychological factors that may contribute to pseudo-psi. My review is not exhaustive. For instance, there is a huge literature on eyewitness testimony that is relevant to spontaneous experiences (e.g. Wells and Loftus 1984). There are also criticisms of the heuristics and biases literature, suggesting that many of the so-called weaknesses in judgement may be eliminated or reduced by altering the experimental methodology (e.g. Gigerenzer 1991a, 1991b). Despite this, clearly it is parsimonious to rule out the potential for such psychological factors before judging that genuine psi has occurred.

Psychology and laboratory parapsychology

It is precisely because of the above-noted difficulties of interpreting spontaneous experiences that parapsychologists conduct laboratory research to increase their understanding of psi. The main feature of this kind of research is an attempt to rule out possible normal channels of information transfer or inference, so that psi is the only means of interacting with the target system. The likelihood of chance coincidence (say, between a target and a receiver's mental impressions) is established with the random selection of the target and its presentation along with a number of decoys. Standard statistical methods are used to determine the extent to which the observed success rate deviates from the success rate that would be expected by chance. The laboratory equivalent of multiple endpoints is avoided by the pre-specification of hypotheses and analyses.

If these and other precautions are put in place, it is possible to be more confident (though never entirely certain, because any scientific research can only provide evidence, not proof) that the results reflect genuine psi. Accepting genuine psi as a working hypothesis, several psychological variables have been found to correlate with psi. This chapter will briefly review three: belief in psi; extraversion and psi; and perception without awareness and psi.

Belief in psi

It is hardly surprising if, in everyday life, people who believe in psi tend to report more psychic experiences than people who don't believe in psi; after all, we typically interpret our experiences so as to confirm our prior beliefs (e.g. Lord *et al.* 1979, Nisbett and Ross 1980). However, this effect seems to persist under controlled conditions. One of the most extensively researched topics in experimental parapsychology is the relationship between belief in ESP and performance at laboratory ESP tasks. A small but reliable effect has been found, showing that believers in ESP tend to perform better at laboratory psi tasks than non-believers (Lawrence 1993, Palmer 1977). It is not simply that non-believers perform at chance levels, but that they perform at levels below chance expectation – suggesting that non-believers are using their psi in a self-defeating way, to detect and then avoid the psi target. This belief–performance relationship appears to be small in size but relatively robust (Lawrence 1993).

Various methods have been used to measure beliefs (Lawrence 1995). Palmer (1971) identified four different criteria of belief in ESP:

1 a belief that ESP could occur in the experiment
2 a belief that ESP exists in the abstract
3 a belief that one has psychic ability
4 a belief that one may be able to perform well at the laboratory psi task.

It is criterion 4 that seems to relate most clearly to actual ESP performance, and subsequent research continues to find this belief–performance relationship (e.g. Smith *et al.* 1997). The effect of belief on ESP outcomes is not limited to the experimental participants. It has also been found that the experimenter's belief may affect the results of psi research. For example, a recent study (Watt and Ramakers 2003) selected individuals with strong belief or disbelief in the paranormal and trained them to conduct experimental sessions with a psi task. Under carefully controlled conditions, it was found that those participants tested by believer experimenters obtained statistically significant psi results, while those tested by disbeliever experimenters obtained chance results. It is important to develop an understanding of these findings, as they are directly relevant to questions of replicability, both in parapsychology and in behavioural research in general.

Extraversion and psi

In their attempts to identify correlates of successful psi performance, and ultimately to understand how psi works, parapsychologists have related various measures of personality to ESP performance, including the personality factor extraversion. Extraverted individuals tend to be sociable and outgoing. Parapsychologists have found that extraversion correlates with ESP performance in experiments, the more extraverted tending to score more highly at ESP tasks (e.g. Honorton *et al.* 1998, Palmer 1977). As with the relationship between ESP beliefs and ESP performance, the size of the extraversion–ESP relationship is small, but statistically significant.

Two explanations have been put forward for the extraversion–ESP relationship. First, extraverts are more sociable than introverts and hence more comfortable in an experimental setting that might be intimidating to introverts. Second, extraverts tend to have lower levels of cortical arousal than introverts, and so would have the reduced physiological arousal that is thought to be psi-conducive (Braud 1975). Also on the question of arousal, Stanford has explored the relation between extraversion/introversion, the intensity of white noise stimulation in the ganzfeld, and ESP performance. (The ganzfeld is an experimental method involving sensory reduction thought to facilitate ESP, with the use of eye-goggles, headphones playing white noise, and physical relaxation.) Stanford found that extraverts enjoyed the relatively loud white noise stimulation and had higher ESP scores than introverts (Stanford *et al.* 1989a, 1989b). However, these findings were not replicated in a study by Stanford and Frank (1991).

Perception without awareness and psi

The term 'perception without awareness' (PWA) refers to people's perception of, and responses to, stimuli that are presented below the levels of conscious awareness. Historically, terms such as subliminal perception and preconscious processing have also been used to refer to the same phenomenon. There has been a great deal of debate in cognitive psychology over whether or not there is evidence for PWA, with some critics of PWA suggesting that in the earlier studies stimuli were not truly being presented below conscious awareness (e.g. Holender 1986). There have been many hysterical and inaccurate media reports suggesting the possibility of subliminal influence by hidden messages, but psychologists have found no evidence to support the idea that subliminal messages can have strong effects on behaviour (Vokey and Read 1985, Merikle 1988, Loftus and Klinger 1992). There is, however, some more recent evidence that stimuli presented below conscious awareness can have subtle and transient effects on conscious judgements and reactions (e.g. Merikle and Cheesman 1987, Debner and Jacoby 1994).

Parapsychologists hope to extend their understanding of ESP by studying the area of overlap between PWA and extrasensory perception. The pioneer of experimental parapsychology, J.B. Rhine stated, 'It is here, in the common unconscious functions of both sensorimotor and extrasensorimotor (or psi) character that parapsychology comes closest to psychology' (Rhine 1977, p. 171). Many parapsychologists have noted the often striking parallels between ESP and subliminal perception (e.g. Beloff 1974, Roney-Dougal 1986). In her book *Parapsychology and Psychology: Matches and Mismatches*, distinguished researcher Gertrude Schmeidler described her 'shock of recognition [which] came from a list of personality variables associated with subliminal sensitivity; they looked just like the variables associated with ESP success' (Schmeidler 1988, p. 22). For example, in her review of the literature on the effect of personality variables on subliminal perception, Roney-Dougal (1986) concluded that 'those susceptible to subliminal stimuli tend to show less repressiveness, more imageability, more "passivity", greater flexibility of report, and less hostility' (p. 416). A state of dispersed attention or relaxation is also known to facilitate sensitivity to subliminal stimulation (Dixon 1981, Fiss 1961, Fisher and Paul 1959). Likewise, it has been suggested that an increased awareness of internal processes, feelings and imagery facilitates extrasensory perception (Honorton 1974). Braud (1975) gives anecdotal and experimental evidence supporting his speculation that 'receptive mode/right hemispheric functioning' may facilitate ESP, and relaxation too has been found to enhance ESP performance (Braud and Braud 1974).

Despite these many apparent similarities, a cautionary note has been sounded. Early PWA research was plagued with methodological problems and new methods have been developed to circumvent these problems. However, much of the parapsychological research into parallels between ESP and PWA seems to have lagged behind in the PWA techniques being used (Wilson 2002). In order to investigate parallels between ESP and PWA effectively, parapsychologists need to become thoroughly acquainted with the latest developments in the PWA field.

Comparing defensiveness and psi performance

Parapsychologists' most systematic explorations of the similarities between PWA and psi perception are in the studies comparing defensiveness and psi performance. 'Defensiveness' can be broadly defined as unconscious resistance to unpleasant or threatening information (Dixon 1981). The most systematic comparisons between subliminal perception and ESP have been into the question of the relationship between defensiveness and psi. Martin Johnson was one of the first parapsychologists to test the hypothesis that 'People who are prone to draw their preconscious blinds in matters of visual perception might act somehow similarly towards perceptions which are extrasensory' (Carpenter 1965, pp. 70–1).

A variety of different measures of defensiveness has been used, the most frequent being the Defence Mechanism Test (DMT). A pre-planned series of ten Icelandic studies comparing DMT scores with performance on a forced-choice ESP task found that, in all but two of the studies, defensive individuals tended to have lower ESP scores than non-defensive individuals. When combined, the overall DMT–ESP relationship is statistically significant (Haraldsson and Houtkooper 1992) and replicates the findings of earlier DMT studies conducted outside of Iceland (Haraldsson *et al.* 1987). However, the most recent DMT–ESP research (Haraldsson *et al.* 2002) identifies an experimenter effect that appears to be linked to Martin

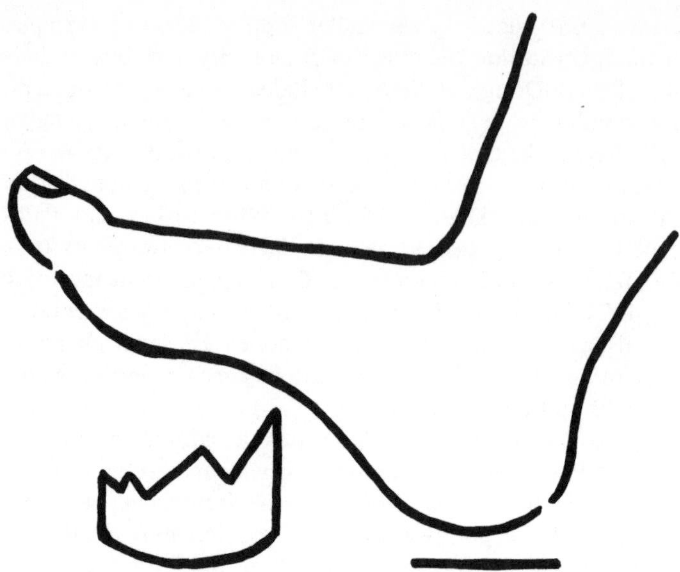

Figure 4.1 Example of threatening stimulus from Watt's studies comparing defensiveness and ESP
Source: C. Watt

Johnson, who scored the DMT protocols in the Icelandic studies. This may cast doubt on the future replicability of the DMT–ESP relationship, as does the fact that the DMT–ESP correlation has declined over time. Two more recent studies involving a different indicator of defensiveness have, however, also found a defensiveness–ESP relationship (Watt and Morris 1995).

Taken as a whole, the evidence for a defensiveness–ESP relationship is consistent with the theory that psi information may initially be perceived at an unconscious level and that this information may be subject to distortions and transformations prior to its emergence in conscious awareness (Tyrrell 1947). There are also preliminary indications of a similar defensiveness–PK relationship (Watt and Gissurarson 1995). The defensiveness–ESP relationship is one example of how psychological factors may contribute to an understanding of parapsychological phenomena.

Conclusion

This brief overview of psychological factors in laboratory parapsychology has highlighted three areas in which a number of studies have identified a relationship between a psychological variable and performance at a controlled laboratory psi task. Such relationships seem to be small in magnitude, and may be moderated by a number of other variables. For instance, the extraversion–ESP relationship appears to be found for studies featuring individual, not group, ESP testing (Palmer and Carpenter 1998). Environmental variables such as global geomagnetic activity and local sidereal time have also been claimed to correlate with psi performance (e.g. Spottiswoode 1997).

Psychology, like parapsychology, is dealing with complex open systems; for example, in both disciplines the experimenter's attitudes and expectations can interact with the participant's expectations, behaviour and performance during an experiment (Rosenthal 1976). Double-blind experimental techniques are therefore necessary to control for participant and experimenter expectancy effects. However, a recent survey of over 1,000 journal articles (Sheldrake 1998) found that only 4.9 per cent of studies of human and animal behaviour used blind methods, compared to 85.2 per cent of parapsychology studies. Perhaps the figures for parapsychology reflect the field's necessary adaptation towards the use of rigorous experimental methods in order to withstand close critical scrutiny from within and outside the field (for alternative interpretations see also Watt and Nagtegaal 2004). Sheldrake's findings suggest psychology could learn from parapsychology's experience. Also, like parapsychology, psychology often deals with relatively weak and unreliable effects. Again through necessity, parapsychologists have led the way in using meta-analytic techniques to aid in the evaluation of the accumulated results of experimental studies. Psychology may benefit from the expertise parapsychologists have developed to deal with questions of replication and statistical analysis (Rosenthal 1986, Utts 1991).

Clearly, parapsychologists have a complex web to untangle in pursuing the challenge posed by psi, both in terms of the difficulties in interpreting everyday paranormal experiences, and in terms of the factors affecting the outcomes of laboratory research. Taking a psychological perspective can be helpful to parapsychologists. In turn, psychology may benefit from the solutions that parapsychologists devise to tackle their challenge.

Recommended reading

Introductory

Irwin, H.J. (2004) *An Introduction to Parapsychology*, 4th edn, Jefferson, NC: McFarland. An up-to-date and balanced introduction to the field, focusing on phenomenology and correlates of spontaneous paranormal experiences.

Marks, D. and Kammann, R. (1980) *The Psychology of the Psychic*, Buffalo, NY: Prometheus. A textbook suggesting psychological explanations for psychic experiences.

Nisbett, R.E. and Ross, L. (1980) *Human Inference: Strategies and Shortcomings of*

Social Judgement, Englewood Cliffs, NJ: Prentice-Hall. A textbook reviewing characteristics of human inference in everyday situations.

Schmeidler, G.R. (1988) *Parapsychology and Psychology: Matches and Mismatches*, Jefferson, NC: McFarland. A survey of the various similarities and dissimilarities that have been found between psychology and parapsychology.

Advanced

Diaconis, P. and Mosteller, F. (1989) Methods for studying coincidences, *Journal of the American Statistical Association*, 84, 853–61. Illustrating basic statistical techniques for studying coincidences.

Palmer, J. (1977) Attitudes and personality traits in experimental ESP research. In B.B. Wolman (ed.) *Handbook of Parapsychology*, New York: Van Nostrand Reinhold, 175–201. Reviewing findings relating individual differences to ESP performance.

Roney-Dougal, S.M. (1986) Subliminal and psi perception: a review of the literature, *Journal of the Society for Psychical Research*, 53, 405–34. A comprehensive though now somewhat dated review comparing subliminal and psi perception.

Watt, C. (1990–1) Psychology and coincidences, *European Journal of Parapsychology*, 8, 66–84. A review of research suggesting possible normal psychological causes for some coincidences.

References

Alvarado, C.S. (1996) The place of spontaneous cases in parapsychology, *Journal of the American Society for Psychical Research*, 90, 1–34.

Ayeroff, F. and Abelson, R. (1976) ESP and ESB: belief in personal success at mental telepathy, *Journal of Personality and Social Psychology*, 34, 240–7.

Beloff, J. (1974) The subliminal and the extrasensory. In A. Angoff and B. Shapin (eds) *Parapsychology and the Sciences*, New York: Parapsychology Foundation Inc.

Benassi, V.A., Sweeney, P.D. and Drevno, G.E. (1979) Mind over matter: perceived success at psychokinesis, *Journal of Personality and Social Psychology*, 37, 1377–86.

Braud, W.G. (1975) Psi-conducive states, *Journal of Communication*, 25, 142–52.

Braud, W.G. and Braud, L.W. (1974) Further studies of relaxation as a psi-conducive state, *Journal of the American Society for Psychical Research*, 68, 229–45.

Carpenter, J.C. (1965) An exploratory test of ESP in relation to anxiety proneness. In J.B. Rhine and associates (eds) *Parapsychology from Duke to FRNM*, Durham, NC: Parapsychology Press.

Conway, M.A. (ed.) (1997) *Recovered Memories and False Memories*, Oxford: Oxford University Press.

Debner, J.A. and Jacoby, L.L. (1994) Unconscious perception: attention, awareness, and control, *Journal of Experimental Psychology: Learning, Memory, and Cognition*, 20, 304–17.

Dixon, N.F. (1981) *Preconscious Processing*, Chichester: John Wiley & Sons.

Falk, R. (1981–2) On coincidences, *The Skeptical Inquirer*, 6, 18–31.

Falk, R. (1989) Judgment of coincidences: mine versus yours, *American Journal of Psychology*, 102, 477–93.

Fischhoff, B. (1975) Hindsight ≠ foresight: the effect of outcome knowledge on judgement under uncertainty, *Journal of Experimental Psychology: Human Perception and Performance*, 1, 288–99.

Fisher, C. and Paul, I.H. (1959) The effect of subliminal visual stimulation on images and dreams: a validation study, *Journal of the American Psychoanalytic Association*, 7, 35–83.

Fiss, H. (1961) State of consciousness and the subliminal effect. Unpublished doctoral dissertation, New York University, New York.

Gigerenzer, G. (1991a) How to make cognitive illusions disappear: beyond 'heuristics and biases'. In W. Stroebe and M. Hewstone (eds) *European Review of Social Psychology*, 2, 83–115.

Gigerenzer, G. (1991b) From tools to theories: a heuristic of discovery in cognitive psychology, *Psychological Review*, 98, 254–67.

Haraldsson, E. and Houtkooper, J.M. (1992) Effects of perceptual defensiveness, personality and belief on extrasensory perception tasks, *Personality and Individual Differences*, 13, 1085—96.

Haraldsson, E., Houtkooper, J.M. and Hoeltje, C. (1987) The Defense Mechanism Test as a predictor of ESP performance: Icelandic study VII and meta-analysis of 13 experiments, *Journal of Parapsychology*, 51, 75–90.

Haraldsson, E., Houtkooper, J.M., Schneider, R. and Bäckström, M. (2002) Perceptual defensiveness and ESP performance: reconstructed DMT-ratings and psychological correlates in the first German DMT–ESP experiment, *Journal of Parapsychology*, 66, 249–70.

Hilgard, E.R. (1965) *Hypnotic Susceptibility*, New York: Harcourt, Brace and World.

Holender, D. (1986) Semantic activation without conscious identification in dichotic listening, parafoveal mision, and visual masking: a survey and appraisal, *Behavioral and Brain Sciences*, 9, 1–66 (and subsequent peer commentary).

Honorton, C. (1974) Psi-conducive states. In J. White (ed.) *Psychic Exploration*, 616–38, New York: Putman.

Honorton, C., Ferrari, D.C. and Bem, D.J. (1998) Extraversion and ESP performance: a meta-analysis and a new confirmation, *Journal of Parapsychology*, 62, 255–76.

Irwin, H.J. (1993) Belief in the paranormal: a review of the empirical literature, *Journal of the American Society for Psychical Research*, 87, 1–40.

Irwin, H.J. (1997) An empirically derived typology of paranormal beliefs, *European Journal of Parapsychology*, 13, 1–14.

Kahneman, D., Slovic, P. and Tversky, A. (eds) (1982) *Judgement Under Uncertainty: Heuristics and Biases*, Cambridge: Cambridge University Press.

Langer, E.J. (1975) The illusion of control, *Journal of Personality and Social Psychology*, 32, 311–28.

Lawrence, T.R. (1993) Gathering in the sheep and goats. A meta-analysis of forced choice sheep–goat ESP studies, 1947–1993, *Proceedings of Presented Papers: The Parapsychological Association 36th Annual Convention*, 75–86.

Lawrence, T.R. (1995) How many factors of paranormal belief are there? A critique of the Paranormal Belief Scale, *Journal of Parapsychology*, 59, 3–26.

Loftus, E.F. and Klinger, M.R. (1992) Is the unconscious smart or dumb? *American Psychologist*, 46, 761–5.

Lord, C., Ross, L. and Lepper, M.R. (1979) Biased assimilation and attitude polarization: the effects of prior theories on subsequently considered evidence, *Journal of Personality and Social Psychology*, 37, 2098–109.

Lyon Playfair, G. (2002) *Twin Telepathy: The Psychic Connection*, London: Vega Books.

McClenon, J. (1994) Surveys of anomalous experience: a cross-cultural analysis, *Journal of the American Society for Psychical Research*, 88, 117–36.

Matlock, J.G. (1990) Past life memory case studies. In S. Krippner (ed.) *Advances in Parapsychological Research 6*, Jefferson, NC: McFarland.

Matthews, R. and Blackmore, S. (1995) Why are coincidences so impressive?, *Perceptual and Motor Skills*, 80, 1121–2.

Merikle, P.M. (1988) Subliminal auditory messages: an evaluation, *Psychology and Marketing*, 5, 355–72.

Merikle, P.M. and Cheesman, J. (1987) Current status of research on subliminal perception. In M. Wallendorf and P. Anderson (eds) *Advances in Consumer Research*, Vol. XIV, Provo, UT: Association for Consumer Research.

Newport, F. and Strausberg, M. (2001) *Americans' Belief in Psychic and Paranormal Phenomena is up over Last Decade*, Princeton: Gallup.

Palmer, J. (1971) Scoring in ESP tests as a function of belief. Part I. The sheep–goat effect, *Journal of the American Society for Psychical Research*, 65, 373–408.

Palmer, J. (1979) A community mail survey of psychic experiences, *Journal of the American Society for Psychical Research*, 73, 221–51.

Palmer, J. and Carpenter, J.C. (1998) Comments on the extraversion–ESP meta-analysis by Honorton, Ferrari, and Bem, *Journal of Parapsychology*, 62, 277–82.

Rhine, L.E. (1953a) Subjective forms of spontaneous psi experiences, *Journal of Parapsychology*, 17, 77–114.

Rhine, L.E. (1953b) The relation of experience to associated event in spontaneous ESP, *Journal of Parapsychology*, 17, 187–209.

Rhine, J.B. (1977) Extrasensory perception. In B. Wolman (ed.) *Handbook of Parapsychology*, New York: Van Nostrand Reinhold.

Rosenthal, R. (1976) *Experimenter Effects in Behavioral Research* (enlarged edn), New York: Irvington Press.

Rosenthal, R. (1986) Meta-analytic procedures and the nature of replication: the ganzfeld debate, *Journal of Parapsychology*, 50, 315–36.

Schouten, S.A. (1982) Analyzing spontaneous cases: a replication based on the Rhine collection, *European Journal of Parapsychology*, 4, 9–48.

Schouten, S.A. (1983) A different approach for analyzing spontaneous cases: with particular reference to the study of Louisa E. Rhine's case collection, *Journal of Parapsychology*, 47, 323–40.

Sheldrake, R. (1998) Experimenter effects in scientific research: how widely are they neglected?, *Journal of Scientific Exploration*, 12, 73–8.

Smith, M.D., Wiseman, R., Machin, D., Harris, P. and Joiner, R. (1997) Luckiness, competition, and performance on a psi task, *Journal of Parapsychology*, 61, 33–43.

Spottiswoode, J. (1997) Geomagnetic fluctuations and free-response anomalous cognition: a new understanding, *Journal of Parapsychology*, 61, 3–12.

Stanford, R.G. and Frank, S. (1991) Prediction of ganzfeld ESP task performance from verbal indicators: a second study, *Journal of Parapsychology*, 55, 349–76.

Stanford, R.G., Frank, S., Kass, G. and Skoll, S. (1989a) Ganzfeld as an ESP-favorable setting. Part I. Assessment of spontaneity, arousal, and internal attention state through verbal transcript analysis, *Journal of Parapsychology*, 53, 1–42.

Stanford, R.G., Frank, S., Kass, G. and Skoll, S. (1989b) Ganzfeld as an ESP-favorable setting. Part II. Prediction of ESP-task performance through verbal-transcript measures of spontaneity, suboptimal arousal, and internal attention state, *Journal of Parapsychology*, 53, 95–124.

Stevenson, I. (1966) *Twenty Cases Suggestive of Reincarnation*, New York: American Society for Psychical Research.

Taylor, S.E. and Fiske, S.T. (1978) Salience, attention and attribution: top of the head phenomena, *Advances in Experimental Social Psychology*, 11, 249–88.

Tsai, A., Loftus, E. and Polage, D. (2000) Current directions in false memory research. In D.F. Bjorklund (ed.) *False-Memory Creation in Children and Adults: Theory, Research, and Implications*, Hillsdale, NJ: Lawrence Erlbaum.

Tversky, A. and Kahneman, D. (1974) Judgement under uncertainty: heuristics and biases, *Science*, 185, 1124–31.

Tyrrell, G.N.M. (1947) The 'Modus Operandi' of paranormal cognition, *Proceedings of the Society for Psychical Research*, Vol. XLVIII, Part 173, 65–120.

Utts, J. (1991) Replication and meta-analysis in parapsychology, *Statistical Science*, 6, 363–403.

Utts, J.M. (1996) *Seeing Through Statistics*, Belmont, CA: Duxbury Press.

Vokey, J.R. and Read, J.D. (1985) Subliminal messages: between the devil and the media, *American Psychologist*, 40, 1231–9.

Watt, C.A. (1994) Making the most of spontaneous cases. In S. Krippner (ed.) *Advances in Parapsychological Research 7*, Jefferson, NC: McFarland.

Watt, C.A. and Gissurarson, L.R. (1995) Research note: exploring defensiveness and psychokinesis performance, *European Journal of Parapsychology*, 11, 92–101.

Watt, C.A. and Morris, R.L. (1995) The relationships among performance on a prototype indicator of perceptual defence/vigilance, personality, and extrasensory perception, *Personality and Individual Differences*, 19, 635–48.

Watt, C.A. and Nagtegaal, M. (2004) Reporting of blind methods: An interdisciplinary survey, *Journal of the Society for Psychical Research*, 68, 105–14.

Watt, C.A. and Ramakers, P. (2003) Experimenter effects with a remote facilitation of attention focusing task: a study with multiple believer and disbeliever experimenters, *Journal of Parapsychology*, 67, 99–116.

Wells, G.L. and Loftus, E.F. (eds) (1984) *Eyewitness Testimony: Psychological Perspectives*, Cambridge: Cambridge University Press.

Wilson, S. (2002) Psi, perception without awareness, and false recognition, *Journal of Parapsychology*, 66, 271–89.

Chapter 5

Scepticism

Christopher C. French

Doubt is not a pleasant mental state, but certainty is a ridiculous one.
Voltaire

Historical roots of scepticism

According to *Chambers English Dictionary* (1988), the word 'scepticism' (or 'skepticism' to use the American spelling) is derived from the Greek words skeptikos, which means 'thoughtful', and skeptesthai, meaning 'to consider'. It is defined as 'that condition in which the mind is before it has arrived at conclusive opinions: doubt [. . .]'. This chapter will discuss the idea of scepticism as it applies to a consideration of paranormal claims. We will begin by considering the philosophical antecedents of modern scepticism (for more detail, see Kurtz 1992).

Hume's essay *Of Miracles*, published in 1748, is particularly relevant to a discussion of scepticism as it relates to the paranormal (Grey 1994). Hume presented a strong argument that one would never be rationally justified in believing that a miracle had occurred. He defined a miracle as an event which violates a law of nature, a definition which would be taken by many as including paranormal events. It is important to realise that Hume was not claiming to have proved that miracles have never occurred, only that we would never be justified in believing that they have. He proposed the following principle:

> No testimony is sufficient to establish a miracle unless that testimony be of such a kind that its falsehood would be more miraculous than the fact which it endeavours to establish.
>
> (Hume pp. 115–16, in Grey 1994, p. 294)

Although this principle allows for the possibility that the evidence in favour of a miracle might outweigh the evidence against it, in practice, Hume argued, this never happens. A number of factors undermine the credibility of miraculous claims, not least of which is the problem of witness reliability. Is it more likely that the person or persons making the claim are deceivers or else themselves deceived or that a law of nature has been violated? Whereas the evidence supporting violations of laws of nature is sparse, possibly even non-existent, we are surrounded by evidence that people sometimes lie and sometimes make mistakes.

Hume's argument against accepting miraculous claims is a particular example of the application of Occam's Razor, a methodological principle commonly attributed to William of Ockham (*c.* 1285–1349), which states that entities should not be multiplied beyond necessity ('Entia non sunt multiplicanda praeter necessitatem'). Essentially, this principle advises that if there are two possible explanations for a particular phenomenon, one of which is in line with known laws of logic and science whereas the other requires the postulation of previously unknown forces, in the interests of parsimony the former is to be preferred. Occam's Razor is one of the fundamental guiding principles of scepticism.

A second fundamental principle is that claims must be falsifiable. Philosophers of science have not found it easy to distinguish science from non-science or pseudoscience. Much has been made of Popper's (1972, 1980) notion of falsifiability in this regard. If a statement is not falsifiable, then it cannot be scientific. This is an important notion and one which can have a profound impact upon one's view of the world if taken to heart. It might appear at first glance that if a particular belief system can account for any outcome, this would indicate its strength. In fact, in scientific terms, such a belief system cannot be thought of as a scientific theory at all. If there is no turn of events that would falsify the belief system, then it clearly lacks any predictive power. It can only apparently account for events retrospectively. Non-falsifiability is a common characteristic of pseudosciences.

Modern scepticism: legitimate and illegitimate

Kurtz has developed his notion of scepticism as a positive constructive approach (e.g. Kurtz 1992, 1994, 1996). He describes his new scepticism as being selective, in that it does not entail doubting everything at once but is limited to the context being considered. It maintains that we are able to develop reliable knowledge about the world. It does not dogmatically reject paranormal claims prior to considering the evidence but is willing to pronounce disbelief if the evidence is found to be inadequate. Paranormal claims should be evaluated through careful scientific investigation using the following criteria: (a) empirical tests based upon observation, (b) logical standards of coherence, and (c) experimental tests in which ideas are judged by their consequences. Kurtz has achieved considerable success in promoting his approach, largely through the activities of the Committee for the Scientific Investigation of Claims of the Paranormal (CSICOP), which he founded in 1976. In addition, Kurtz is president of Prometheus Books, a publishing house which specialises in the publication of sceptical books.

However, it is not only those who doubt the existence of paranormal forces that have promoted the judicious application of scepticism. Parapsychologist John Palmer (1986) has made the important point that those traditionally labelled as 'sceptics' regarding the paranormal are often not true sceptics at all. They tend to uncritically accept any non-paranormal explanation for an ostensibly paranormal event (OPE), no matter how far-fetched, and only adopt a sceptical approach when considering explanations which would imply the existence of paranormal forces. Palmer suggests that such critics might more accurately be described as conventional theorists (CTs), a term intended to convey the belief of this group that ultimately all OPEs will be explained in terms of conventional scientific concepts. A true sceptic, according to Palmer, would adopt an attitude of doubt towards all unproven explanations of OPEs. Despite the importance and value of Palmer's (1986) arguments, it is unlikely that the phrase 'conventional theorist' will enter into common usage. 'Sceptic' is a handy, if imprecise, description of CTs and will be used in this sense for the remainder of this chapter.

Palmer (1986) calls for the adoption of a new approach which he calls progressive scepticism. This would require a critical attitude towards all unproven explanations of OPEs and rigorous scientific research from both the paranormal and conventional perspectives in attempting to provide definitive explanations. The burden of proof with respect to paranormal claims should not be seen as resting solely with the proponents of the paranormal. Those offering non-paranormal accounts should also be required to produce empirical evidence in support of their arguments.

Sceptical organisations

Numerous organisations now exist, both nationally and internationally, to promote a sceptical approach to paranormal and related claims (see website below). Probably the most influential organisation is the Committee for the Scientific Investigation of Claims of the Paranormal (CSICOP, pronounced 'sigh cop'). Kendrick Frazier (1996), a member of CSICOP's Executive Council, provides a sympathetic account of the aims and achievements of the group (but see Hansen 1992 for a more critical assessment). Frazier (1996, p. 168) describes CSICOP as 'an independent, non-profit organization that evaluates paranormal and fringe-science claims from a scientific viewpoint and attempts to provide the public and scholars with scientifically reliable information about them. It also encourages an appreciation of scientific thinking and the application of science and reason to important public issues'.

The means by which CSICOP attempts to achieve its objectives as indicated in their journal are: to maintain a network of people interested in critically examining paranormal, fringe-science, and other claims, and in contributing to consumer education; to prepare bibliographies of published materials that carefully examine such claims; to encourage research by objective and impartial enquiry in areas where it is needed; to convene conferences and meetings; to publish articles that examine claims of the paranormal; not to reject claims on a priori grounds, antecedent to enquiry, but to examine them objectively and carefully. CSICOP also responds to media enquiries by providing contacts with informed sceptics to comment upon paranormal and pseudoscientific claims.

There is little doubt that CSICOP has had considerable success in disseminating its message. The *Skeptical Inquirer* currently has a circulation in excess of 50,000, including 35,000 subscribers, with readers in seventy-two countries. CSICOP has also been successful in inspiring the formation of local or regional sceptical groups in the majority of American states as well as in twenty-eight countries (including the UK).

Whereas CSICOP and its supporters often view themselves as lonely defenders of rationalism and common sense, their critics often see them as self-appointed 'scientific vigilantes'. The truth is that some sceptics do seem to over-emphasise the dangers in what they see as 'a rising tide of irrationalism' in modern society and to have an inordinate fondness for military metaphors when describing their 'battles' against this threat. There is also some truth in the criticism that CSICOP sometimes fails to make distinctions between its targets, attacking the trivial and the serious with equal vigour.

However, although recognising CSICOP's imperfections, it is probably fair to say that most moderates on both sides of the psi debate acknowledge the vital role played by this organisation and its many positive achievements. There have recently been signs that CSICOP has mellowed somewhat in its attitude to serious experimental parapsychologists. One notable example of this constructive approach is the joint communiqué from critic Ray Hyman and parapsychologist Charles Honorton with respect to the ganzfeld studies (Hyman and Honorton 1986). Both agreed that the data set from these studies demonstrated a real effect, but there was disagreement regarding whether or not psi had been the cause of the effect. Perhaps more importantly, the communiqué included a detailed list of guidelines for the conduct of future research using that technique. Such constructive criticism can only help serious researchers to improve the quality of their evidence.

It is undoubtedly the case, however, that many of the targets of CSICOP's criticism would not be seen by serious parapsychologists and psychical researchers as likely candidates for providing convincing evidence of paranormal forces. To criticise CSICOP for this, however, is to ignore the fact that the organisation explicitly sees public education as one of its main roles. Although many serious proponents of the paranormal may be unimpressed by the feats of psychic superstars such as Uri Geller or the claims of psychic detectives and psychic healers, many members of the public are convinced by uncritical media portrayals of such individuals. Similarly, even though many professional astrologers would condemn newspaper horoscopes, many members of the public take them quite seriously. CSICOP's criticisms of such areas are useful in providing an alternative point of view, particularly in the realm of media discussions. Furthermore, it is obviously in the public interest that charlatans claiming healing powers are exposed as dangerous frauds. One example would be the Reverend Peter Popoff who claimed to receive messages directly from God informing him of details of congregation members' illnesses. In fact, details were relayed by Popoff's wife via a tiny radio receiver in Popoff's ear (Randi 1987). Another would be the Filipino surgeons who use sleight of hand and animal tissue to fool cancer victims into believing that malignant tumours are being removed from their bodies without the use of surgical instruments.

The psychology of belief and disbelief

Sceptics are not convinced by the evidence put forward in support of the existence of psi. With respect to attempts to establish psi scientifically, they emphasise various problems that have historically plagued parapsychology, including methodological sloppiness, fraud on the part of participants and experimenters, and inability to replicate effects (Hyman 1985). In fairness, the recent evidence presented by parapsychologists relating to the autoganzfeld technique (Bem and Honorton 1994) and remote viewing (Utts 1996, Hyman 1996) presented a strong challenge to those sceptical of the existence of paranormal forces (see Chapter 3 on the parapsychology meta-analyses). However, it is often wise to withhold judgement for a while where controversial claims are concerned. After all, it took four decades to conclusively establish that Soal's positive results could not be taken at face value (Hyman 1985). A subsequent meta-analysis by Milton and Wiseman (1999) of ganzfeld studies carried out after those reviewed by Bem and Honorton failed to find any significant deviation from mean chance expectation. Furthermore, remote viewing studies have been severely criticised by Marks (2000). It can reasonably be argued that psi has not yet been established in the laboratory beyond reasonable doubt.

Most people, of course, do not base their belief in the paranormal upon an assessment of the scientific evidence. Many surveys have shown that one of the main reasons given for believing in the paranormal is personal experience of ostensibly paranormal events (along with reports of similar experiences from trusted others and the media). Although sceptics are always aware of the possibility of hoaxes, in general they do not doubt the sincerity of individuals reporting such experiences. It is not the experiences which sceptics question, but the interpretation of the experiences as necessarily involving psi. There is no doubt that many situations may appear to reflect the operation of paranormal forces when in fact known psychological and physical factors are all that is required to explain them (Alcock 1981, Blackmore 1990, French 1992, Hines 2003, Hoggart and Hutchinson 1995, Zusne and Jones 1989; see also Chapter 4 on psychological factors in parapsychology).

This raises the interesting possibility that believers and sceptics may be psychologically different in important ways. Certain types of ostensibly paranormal experience may be explained in terms of the operation of universal cognitive biases. French (1992) discusses several relevant psychological factors including the illusion of control, the tendency to seek confirmatory evidence for our beliefs, poor appreciation of the probability of coincidences, and lack of knowledge of conjuring techniques. There is suggestive evidence that believers in the paranormal may be more prone to these biases, even though they affect virtually everyone to a greater or lesser extent. Many parapsychologists, most notably Harvey Irwin (e.g. Irwin 1993) and Michael Thalbourne (e.g. Thalbourne and Delin 1994), have also carried out extensive research in this area.

Sceptical researchers are likely to draw different conclusions from those of proponents of the paranormal when psychological differences between believers and sceptics are found. For example, the sceptic is likely to argue that because believers are more fantasy-prone than sceptics (e.g. Irwin 1993), many ostensibly paranormal experiences are simply fantasies. Proponents of the paranormal, on the other hand, are likely to give serious consideration to the possibility that fantasy-prone individuals might possess psychological characteristics which make it more likely that they will experience genuine paranormal events (see, for example, Thalbourne 1996).

Relatively little attention has been paid directly to the psychology of disbelief, the implicit assumption being that it is paranormal belief which requires explanation. From a sceptical perspective, this is of course quite reasonable. In general, when proponents of the paranormal have considered the psychology of scepticism, they have mainly emphasised negative psychological characteristics, just as sceptics have done when considering paranormal belief. Irwin (1989), for example, considers a number of psychodynamic accounts of the extreme emotional commitment to 'the cause' which some sceptics appear to demonstrate. Many of these psychodynamic accounts involve the unsubstantiated idea that 'paranormal belief stirs certain repressed fantasies and perceptions of our early childhood'. The related idea that sceptics are afraid of the paranormal is also frequently voiced. Although this may apply in some cases, it cannot apply to all. Many sceptics, including Susan Blackmore, Anthony Flew, Chris Scott, John Taylor and me, were once believers with a very positive attitude towards the paranormal.

Sceptics frequently report, on the basis of well-controlled experiments, that believers tend to distort evidence in such a way that it appears to offer support for their paranormal beliefs. However, proponents of psi can also cite instances of sceptics distorting the scientific evidence in such a way that it appears to offer less support for the paranormal than it actually does. Keil (1990) claims that Gardner misrepresented investigations of Pavel Stepanek's alleged psychic powers and both Child (1985) and Palmer (1986) discuss the ways in which the experiments at Maimonides Medical Center on possible ESP in dreams have been misreported by sceptics (e.g. Zusne and Jones 1982; note that no such misrepresentation of these studies is to be found in the second edition of this book (Zusne and Jones 1989).

We should not be surprised that both sides in the psi debate will occasionally misrepresent the evidence in such a way that their own position appears to be somewhat stronger than it actually is. After all, to err is human and a great deal of psychological research shows that we are far more likely to notice errors in an argument if we disagree with its conclusions than if we agree with them. The fact that errors of reporting occur should not necessarily be taken as a deliberate attempt to mislead. Clearly, it is reasonable to place less faith in a commentator who has repeatedly demonstrated such academic sloppiness, but there are probably few of us who have not noticed the occasional error in our own previous writings.

Edge *et al.* (1986) have pointed out several negative characteristics shared by extremists on both sides of the psi debate:

> Each is trying to persuade others and thus may make liberal use of the techniques of persuasion. Frequently used ploys include: emotional rhetoric; *ad hominem* arguments, including unsupported charges of incompetence; ridicule; guilt by association; generalizing to the whole from the faults of the part, including focusing on extremists in the 'opposing camp' and generalizing to those of moderation; obviously fallacious reasoning; and ignoring or superficially dismissing information counter to the strongly held position. Experimental research may occasionally be conducted, with unwarranted generalizations drawn from little data or from data that could obviously be affected by experimenter bias. Extreme advocates and counteradvocates [of the existence of psi] may claim that their position needs no external support, that it is intuitively obvious to those willing to take it seriously; others are too biased or incompetent.
>
> (Edge *et al.* 1986, p. 322)

Conclusion

On the positive side, moderates in the psi debate also share many characteristics, including a commitment to the scientific method as the best means to resolve the issue and a recognition of the necessity for a constructively sceptical approach. Meaningful dialogue between moderate proponents of the paranormal and moderate sceptics is essential for the future progress of parapsychology.

Recommended reading

Introductory

Hoggart, S. and Hutchinson, M. (1995) *Bizarre Beliefs*, London: Richard Cohen Books. Beautifully illustrated and highly readable – at last, a coffee-table book for sceptics!

Randi, J. (1982) *Flim-Flam! The Truth about Unicorns, Parapsychology and Other Delusions*, Buffalo, NY: Prometheus. Entertaining exposé of a wide range of pseudoscientific topics.

Advanced

Alcock, J.E. (1981) *Parapsychology: Science or Magic?* Oxford: Pergamon Press. Well-argued sceptical critique of parapsychology by a leading social psychologist.

Cardena, E., Lynn, S.J. and Krippner, S. (eds) (2000) *Varieties of Anomalous Experience: Examining the Scientific Evidence*, Washington, DC: American Psychological Association. Comprehensive review chapters of relevant topics.

Dawkins, R. (1998) *Unweaving the Rainbow: Science, Delusion and the Appetite for Wonder*, London: Penguin. Passionately argued case in favour of science and against pseudoscience as the best means for gaining true insight into the nature of the universe.

Hines, T. (2003) *Pseudoscience and the Paranormal.* 2nd edn, Amherst, NY: Prometheus. Entertaining critical overview of pseudoscience and the paranormal.

Kurtz, P. (ed.) (1985) *A Skeptic's Handbook of Parapsychology*, Buffalo, NY: Prometheus. A highly readable collection of critical essays on parapsychology, mainly from a sceptical perspective.

Vyse, S.A. (1997) *Believing in Magic: The Psychology of Superstition*, New York: Oxford University Press. Well-written summary of psychological research into the formation and maintenance of superstitious thinking.

Skeptiks < http://www.skeptiks.com.au/features/links/skeporg.htm > Offers links to over fifty websites of sceptical organisations.

References

Baker, R.A. and Nickell, J. (1992) *Missing Pieces: How to Investigate Ghosts, UFOs, Psychics and Other Mysteries*, Buffalo, NY: Prometheus.

Bem, D.J. and Honorton, C. (1994) Does psi exist? Replicable evidence for an anomalous process of information transfer, *Psychological Bulletin*, 115, 4–18.

Blackmore, S. (1990) The lure of the paranormal, *New Scientist*, 22 September, 62–5.

Blackmore, S.J. (1993) *Dying to Live: Science and the Near-Death Experience*, London: Grafton.

Buckman, R. and Sabbagh, K. (1993) *Magic or Medicine? An Investigation into Healing*, London: Macmillan.

Child, I.L. (1985) Psychology and anomalous observations: the question of ESP in dreams, *American Psychologist*, 40, 1219–30.

Edge, H.L., Morris, R.L., Rush, J.H. and Palmer, J. (1986) *Foundations of Parapsychology: Exploring the Boundaries of Human Capability*, Boston: Routledge & Kegan Paul.

Frazier, K. (ed.) (1981) *Paranormal Borderlands of Science*, Buffalo, NY: Prometheus.

Frazier, K. (ed.) (1986) *Science Confronts the Paranormal*, Buffalo, NY: Prometheus.

Frazier, K. (ed.) (1991) *The Hundredth Monkey and Other Paradigms of the Paranormal*, Buffalo, NY: Prometheus.

Frazier, K. (1996) Committee for the Scientific Investigation of Claims of the Paranormal (CSICOP). In G. Stein (ed.) *The Encyclopedia of the Paranormal*, Amherst, NY: Prometheus, 168–80.

Frazier, K. (ed.) (1998) *Encounters with the Paranormal: Science, Knowledge, and Belief*, Amherst, NY: Prometheus.

French, C.C. (1992) Factors underlying belief in the paranormal: do sheep and goats think differently? *The Psychologist*, 5, 295–9.

Gardner, M. (1957) *Fads and Fallacies in the Name of Science*, New York: Dover.

Gardner, M. (1981) *Science: Good, Bad and Bogus*, Buffalo, NY: Prometheus.

Grey, W. (1994) Philosophy and the paranormal. Part 2: Skepticism, miracles, and knowledge, *Skeptical Inquirer*, 18, 288–94.

Hansen, G.P. (1992) CSICOP and the skeptics: an overview, *Journal of the American Society for Psychical Research*, 86, 19–63.

Hyman, R. (1985) A critical historical overview of parapsychology. In P. Kurtz (ed.) *A Skeptic's Handbook of Parapsychology*, Buffalo, NY: Prometheus, 3–96.

Hyman, R. (1996) Evaluation of a program on anomalous mental phenomena, *Journal of Scientific Exploration*, 10, 31–58.

Hyman, R. and Honorton, C. (1986) A joint communiqué: the psi ganzfeld controversy, *Journal of Parapsychology*, 50, 351–64.

Irwin, H.J. (1989) On paranormal disbelief: the psychology of the sceptic. In G.K. Zollschan, J.F. Schumaker and G.F. Walsh (eds) *Exploring the Paranormal: Perspectives on Belief and Experience*, Bridport, Dorset: Prism Press, 305–12.

Irwin, H.J. (1993) Belief in the paranormal: a review of the empirical literature, *Journal of the American Society for Psychical Research*, 97, 1–39.

Keil, J. (1990) How a skeptic misrepresents the research with Stepanek: a review of Martin Gardner's *'How Not to Test a Psychic'*, *Journal of Parapsychology*, 54, 151–67.

Kurtz, P. (1992) *The New Skepticism: Inquiry and Reliable Knowledge*, Buffalo, NY: Prometheus.

Kurtz, P. (1994) The new skepticism, *Skeptical Inquirer*, 18, 134–41.

Kurtz, P. (1996) Skepticism and the paranormal. In G. Stein (ed.) *The Encyclopedia of the Paranormal*, Amherst, NY: Prometheus, 684–701.

Marks, D. (2000) *The Psychology of the Psychic*, 2nd edn, Amherst, NY: Prometheus.

Milton, J. and Wiseman, R. (1999) Does psi exist? Lack of replication of an anomalous process of information transfer, *Psychological Bulletin*, 125, 387–91.

Palmer, J. (1986) Progressive skepticism: a critical approach to the psi controversy, *Journal of Parapsychology*, 50, 29–42.

Popper, K. (1972) *Conjectures and Refutations: The Growth of Scientific Knowledge*, 4th edn, London: Routledge and Kegan Paul.

Popper, K. (1980) *The Logic of Scientific Discovery*, 10th edn, London: Hutchinson.

Randi, J. (1982) *The Truth About Uri Geller*, Buffalo, NY: Prometheus Books.

Randi, J. (1987) *The Faith Healers*, Buffalo, NY: Prometheus.

Sagan, C. (1996) *The Demon-Haunted World: Science as a Candle in the Dark*, New York: Random House.

Stein, G. (ed.) (1996) *The Encyclopedia of the Paranormal*, Amherst, NY: Prometheus.

Thalbourne, M.A. (1996) An attempt to predict precognition scores using transliminality-relevant variables, *Journal of the Society for Psychical Research*, 61, 129–40.

Thalbourne, M.A. and Delin, P.S. (1994) A common thread underlying belief in the paranormal, creative personality, mystical experience and psychopathology, *Journal of Parapsychology*, 58, 3–38.

Utts, J. (1996) An assessment of the evidence for psychic functioning, *Journal of Scientific Exploration*, 10, 3–30.

Wiseman, R. (1997) *Deception and Self-Deception: Investigating Psychics*, Amherst, NY: Prometheus.

Zusne, L. and Jones, W.H. (1982) *Anomalistic Psychology*, Hillsdale, NJ: Erlbaum.

Zusne, L. and Jones, W.H. (1989) *Anomalistic Psychology: A Study of Magical Thinking*, 2nd edn, Hillsdale, NJ: Erlbaum.

Paranormal cognition

Chapter 6

Second sight

Shari A. Cohn-Simmen

Second sight is the name of a special psychic ability which is believed to be an inborn natural faculty of mind. For some it is believed to be a spiritual gift from God, for others, a hereditary gift which runs in particular families. There has been a long tradition of second sight, especially in the Highlands and Western Isles of Scotland, but it is also known to be experienced in other parts of the United Kingdom as well as in other cultures (Martin 1703, Schmëing 1950, Grober-Glück 1973, Shaw 1987, Virtanen 1990). There are many expressions pertaining to the faculty in the Gaelic language spoken by people indigenous to these areas (MacInnes 1989). The most common is An Dà Shealladh which literally means 'two sights'. One is the normal sight and the other is the ability to have prophetic visions.

Accounts of second sight from the seventeenth century onwards are consistent with modern-day accounts and reflect the cycle of birth, life and death. Though most visions are experienced in an awake state, some are experienced in a hypnagogic or dream state. The prophetic visions are experienced through various forms of imagery and usually concern sad events. Many classical accounts of second sight experiences reflect the burial customs of the time and can take the form of a direct representation of a person's fate. For example, a person literally sees a funeral procession at night and, by recognising the people carrying the coffin, knows who will die. Alternatively, the accounts can take a symbolic form. For example, a death shroud is seen on a person before that person dies. How much of the body is covered may be taken to indicate how soon the person will die. Other visions are of a person before, at the moment, or after they have died. For example, a woman saw a huge wave engulf a fisherman before he and his crew were drowned. In another case a woman had a vision of her neighbour in solid form in front of her house, and only later found he had died many miles away at the same time as she saw him. Some visions can involve people seeing their own *doppelgänger*, and tradition suggests this means you will soon die. Many accounts concern foreseeing accidents. For example, a man had a vision of his colleague falling off a roof on to spiked railings below. Although the man warned his colleague to be careful, his warnings went unheeded, and several days later his colleague was injured in the manner foreseen. For details of the accounts, see Cohn (1996).

The visions need not be exclusively visual; they can be expressed through the other senses as well. For example, a fisherman heard a woman's crying quite close to him. He searched all around but could find no trace of her. Three months afterwards, a young lad was drowned at the very spot, and his mother was crying there when the body was found (Cohn 1996). Some experiences bring good news. For example, the percipient has a vision of an apparition of a living person whom they do not recognise but eventually meet and marry.

Research

Many of the investigators, from the seventeenth century onwards, have collected accounts of second sight from the person directly (Kirk 1691, Fraser 1707, Theophilus Insulanus 1763), using what would now be considered the process-oriented approach to spontaneous case research in parapsychology. Others tried to record additional testimony from witnesses (e.g. Martin 1703) akin to today's proof-oriented approach. Some investigators' central aim was to prove to atheists that these accounts were evidence for a spiritual dimension of the mind in accordance with the Christian faith (Kirk 1691, Theophilus Insulanus 1763, Fraser 1707). Some investigators also maintained that second sight was hereditary, though they differed in their observations of the transmission patterns. Reverend Kirk, from Perthshire, observed that second sight was transmitted from father to son (Kirk 1691). However, Reverend Fraser, minister of the islands of Tiree and Coll, could not find any evidence to support such a transmission pattern (Fraser 1707). Aubrey (1696) published the first questionnaire-style investigation of second sight. He was informed by a correspondent that in several families in the Isle of Skye second sight was passed down from parents to their children. However, Martin (1703), who was himself born in Skye and trained in medicine, observed several cases where either parents or children appeared to possess second sight but not both. Much later, Campbell (1902) observed that second sight generally ran in families but there were a few cases in which only one person possessed the gift. Campbell was unusual for his time in that he was a sceptic, maintaining that second sight was due to hallucinations caused by disease.

More recent investigators from the School of Scottish Studies in the University of Edinburgh have recorded numerous accounts of second sight from the 1950s onwards as part of a wider effort to study the ethnology – the customs, languages, beliefs and ways of life – of diverse communities (Bennett 1989). The people interviewed came from the Highlands, Western Isles, Shetland and Orkney, and the Lowlands of Scotland as well as from North America. The interviews are generally recorded and care is taken over the confidentiality of the material. Some informants gave permission for their accounts to be published in a School of Scottish Studies journal, *Tocher* (McDermitt 1986, Whyte 1976, Bruford 1972, MacDonald 1972, MacLeod 1972). Autobiographical accounts of those who claim to possess second sight can be found in Watt (1989) and Whyte (1979). (For a comprehensive review of previous investigations, see Cohn 1999a, Hunter 2001a, 2001b.)

Cohn (1996) used a multidisciplinary approach to study second sight, applying methods from ethnology, parapsychology and human genetics. Drawing on interviews with people in different parts of Scotland, and questionnaire, survey and family history data, Cohn examined the prevalence of second sight, the nature of the experiences and whether there is any evidence to support the belief that second sight is hereditary. As there are few questionnaire studies (Aubrey 1696, Campbell and Hall 1968), Cohn (1996) devised a new questionnaire covering the different types of second sight experiences found in the historical accounts and biographical and family history information, which was sent to people who expressed an interest in the study. The 208 responses – mostly from Scotland – indicated that second sight is experienced by people of diverse ages, occupations, and religious and cultural traditions. An important factor related to having second sight was having had a religious experience. Women tended to report more experiences than men (Cohn 1999c). This sex difference is also found in reports of psychic and synchronistic experiences generally (Henry 1993).

Seventy people were interviewed and over 500 accounts were collected. The aim was to look for patterns in the large collection of cases. This approach made it impractical to authenticate every case, although often additional interviews were arranged with the informant and other family members. A consistent feature is that the imagery, whether visual, auditory, tactile or olfactory, was described as real and not originating purely in the mind. Some visions were seen as quick 'film-like' images through the mind, others appeared as projected three-dimensional images which became the central focus of perception. Projected 3-D imagery is also a key element in eidetic imagery. It was proposed that people with second sight could have an eidetic-like imagery (Cohn 1996). Schmëing (1950, 1954), who collected accounts of second sight in Germany, also observed such a relationship.

A significant finding from a recent large-scale random mail survey was that, throughout Scotland, people who reported second sight were significantly more likely to report second sight in blood-related family members (Cohn 1994). This gives empirical support to the traditional belief that second sight runs in families – but is it hereditary? To explore this, 130 pedigrees from families with a history of second sight were constructed and analysed for known inheritance patterns in consultation with a geneticist who is a sceptic regarding psychic phenomena (Cohn 1996, 1999b). The results are consistent with second sight having a possible genetic component, though certain aspects of the data favoured a social and cultural explanation.

Explanation

Sceptics regard second sight experiences as hallucinations, with any correspondence to real-world events being attributable to coincidence or rational inference about likely events. In this view, second sight runs in families due to oral tradition: the interpretation that experiences are psychic is handed down in the family.

The alternative view is that second sight is a genuine mental ability where the capacity to have psychic experiences is hereditary but the way the experiences are expressed is influenced by cultural factors. This would raise philosophical questions about the nature of mind, its relationship to time and how such an ability could be hereditary. To see which explanation is more likely, other family studies need to be done. If similar inheritance patterns are observed from different cultures, second sight could be a creative inborn mental process.

Conclusion

Experiences of second sight today may differ little from those of the seventeenth century. Whether they are examples of remarkable coincidences or instances of 'psychic' communication, they have a meaningful and often transformative effect on the lives of the people who have them. Second sight experiences offer us a window into the nature of mind and its exceptional abilities.

Recommended reading

Introductory

Bennett, M. (1989) *Scottish Customs: From the Cradle to the Grave*, Edinburgh: Polygon.

Campbell, J.G. (1902) *Witchcraft and Second Sight in the Highlands and Islands of Scotland*, Glasgow: James Maclehose & Sons.

Cohn, S.A. (1999a) A historical review of second sight: the collectors, their accounts and ideas, *Scottish Studies*, 33, 146–85.

Davidson, H.E. (ed.) (1989) *The Seer in Celtic and Other Traditions*, Edinburgh: John Donald.

Advanced

Cohn, S.A. (1999b) Second sight and family history: pedigree and segregation analyses, *Journal of Scientific Exploration*, 13, 3, 351–72.

Hunter, M. (2001a) *The Occult Laboratory: Magic, Science, and Second Sight in Late Seventeenth Century Scotland*, Woodbridge: Boydell Press.

Kirk, R. (1691) *The Secret Commonwealth of Elves, Fauns and Fairies and A Short Treatise of Charms and Spels* (1976 edition), Cambridge: D.S. Brewer Ltd and Rowan & Littlefield for the Folklore Society.

Martin, M. (1703) An account of the second sight. In *A Description of the Western Isles of Scotland*, London: Andrew Bell, 300–35.

References

Aubrey, J. (1696) *Miscellanies*, London: E. Castle.

Bruford, A. (1972) Second sight, *Tocher*, 6, 199–200.

Campbell, J.G. (1902) *Witchcraft and Second Sight in the Highlands and Islands of Scotland*, Glasgow: James Maclehose & Sons.

Campbell, J. and Hall, T. (1968) *Strange Things*, London: Routledge & Kegan Paul.

Cohn, S.A. (1994) A survey of Scottish second sight, *Journal of the Society for Psychical Research*, 59, 835, 385–400.

Cohn, S.A. (1996) The Scottish tradition of second sight and other psychic experiences in families. Unpublished Ph.D. dissertation, Dept of Psychology, University of Edinburgh.

Cohn, S.A. (1999c) A questionnaire study on second sight experiences, *Journal of the Society for Psychical Research*, 63, 855, 129–57.

Fraser, J. (1707) *Deuteroscopia: A Brief Discourse Concerning the Second Sight*, Edinburgh: A. Symson.

Grober-Glück, G. (1973) Second sight in Northern Germany: traditional popular belief and precognition. In A. Angoff and D. Barth (eds) *Parapsychology and Anthropology: Proceedings*, New York, 180–202.

Henry, J. (1993) Coincidence experience survey, *Journal of the Society for Psychical Research*, 59, 97–108

Hunter, M. (2001b) The discovery of second sight in late 17th-century Scotland, *History Today*, June, 48–53.

Insulanus, T. (1763) A treatise on the second sight. In *Miscellanea Scotica: A Collection of Tracts Relating to the History, Antiquities, Topography, and Literature of Scotland* (1820 edn), Glasgow: John Wylie and Co.

McDermitt, B. (1986) Stanley Robertson, *Tocher*, 40, 170–86.

MacDonald, A.J. (1972) Second sight, *Tocher*, 6, 192–5.

MacInnes, J. (1989) The seer in Gaelic tradition. In H.E. Davidson (ed.) *The Seer in Celtic and Other Traditions*, Edinburgh: John Donald, 9–24.

MacLeod, M. (1972) Second sight, *Tocher*, 6, 196–7.

Schmëing, K. (1950) *Geschichte des Zweiten Gesichts*, Bremen-Horn: Walter Dorn Verlag.

Schmëing, K. (1954) *Seher und Seherglaube Soziologie und Psychologie des 'Zweiten Gesichts'*, Darmstadt-Eberstadt: Themis-Verlag.

Shaw, J. (1987) *Tales until Dawn: The World of a Cape Breton Gaelic Story-Teller*, Kingston: McGill-Queen's University Press.

Virtanen, L. (1990) *'That Must Have Been ESP!': An Examination of Psychic Experiences*, Bloomington: Indiana University Press.

Watt, E. (1989) Some personal experiences of the second sight. In H.E. Davidson (ed.) *The Seer in Celtic and Other Traditions*, Edinburgh: John Donald, 25–36.

Whyte, B. (1976) Bessie Whyte, *Tocher*, 23, 249–76 (with contributions from Linda Headlee and Alan Bruford).

Whyte, B. (1979) *The Yellow on the Broom*, London: Futura.

Chapter 7

Extrasensory perception

John Beloff with Jane Henry

The expression extrasensory perception or ESP was introduced by J.B. Rhine when he set up a parapsychology laboratory at Duke University in the 1930s. It was intended to cover mind to mind communication cases known as 'telepathy' (defined as non-sensory communication between separated individuals), 'clairvoyance' (non-sensory awareness of some scene or object) and 'precognition' (non-inferential awareness of some future event or state of affairs). Retrocognition was subsequently introduced to refer to non-inferential awareness of a past event. ESP was contrasted with PK (psychokinesis) which implies the influence of the individual on the external world otherwise than by the use of the limbs and body (mind over matter). The terms 'telepathy', 'clairvoyance', 'precognition' and 'retrocognition' were retained to denote the particular mode of ESP in operation. Many experiments use telepathic, clairvoyant and precognitive variants of the same basic protocol, for example card guessing or the ganzfeld technique.

The following are some of the questions which parapsychologists have addressed concerning the nature and *modus operandi* of ESP.

1 Is it, like sense-perception, limited by space, time and situation or is it, potentially, independent of space–time and situational limitations?
2 Is it an acquired skill which anyone could, with practice, hope to attain? Or is it, like genius in music or mathematics, something one is born with?
3 Can it be explained in the sort of way that we can now explain sensory perception?
4 Are ESP experiments replicable?

Like most questions in parapsychology, or, indeed, in psychology, there are no universally agreed answers; the first author's answers to these questions follow:

1 Unlike normal perception, ESP does not appear to be limited by spatial and temporal factors.

2 Although some improvement may be expected with practice, ESP ability, much like musical ability, is a gift.
3 There is no agreed explanation in psychophysiological terms, as there is for sense-perception, hence we still categorise ESP as 'paranormal'.
4 Meta-analyses are beginning to provide evidence to suggest that certain forms of ESP may be replicable.

Research methods

Research into ESP can be divided into forced-choice and free-choice experiments. In the former the number of targets is restricted. In the latter each potential target is open (in the sense that in principle the target might be any picture or location).

Forced choice

Card guessing

J.B. Rhine (1947), at Duke University, introduced the use of a special pack of 'ESP cards' (known as 'Zener cards') consisting of twenty-five cards composed of five sets of five symbols, namely circle, cross, wavy-lines, square and star. These differ in the number of lines they comprise, from one for the circle to five lines for the star. By chance alone, a subject can be expected to guess correctly on average five times out of the twenty-five.

In the early days of the Rhine laboratory several 'high-scoring' subjects emerged, notably Hubert Pearce, Charles Stuart and A.J. Linzmayer, capable of averaging around seven hits per run over a large number of runs, thereby producing enormous odds against chance. Of particular note were the experiments conducted by J. Gaither Pratt with Pearce in 1954 where sender and subject were in different buildings on the Duke campus. The mean number of hits per run in 74 runs was 7.1 giving odds against chance of 10^{-23}. But later such subjects were hard to come by. One was Bill Delmore (discussed in Chapter 1, pp. 12–13), a law student from Yale who had unusual vivid imagery. He was tested intensively by Edward Kelly and B.K. Kanthamani (an Indian woman who worked for a period with Rhine) who published their findings in 1972. (For a critical view of Delmore's work see Hansen 1992.)

In Britain, the foremost exponent of card-guessing ESP was S.G. Soal who, after spending many years trying in vain to replicate Rhine's findings, discovered two outstanding subjects, Basil Shackleton and Gloria Stewart, with whom he worked during the 1940s. Unfortunately, Soal's work came under a cloud when, after he died in 1975, the researcher and statistician, Betty Markwick, published evidence suggesting that Soal had been guilty of falsifying some of his results in the Shackleton experiments.

The next card-guessing subject to make parapsychological history was Pavel Stepanek, a library clerk who lived in Prague. He was discovered by the Czech parapsychologist, Milan Ryzl, who at the time was interested in using hypnosis to boost ESP scoring. However, Stepanek soon functioned just as well in the waking state. The task at which he made his name consisted of guessing whether the green side or the white side of a coloured card was uppermost when the card was presented to him inside an opaque envelope. As against the 50 per cent correct to be expected by chance, Stepanek would average about 55 per cent correct over long sequences. Eventually, J.G. Pratt, a former associate of Rhine's, took charge of the investigation and brought Stepanek over to the United States for testing in his own laboratory, where the scoring continued as before. Over a ten-year period, some eighteen different investigators were involved giving rise to some twenty-seven research reports. Stepanek finally achieved a kind of immortality when he was included in the *Guinness Book of Records* as having registered more card guesses than any other individual in history!

Automated ESP

When, in the 1960s, Helmut Schmidt took over as director of research at the Duke Laboratory, he introduced automated methods of scoring using a machine of his own devising where the subject presses a button to indicate which of five lamps will next come on. The randomicity of the target sequence was determined by the random emission of electrons from a radioactive source. Three specially selected subjects were used in the initial experiments with this device and results showed that, although the hit rate was a mere 26.7 per cent as against the 25 per cent expected by chance, the odds over 15,000 trials were astronomically beyond chance. Like Rhine, he, too, found his most successful subjects early in his career.

Free-choice protocols

Since the 1960s, the so-called 'free-response' paradigm has dominated ESP research. The three most successful techniques using a free-response paradigm were:

1. 'Remote-viewing' as developed by Russell Targ and Hal Puthoff (1977) at the S.R.I. in San Francisco.
2. The 'ganzfeld' technique as developed by the late Charles Honorton at his own Psychophysical Research Laboratory at Princeton.
3. The dream-telepathy technique as developed by Montague Ullman and Stanley Krippner at the Maimonides Hospital, New York.

In all such free-response procedures the choice of target is arbitrary.

Remote viewing

In a remote-viewing trial, the target is some place or object selected at random by the experimenter from a range of such targets and the subject is encouraged to try visualising the target and to make sketches before eventually being asked to identify the place or object chosen as target for that trial (e.g. Mumford *et al.* 1995, Wiseman and Milton 1999). A brief outline of some of Targ and Puthoff's experiments may be found on p. 14.

The 'remote-viewing' program which came under the direction of Edwin May in 1985 was, perhaps, the first parapsychological research program to be funded by government agencies, notably the Science Applications International Corporation (SAIC) with funding from the Army, the Navy, NASA and the CIA, all of whom appreciated the possibilities it seemed to offer for spying purposes.

Radin (1997) has drawn attention to the following conclusions for parapsychology arising out of the government review committee's report in the wake of the SAIC remote-viewing program:

1 The free-response method is much more successful than the forced-choice method (where the subject has to choose between a given set of targets).
2 Subjects selected on the basis of their past performance were far more successful than randomly selected subjects.
3 Only about 1 per cent of subjects tested proved to be consistently successful, showing that, like musical or mathematical ability, psi ability is a rare gift.
4 Practice makes little difference to the rate of success.
5 Feedback is not strictly necessary though it can be psychologically rewarding.

Finally, and of special theoretical interest in this context, the distance between subject and target seems to make no difference to the accuracy of the results, nor does the electromagnetic shielding of the subject.

The ganzfeld technique

In the ganzfeld technique the subject is cut off from his/her surroundings by being put in a secluded place and having his/her eyes covered with translucent goggles to produce a uniform visual field (the 'ganzfeld') as a means of generating vivid visual imagery. Later the subject is shown four pictures and asked to identify the one which corresponds most closely to the imagery which he/she has been experiencing (Honorton *et al.* 1990). See p. 15 for a fuller description of this approach and Chapter 3 for a detailed account of the meta-analysis of the ganzfeld experiments over the years.

Dream-telepathy

Many spontaneous psi experiences, perhaps as many as half of those reported, occur during sleep in the course of dreaming. At the Maimonides Medical Center in Brooklyn, New York, Montague Ullman, a psychiatrist, and Stanley Krippner, a psychologist, decided to exploit this fact by getting volunteers to sleep at the laboratory where they would be awakened after each dream-phase (which can be identified by the rapid eye movements (REMs) that accompany dreaming and are discernible under the eyelids) and asked to recount their dream. An experimenter in another room would be looking at a picture and attempting to influence telepathically the dream content so as to reflect the content of the target picture. Eventually, independent judges would be asked to match a set of dream protocols for the successive nights with a set of such target pictures. The Maimonides experiments, which broke new ground in parapsychology, lasted from 1966 to 1972 (Ullman *et al.* 1973).

The 'ganzfeld', the 'remote-viewing' and the dream-telepathy techniques have all been replicated elsewhere although seldom with as much success as by their pioneers; pioneering, we must remember, is always more exciting than replicating the work of others. However, Marilyn Schlitz, of the Institute of Noetic Sciences, California, who has distinguished herself both as experimenter and as subject, achieved notable successes as a subject in remote-viewing experiments. At all events, meta-analyses of the results for each of these three techniques suggest that more than chance is operating (see Chapter 3 on meta-analyses in parapsychology).

While most targets are visual, other types of target have been tried, including musical targets and smell. Recently there has been increased interest in physiological measures as indicators of ESP. William Braud (1981) has made a major contribution to their use. For example, the electrical conductivity of the skin (the galvanic skin response or GSR) is a sensitive measure of emotional arousal. There is evidence that it will respond to an ESP signal when, for example, an agent in another room is given an emotionally arousing stimulus (Schlitz and LaBerge 1997, see also pp. 51–2). Braud also tested the folk belief that people can tell when they are being stared at from behind using closed circuit television in the test situation. This topic is discussed at length in Sheldrake (1994; 2003) and Schmidt *et al.* (2004).

Personality

Is there any way we can tell in advance which subjects will succeed and which will fail at a given task? In the 1950s, Gertrude Schmeidler and Bob McConnell worked on the 'sheep–goat' effect comparing the performance of believing *sheep* and doubting *goats*. Essentially, it has been shown that those who believe in ESP, the 'sheep', will do better than those who do not believe in ESP, the 'goats', who may even score significantly in the negative direction (Schmeidler 1988). Belief seems to be an important predictor of success in psi experiments. There is also evidence that *extraverts* make better subjects than introverts and the Eysenck Personality Inventory has been used in this connection (as discussed in Chapter 3, p. 55).

There is further evidence that subjects will do better in tests of ESP when in a *relaxed* condition, and pioneering work has been done in this connection by William Braud and Lendell Braud using the technique they call 'progressive relaxation'. Other work has looked at defensiveness (see p. 73) and hypnotic susceptibility.

Explanations

At present there is no accepted mechanism which could explain ESP. Some explanations attempt to explain the phenomenon away, and others speculate about possible mechanisms which might account for the phenomenon. A brief summary of some of the key explanations follows. Chapter 1 (pp. 19–24) offers a fuller account of explanations for parapsychological phenomena.

Fraud

One explanation for ESP is fraud. The role of fraud has been raised in relation to certain subjects and experimenters – see, for example, Hansen's (1992) article on the work with Delmore. However, modern experimental controls effectively rule out the possibility of fraud through devices such as automated target-setting and result recording and independent judging.

Psychological predisposition

It has been proposed that certain people are predisposed to ESP experiences. Those who experience ESP spontaneously have a tendency to score high on measures of dissociation (Zingrone and Alvarado 1994). The fantasy-prone report a high frequency of ESP experiences (Wilson and Barber 1983). High absorption is built into ESP experiments like the ganzfeld and dream research and appears to facilitate ESP.

Physical mechanism

The mechanisms underlying ESP are not understood. Some researchers have suggested a role for the temporal lobe, or pineal gland, others that a synaesthetic-like component may be involved, but none of these seems adequate to account for all ESP experiences. Some researchers believe that some as yet unexplained physical phenomenon can account for ESP, others believe that if ESP proves to be substantiated it throws into question our materialist assumptions.

Experimenter effect

Even if ESP is accepted there is the question of the source of the ESP. The success of certain experimenters (such as Honorton, Schmidt and Schlitz) in obtaining positive results while others, using ostensibly the same techniques, are unsuccessful, has led some people to suggest that in certain cases the source of the ESP may be the experimenter rather than the subject.

Paraphysics

Even people who believe that telepathy and clairvoyance will be explained at some time in the future often have problems with precognition. This appears to violate the laws of nature. Paraphysicists have suggested various mechanisms through which such communication might theoretically be possible; however, these are purely speculative hypotheses (see Rush 1986 for a review).

Conclusion

What conclusions, then, can we draw from the evidence for ESP? On the one hand, we can never be certain that, simply by following a tried procedure, we will obtain significant results. Hence most sceptics are reluctant to devote time to replicating such experiments and can still fall back on the plea that, until they can be confident of reproducing the given phenomenon in their own laboratory, they will continue to ignore parapsychological findings and refuse to grant that ESP (whether telepathic or clairvoyant) is established.

There is, however, a deeper reason for the refusal of the scientific establishment to credit paranormal phenomena. For, as has been pointed out, 'paranormality' implies that there is no agreed explanation within current understanding of what is possible, that is, in terms of the physico-chemical processes which are assumed to underlie all natural phenomena. Once we accept ESP (or, indeed, any paranormal phenomenon) we may have to step outside that arena where we can fall back on mechanistic explanations.

This chapter has given only a brief outline of some of the main lines of work on ESP. The other chapters in the first two sections of the book (Chapters 1 to 9) also address various differing aspects of ESP and serve to amplify the outline given here.

Recommended reading

Introductory

Broughton, R.S. (1991) *Parapsychology: The Controversial Science*, New York: Ballantine Books. Accessible account of parapsychology.

Inglis, B. (1985) *The Paranormal: An Encyclopedia of Psychic Phenomena*, London: Paladin. Popular introduction to psi.

Irwin, H.J. (1999) *An Introduction to Parapsychology*, 3rd edn, Jefferson, NC: McFarland. More academic account of the field.

Sheldrake, R. (1994) *Seven Experiments that Could Change the World*, London: Fourth Estate. Interesting and provocative.

Advanced

Edge, H.L., Morris, R.L., Rush, H. and Palmer, J. (1985) *Foundations of Parapsychology*, London and Boston: Routledge & Kegan Paul. A parapsychology textbook by authors who have done pioneering work in the field.

Nash, C.B. (1986) *Parapsychology: The Science of Psiology*, Springfield. IL: Charles C Thomas. By a distinguished parapsychologist.

Radin, D. (1997) *The Conscious Universe: The Scientific Truth of Psychic Phenomena*, San Francisco: Harper Edge. Authoritative and sophisticated review of the evidence on experimental ESP and PK.

Ramakrishna Rao, K. (1984) *The Basic Experiments of Parapsychology*, Jefferson, NC: McFarland. By a distinguished parapsychologist.

Wolman, B.J. (ed.) (1977) *Handbook of Parapsychology*, New York: Van Nostrand Reinhold. Encyclopedia of paranormal phenomena, good but dated.

References

Braud, W. (1981) Psi performance and autonomic nervous system activity, *Journal of the American Society for Psychical Research*, 75, 1–35.

Hansen, G. (1992) The research with B.D. and the legacy of magical ignorance, *Journal of Parapsychology*, 56, 4, 307–33.

Honorton, H., Berger, R.E., Varvoglis, M., Quant, M., Derr, P., Schechter, E.I. and Ferrari, D.C. (1990) Psi communication in the ganzfeld, *Journal of Parapsychology*, 54, 99–139.

Irwin, H.J. (1994) *An Introduction to Parapsychology*, 2nd edn, Jefferson, NC: McFarland.

Mumford, M.D., Rose, A.M. and Goslin, D.A. (1995) *An Evaluation of Remote Viewing*, American Institutes of Research.

Rhine, J.B. (1947) *The Reach of the Mind*, New York: Sloane.

Rush, J.H. (1986) Physical and quasi-physical theories of psi. Chapter 11 in H. Edge, R.L. Morris, J. Palmer and J.H. Rush (1986) *Foundations of Parapsychology*, Boston: Routledge and Kegan Paul.

Schlitz, M. and LaBerge, S. (1997) Covert observation increases skin conductance in subjects unaware they are being stared at, *Journal of Parapsychology*, 61, 3, 185–96.

Schmeidler, G.R. (1988) *Parapsychology and Psychology: Matches and Mismatches*, Jefferson, NC: MacFarland.

Schmidt, S., Schneider, R., Utts, J. and Walach, H. (2004) Distant intentionality and the feeling of being stared at: Two meta-analyses, *British Journal of Psychology*, 95, 235–47.

Sheldrake, M. (2001) The sense of being stared at: elimination of possible artefacts, *Journal of the Society for Psychical Research*, 65, 122–37.

Sheldrake, M. (2003) *The Sense of Being Stared at*, London: Hutchinson.

Targ, R. and Puthoff, H. (1977) *Mind-Reach*, New York: Delacorte.

Ullman, M., Krippner, S. and Vaughan, A. (1973) *Dream Telepathy*, London: Turnstone.

Wilson, S.C. and Barber, T.X. (1983) The fantasy-prone personality. In A.A. Sheikh (ed.) *Imagery: Current Research, Theory and Application*, New York: Wiley, 340–87.

Wiseman, R. and Milton, J. (1999) Experiment one of the SAIC remote viewing program: a critical re-evaluation: reply to May, *Journal of Parapsychology*, 63, 1, 3–14.

Zingrone, N.L. and Alvarado, C.S. (1994) Psychic and dissociative experiences. Paper presented to the 37th Annual Convention of the Parapsychological Association.

Chapter 8

Precognition and premonitions

Keith Hearne and Jane Henry

A *premonition* (forewarning) is an experience which appears to anticipate a future event and which could not reasonably have been inferred from information available before that later event. The premonition may consist of apparent actual detailed knowledge of a later event, or a non-specific feeling of foreboding that something will happen. The more neutral term precognition (foreknowing) is often applied in scientific literature.

The following example of a premonition exemplifies the media-announcement variety, where it is reported that future information comes in the form of some official statement. At about noon on 1 June 1974, a woman living near Grimsby in South Humberside, England, was watching TV alone, when the word 'Newsflash' appeared on the screen and a voice-over stated that an explosion had occurred at the Flixborough chemical plant, some 40 km away. The woman knew no one who worked at the plant, and the place meant little to her. She told two reliable witnesses shortly afterwards when they came in for lunch. A few hours later, at 4.53 p.m. that same afternoon, a massive explosion at the site killed twenty-eight people and caused extensive damage, when a bypass pipe ruptured unexpectedly. According to the official report of the disaster, there was no particular technical problem at the plant when the shifts changed over at 3 p.m. that afternoon. None of the TV stations had put out a Newsflash of any kind that lunch time (Hearne 1982a).

Precognition has been a persistently recognised phenomenon throughout chronicled history (Dodds 1971). Cases were noted in the ancient civilisations of the Egyptians, Assyrians, Babylonians, Greeks, Romans and others, and have continued to be reported to the present time. A dramatic example is provided by the case of Mrs Grant who having become increasingly agitated throughout the day persuaded her husband General Grant not to accompany Lincoln out on the evening he was assassinated. It subsequently emerged that Grant had been an intended victim that night (Radin 1997, pp. 112–13).

Prophetic dreams are mentioned in the Bible, perhaps the most famous being that of the Pharaoh who dreamed of seven years of abundance followed by seven years of famine, as interpreted by Joseph (Genesis 41).

Other phenomena involving apparent foreknowledge include omens and divination. An *omen* is a happening that precedes an event and which seems to reflect unfavourably, or favourably, on it by way of symbolism. For instance, the head of the staff of King Charles I fell off at his trial. The king was indeed later executed.

Divination entails attempting to foretell the future. An augury is a form of divination based on a chance outcome such as inspecting entrails, reading tea-leaves, throwing bones, the I Ching and the Runes. A universally employed technique of seeing future events, termed scrying, uses a surface that encourages the formation of visual imagery, for example hydromancy (water with a little oil added) and crystal gazing. A famous book of prophecies, in the form of 942 quatrains (obtained by the scrying method), was compiled by the Frenchman Nostradamus in the sixteenth century. However, the prophecies are not in chronological order, and are vague and ambiguous (Cheetham 1973).

Research

Surveys

Surveys suggest that premonitions are quite common. Louisa Rhine (1955) found that 40 per cent of anecdotal psi effects concern precognition in some form. According to a large-scale survey in Britain, about one in four of the sample asserted that they had experienced a premonition and some two-thirds of those questioned accepted the occurrence of premonition dreams (Haraldsson 1985).

Hearne (1984) determined that premonitions were reported to emerge from four basic states, in the following descending order of frequency: dreams (44 per cent), waking thoughts (34 per cent), waking imagery (12 per cent) and sleep-onset imagery (10 per cent). When categorised, the frequencies of themes were: death (53 per cent), unpleasant events (32 per cent), pleasant events (8 per cent) and neutral events (7 per cent). About 90 per cent of the premonition cases reported were submitted by females. Some individuals reported having experienced very many premonitions. A number of other studies of accounts have found that a high proportion (three-fifths and three-quarters) of precognitive cases occur in dreams (e.g. Sannwald 1963, Rhine 1962).

A number of researchers have attempted to investigate cases of reported premonition (Saltmarsh 1938, Rhine 1962, Hearne 1982b, Sondow 1989). For example, Barker (1967) retrospectively sought premonitions of the

Aberfan coal disaster and appeared to receive a small number of impressive accounts he subsequently verified with witnesses. For example, one woman's dream of 'screaming children and a creeping black substance' fourteen days prior to the event was confirmed by her husband. The occasional striking correspondence between, say, dreams and future events is likely, given the large number of people in the world and the fact that we dream every night.

Cox (1956) wondered if forebodings could affect action without reaching conscious awareness. He found that the occupancy rate on trains having serious accidents was lower than the occupancy rate on the day before. He interpreted this as suggesting that some people unconsciously used psi to avoid the accident. An alternative theoretical explanation is that bad weather may have kept some people away on the day of the accident and possibly made the accident itself more likely.

Experiments

Experimental investigation of precognition has involved, among other research, card-guessing (Rhine 1964), random number generator (RNG) studies (Schmidt 1969), animal researches (Duval and Montredon 1968) and dreams (Ullman *et al.* 1973).

Honorton and Ferrari's (1989) meta-analysis of all the 'forced-choice' precognition experiments conducted in the previous fifty years involved dice, Zener cards or lamp colours. The participant had to guess which of a limited number of symbols would be selected. Some of the future targets were selected in informal ways by dice tossing and card shuffling, others were selected randomly through the use of random number tables or electronic random number generation. This database includes over 300 studies by 60 odd investigators, 23 of whom reported successful results. The result was extremely significant with the odds of 10^{25} to 1 against this occurring by chance. Steinkamp *et al.* (1998) undertook a meta-analysis of all the forced-choice experiments published in reputable parapsychology journals between 1935 and 1997 that compared clairvoyance and precognition. They found essentially no difference in the effect size between the two protocols. (See pp. 50–1 for amplification of these studies.)

The precognitive dream-telepathy experiments conducted by Ullman *et al.* (1973) were highly successful. For example, Malcolm Bessent, a British sensitive, slept in the laboratory and described his dreams to an experimenter before the target was chosen. Judges subsequently matched the dream descriptions to one of eight possible targets. Bessent got the target correct in ten out of sixteen sessions, a highly significant result.

Recent experiments by Radin (1997) seem to show a presentiment effect in physiological measures such as electrodermal activity (EDA). Typically participants are shown either calm or emotionally arousing pictures. EDA normally goes up after viewing emotional pictures and slightly down after calm ones. Heart rate also drops after seeing a calm picture. Amazingly in these experiments participants appeared to anticipate the nature of the future card, as not only did their EDA begin to change differentially a few seconds before they saw the picture (as they anticipated seeing it), but their EDA rose more on average before an emotional picture than before a calm picture. Most participants were unaware of this change in themselves, suggesting that any presentiment was largely unconscious. Bierman (2002) has replicated this phenomenon. Earlier Klintman (1983, 1984) had reported an unexpected apparent precognitive effect in a series of perceptual priming experiments.

The results from laboratory precognition experiments appear to be as successful as parapsychology experiments undertaken in real time.

Explanation

Normal

Attempts to account for premonitions through normal explanations include: inference, coincidence, preferential selection, self-fulfilling prophecies and psychological abnormality. (See Chapter 4 for elaboration on the possible role of psychological factors in accounting for apparently parapsychological phenomena.)

Supernormal

Supernormal explanations, falling short of accepting precognition *per se*, include: simultaneous telepathy/clairvoyance (Stevenson 1970), psychokinetic forces causing the later event (Tanagras 1949), information carried via sub-atomic particles (Feynmann 1949), and an extended 'specious present' (Saltmarsh 1938). For example, if someone foretells which car will win a race they might have clairvoyantly intuited the superiority of the mechanics of the vehicle in the present and realised that would lead the car to win, or alternatively the fact that they believed the car would win might have had some PK effect assisting its passage to the winning position. Other theories proffer notions of multiple time-dimensions (Dunne 1927), space-time folds (Schmeidler 1971), psi fields (Roll 1957–64), and acausality (Jung and Pauli 1955).

Precognition

The 'precognitive' explanation suggests that information can somehow travel across time. Of those prepared to entertain the idea of precognition some feel that premonitions can foretell the future as it will happen and others that premonitions only indicate a probable future outcome which may not necessarily come to pass. Some parapsychologists accept telepathy but find precognition hard to envisage. The particular and unique philosophical problem concerning precognition is that the apparent law of cause and later effect is violated by such phenomena, resulting in 'backwards causation'. Taking the current philosophical attitude of standard realism, many scientists have dismissed precognition as simply impossible. However, some theorists have asserted that if precognition occurs, then the materialistic universe must be rethought (Hearne 1989).

Conclusion

Considering the fundamental implications for science if precognition is a real phenomenon, the strong persistence of premonition reports over a long historical period and positive precognition experimental results, more research into precognition, premonition and presentiment seems justified.

Recommended reading

Introductory

Radin, D. (1997) Perception through time. Chapter 7 in D. Radin, *The Conscious Universe*, New York: Harper Collins, 11–124. Clear and interesting introduction to premonitions and precognition, strong on experimental data.

Advanced

Dunne, J.W. (1927) *An Experiment with Time*, London: Faber. A detailed account of a series of premonitions.

References

Barker, J.C. (1967) Premonitions of the Aberfan disaster, *Journal of the Society for Psychical Research*, 44, 169–81.

Bierman, W. (2002) Anomalous anticipatory behaviour. Presentation to Towards a Science of Consciousness Conference, Tucson.

Cheetham, E. (1973) *The Prophecies of Nostradamus*. Pedigree Books: NY.

Cox, W.E. (1956) Precognition: an analysis II, *Journal of the American Society for Psychical Research*, 50, 99–109.

Dodds, E.R. (1971) *The Prophecies of Nostradamus*, London: Corgi Books.

Duval, P. and Montredon, E. (1968) ESP experiments with mice, *Journal of Parapsychology*, 32, 153–66.

Feynmann, R.P. (1949) The theory of positrons, *Physical Review*, 76, 749–59.

Haraldsson, E. (1985) Representative national surveys of psychic phenomena, *Journal of the Society for Psychical Research*, 52, 796, 261–70.

Hearne, K.M.T. (1982a) An ostensible precognition of the 1974 Flixborough disaster, *Journal of the Society for Psychical Research*, 51, 790, 210–13.

Hearne, K.M.T. (1982b) Three cases of ostensible precognition from a single percipient, *Journal of the Society for Psychical Research*, 51, 791, 288–91.

Hearne, K.M.T. (1984) A survey of reported premonitions and those who have them, *Journal of the Society for Psychical Research*, 53, 801, 261–70.

Hearne, K.M.T. (1989) *Visions of the Future*, Wellingborough: Aquarian Press.

Honorton, C. and Ferrari, D.C. (1989) Fortune telling: a meta-analysis of forced choice precognition experiments, 1935–87, *Journal of Parapsychology*, 53, 281–308.

Jung, C.G. and Pauli, W. (1955) *The Interpretation of Nature and the Psyche: Synchronicity; and the Influence of Archetypal Ideas on the Scientific Theories of Kepler*, New York: Pantheon.

Klintman, H. (1983) Is there a paranormal precognitive effect in certain types of perceptual sequences? Part 1, *European Journal of Psychology*, 5, 19–49.

Klintman, H. (1984) Is there a paranormal precognitive effect in certain types of perceptual sequences? Part 2, *European Journal of Psychology*, 5, 125–40.

Rhine, L.E. (1954) Frequencies of types of experiences in spontaneous precognition, *Journal of Parapsychology*, 18, 93–123.

Rhine, L.E. (1955) Precognition and intervention, *Journal of Parapsychology*, 19, 34.

Rhine, L.E. (1962) Psychological processes in ESP experiences, Part 1, *Journal of Parapsychology*, 26, 88–111

Rhine, J.B. (1964) *Extra-sensory Perception*, Boston: Branden.

Roll, W.G. (1957–64) The psi-field, *Proceedings of the Parapsychological Association*, 1, 32–65.

Saltmarsh, H. (1938) *Foreknowledge*, London: G. Bell.

Sannwald, G. (1963) On the psychology of spontaneous paranormal phenomena, *International Journal of Parapsychology*, 5, 274–92.

Schmeidler, G. (1971) Respice, adspice ~ prospice, *Proceedings of the Parapsychological Association*, 8, 117–45.

Schmidt, H. (1969) Precognition as a quantum process, *Journal of Parapsychology*, 33, 99–108.

Sondow, N. (1989) The decline of precognized events with the passage of time: evidence from spontaneous dreams, *European Journal of Psychology*, 82, 1, 33–51.

Steinkamp, F., Milton, J. and Morris, R.L. (1998) A meta-analysis of forced-choice experiments comparing clairvoyance and precognition, *Journal of Parapsychology*, 62, 3, 193–218.

Stevenson, I. (1970) Precognition of disasters, *Journal of the American Society for Psychical Research*, 64, 2, 187–210.

Tanagras, A. (1949) The theory of the psychobolie, *Journal of the American Society for Psychical Research*, 43, 151–4 .

Ullman, M., Krippner, S. and Vaughan, A. (1973) *Dream Telepathy*, New York: Macmillan.

Chapter 9

Animal psi

Rupert Sheldrake

For many years animal trainers, pet owners and naturalists have reported various kinds of perceptiveness in animals that suggest the existence of animal psi. Surprisingly little research has been done on these phenomena. Biologists have been inhibited by the taboo against 'the paranormal', and psychical researchers and parapsychologists have with few exceptions confined their attention to human beings (exceptions include Duval and Montredon 1968 and Schmidt 1970). At one time there was more interest in animal psi among parapsychologists but a prominent case of possible fraud concerning the work of Levy seems to have left the field under a bit of a cloud (Beloff 1993, pp. 145–6). The main line of research in this area currently is work with pets and pet owners.

Three kinds of unexplained perceptiveness

There are three major categories of unexplained perceptiveness by animals that suggest the existence of psi, namely telepathy, the sense of direction, and premonitions.

Telepathy

Recent random household surveys in England and the United States have shown that many pet owners believe their animals are sometimes telepathic with them. An average of 48 per cent of dog owners and 33 per cent of cat owners said that their pets responded to their thoughts or silent commands (Sheldrake *et al.* 1998). Many horse trainers and riders believe that their horse can pick up their intentions telepathically. Some companion animals seem to know when a particular person is on the telephone. Some react when their owner is in distress in a distant place, or dying.

Many pet owners have also observed that their animals seem to anticipate the arrival of a member of the household, sometimes ten minutes or more in advance. The pets typically show their anticipation by going to wait at a door or window. In the random household surveys, 51 per cent of dog owners said they had noticed such anticipatory behaviour, and 30 per cent of cat owners (Sheldrake 1999). Some parrot and parakeet owners have also observed that their birds become excited before a member of the family returns.

In many cases the animal's anticipation of their owner's return cannot be explained in terms of routine, clues from people at home, or hearing familiar cars approaching (Sheldrake 1999). In videotaped experiments, dogs can still anticipate their owner's return at randomly chosen times, even when they are travelling in taxis or other unfamiliar vehicles (Sheldrake and Smart 1998, 2000a). The animals seem to pick up telepathically their owner's intention to come home.

The sense of direction

Homing pigeons can find their way back to their loft over hundreds of miles of unfamiliar terrain. Migrating European swallows travel thousands of miles to their feeding grounds in Africa, and in the spring return to their native place, even to the very same building where they nested before. Their ability to navigate towards distant destinations is still unexplained and cannot be accounted for in terms of smell, or any of the known senses, or even a compass sense.

Some dogs, cats, horses and other domesticated animals also have a good sense of direction and find their way home from unfamiliar places many miles away.

Sometimes animals 'home' not to places but to people. Some dog owners who have gone away and left their pet behind are found by the animal in distant places to which the animal has never been before. Tracking the person by smell may explain some cases when the distances are short, but in others the only feasible explanation seems to be an invisible connection between the animal and the person to whom they are bonded (Sheldrake 1999).

Premonitions

Some premonitions may be explicable in terms of physical stimuli: for example, animals that become disturbed before earthquakes may be reacting to subtle electrical changes, or dogs that alert their epileptic owners to an impending fit may notice subtle muscular tremors or unusual odours. But other premonitions seem to involve mysterious forebodings that challenge our usual assumptions about the separation of past, present and future.

All three types of perceptiveness – telepathy, the sense of direction and premonitions – seem better developed in non-human species such as dogs than they are in people. Nevertheless they occur in the human realm too.

Human psychic powers or a 'sixth sense' look more natural, more biological, when they are seen in the light of animal behaviour. Much that appears 'paranormal' at present looks normal when we expand our ideas of normality.

Animal psychokinesis

Unlike the kinds of perceptiveness whose existence is implied by a great wealth of anecdotal evidence, there is little or no anecdotal evidence that suggests the existence of psychokinesis (PK) by animals, perhaps because such 'mind over matter' effects, if they occurred, would be hard to recognise. The evidence for animal PK comes from laboratory experiments involving random number generators, and is discussed below.

Research on the unexplained powers of animals

Animal telepathy

Much of the evidence for animal telepathy is anecdotal, in the sense that it consists of unpublished stories. I have built up a large database of such stories, and they provide the basis for a natural history of what people believe about the perceptiveness of animals.

The commonest kinds of seemingly telepathic response are: the anticipation of owners coming home; the anticipation of owners going away; the anticipation of being fed; cats knowing when their owners intend to take them to the vet, and disappearing; dogs knowing when their owners are planning to take them for a walk; and animals that get excited when their owner is on the telephone, even before the telephone has been answered, while they ignore calls from other people.

As sceptics rightly point out, some of these responses could be explained in terms of routine expectations, subtle sensory cues, chance coincidence and selective memory, or could be put down to the imaginations of doting pet owners. To test these possibilities, it is necessary to do experiments.

I and my colleagues have concentrated on the phenomenon of dogs that know when their owners are coming home. Dogs cannot be reacting to sensory cues from their owners when the people are miles away. In these experiments, the place where the dog waits for its owner is continuously recorded on time-coded videotape for the whole duration of the experiment. The person then returns at a randomly selected time unknown to the people at home and travels in an unfamiliar vehicle.

Over 150 experiments with a dog called Jaytee, belonging to Pam Smart, of Ramsbottom, Lancashire (Figure 9.1), have shown that the dog did indeed anticipate her return by fifteen minutes or more even when she was returning at randomly selected times in a taxi from over 6 km away, and

Figure 9.1 Pam Smart with Jaytee
Source: Gary Taylor © Rupert Sheldrake

when no one at home knew when to expect her. The dog usually reacted before she actually began her journey and seemed to be responding to her *intention* to return. However, Jaytee sometimes failed to anticipate Pam's return, especially when he was sick or distracted by a bitch on heat in a nearby flat. Nevertheless, taking all the results together, this effect was highly significant statistically, with odds against it being a chance effect of more than 100,000 to one. Jaytee showed the same anticipatory behaviour even when tested by sceptics (Sheldrake and Smart 2000a), although the sceptics themselves (Wiseman *et al.* 1998) claimed that the dog had failed their tests. However, they were only able to make this claim by ignoring most of their own data (Sheldrake 1999b, 2000; see also the reply of Wiseman *et al.* 2000).

Although Jaytee is the dog that has been investigated most, I and my colleagues have obtained very similar results in videotaped experiments with several other dogs.

Other kinds of animal telepathy can also be investigated experimentally, for example the apparent ability of dogs to know when they are going to be taken for a walk. In these experiments the dogs are kept in a separate room or outbuilding and videotaped continuously while their owner, at a randomly selected time, thinks about taking them for a walk and then five minutes later does so. Preliminary experiments have shown dogs exhibiting obvious excitement when their owner is thinking about taking them out, although they could not have known this by normal sensory means. They did not manifest such excitement at other times.

There is much potential for further research on animal telepathy. If domestic animals are telepathic with their human owners, then it seems very likely that animals are telepathic with each other, and that this may play an important part in the wild. Some naturalists have already suggested that the co-ordination of flocks of birds and herds of animals may involve something like telepathy, as may communication between members of a pack of wolves.

Research into animal telepathy should enable human telepathy to be seen in an evolutionary light. The investigation of animal telepathy would also build bridges between parapsychology and biology to their mutual benefit.

The sense of direction

Most research on animal navigation has been carried out with homing pigeons, and this research over many decades has served only to deepen the problem of understanding their direction-finding ability. Navigation is goal-directed, and this implies that the animals know where their home is even when they are in an unfamiliar place and have to cross unfamiliar terrain.

Pigeons do not know their way home by remembering the twists and turns of the outward journey, because birds taken in closed vans by devious routes find their way home perfectly well, as do birds that have been anaesthetised on the outward journey, or transported in rotating drums. They do not navigate by the sun, because pigeons can home on cloudy days and can even be trained to navigate at night. However, they may use the sun as a simple compass to keep their bearings. Although they use landmarks in familiar terrain, they can home from unfamiliar places hundreds of kilometres from their home, where no familiar landmarks are visible. They cannot smell their home from hundreds of miles away, especially when it is downwind, although smell may play a part in their homing ability when they are close to familiar territory. Pigeons deprived of their sense of smell by researchers were still able to find their homes. (Sheldrake 1988 offers a review of work aiming to understand homing.)

Some biologists hope that the homing of pigeons might turn out to be explicable in terms of a magnetic sense. But even if pigeons have a compass sense (which is not proven), this could not explain their ability to navigate. If you were taken blindfold to an unknown destination and given a compass, you would know where north was, but not the direction of your home.

The failure of conventional attempts to explain pigeon homing and many other kinds of animal navigation implies the existence of a sense of direction as yet unrecognised by institutional science. This could have major implications for the understanding of animal migrations, and would shed light on the human sense of direction, much better developed in traditional peoples, such as the bushmen of the Kalahari or Polynesian navigators, than in modern urban people.

Premonitions

Very little research has been done on animal premonitions, even in the case of earthquakes where such warnings could prove very useful.

Some forewarnings might be explicable in terms of physical clues, such as electrical changes before earthquakes and storms. Other premonitions are more mysterious, as in the case of animals that anticipated air raids during the Second World War long before they could have heard enemy planes approaching, or animals that become agitated before unforeseeable accidents. Here precognition or presentiment may be involved, implying either an influence passing backwards in time, or a blurring of the distinction between future, present and past.

Psychokinesis

Most recent research on human psychokinesis (PK) has involved the use of random event generators (see Chapter 10). In some astonishing experiments with young chicks, the French researcher René Peoc'h has demonstrated an effect of chicks' desires on random events at a distance (Peoc'h 1988a, 1988b). His experiments involved young chicks bonding to a machine instead of their mother.

Newly hatched chicks, like newly hatched ducklings and goslings, 'imprint' on the first moving object they encounter and follow it around. Normally this imprinting instinct causes them to bond with their mother, but if the eggs are hatched in an incubator and young birds first meet a person, then they will follow that person around instead. In laboratory experiments they can even be induced to imprint on moving balloons or other inanimate objects.

In his experiments, Peoc'h used a small robot that moved around on wheels in a series of random directions. At the end of each movement, it stopped, rotated through a randomly selected angle, and moved in a straight line for a randomly determined period before stopping and rotating again, and so on. These random movements were determined by a random number generator (RNG) inside the robot. The path it traced out was recorded. In control experiments, its movements were indeed random.

Peoc'h (1988a, 1988b) exposed newly hatched chicks to this robot, and they imprinted on this machine as if it were their mother. Consequently they wanted to follow it around, but Peoc'h stopped them doing so by putting them in a cage from which they could see the robot. The chicks could not move towards it; instead, they made the robot move towards them. Their desire to be near the robot somehow influenced the random number generator so as to keep the robot close to the cage. Chicks that were not imprinted on the robot had no such effect on its movement.

In other experiments, Peoc'h kept non-imprinted chicks in the dark. He put a lighted candle on the top of the robot, and put the chicks in the cage where they could see it. Chicks prefer being in the light during the daytime, and they 'pulled' the robot towards them, so that they received more light.

Peoc'h also carried out experiments in which rabbits were put in a cage where they could see the robot. At first they were frightened of it, and the robot moved away from them: they repelled it. But rabbits exposed to the robot daily for several weeks were no longer afraid of it and tended to pull it towards themselves.

Thus the desire or fear of these animals influenced 'random' events at a distance so as to attract or repel the robot. This would obviously not be possible if animals' desires and fears were confined to the inside of their brains. Instead, their intentions reached out to affect the behaviour of this machine.

As far as I know, no one has yet repeated Peoc'h's experiments. It is possible that they involve some technical flaw that no one has yet spotted. But if they are reliable and repeatable, then they are very important indeed. They imply that animals, both domesticated and wild, may through their fears and desires be able to influence what happens around them by psychokinesis.

Possible explanations

Explanations for animal psi include normal explanations (such as subtle sensory cues, coincidence, selective memory and imagination) and some form of telepathy on the part of the animal and/or human keeper.

It has been suggested that some animal psi may be a result of an experimenter effect on the part of the human experimenter rather than a telepathic ability in the animal. This is one possible explanation for Schmidt's surprising finding that the cockroaches in his PK experiments ended up receiving more than the expected number of electric shocks. Schmidt, an experimenter with a positive record of results in psychokinesis experiments, admitted that he disliked cockroaches and wondered if he could have inadvertently been influencing the RNG himself (Schmidt 1970). Human telepathy may explain some other animal psi phenomena (Randall 1998).

Telepathy from people to animals usually occurs only when there are close emotional bonds. This may well be an important factor in human telepathy too. My own hypothesis is that these bonds depend on fields that link together members of a social group, called social fields. These are one type of a more general class of fields called morphic fields (described in detail in Sheldrake 1988). These bonds continue to link members of the social group together even when they are far apart, beyond the range of sensory communication, and can serve as a medium through which telepathic communications can pass. The alternatives to the idea of morphic fields are the theories of telepathy and ESP discussed in Chapter 7.

Morphic fields may also underlie the sense of direction. Animals are linked not only to members of their social group by morphic fields, but also to significant places, such as their home. These fields continue to connect them to their home even when they are far away, rather like invisible elastic bands. These bonds can consequently give directional information, 'pulling' the animal in a homewards direction.

Morphic fields do not, however, provide any straightforward explanation for precognition (see Chapter 8 on precognition).

Perhaps animal psychokinesis is explicable in terms of morphic fields that project out to the focus of the animal's attention, connecting them to it and influencing 'random' events within it in accordance with their fears and desires.

Recommended reading

Introductory

Sheldrake, R. (1999) *Dogs That Know When Their Owners Are Coming Home, and Other Unexplained Powers of Animals*, London: Hutchinson. An extensive survey of this field and a summary of research on the unexplained powers of animals.

Advanced

Morris, R.L. (1977) Parapsychology, biology and ANPSI. In B.B. Wolman (ed.) *Handbook of Parapsychology*, New York: Van Nostrand Reinhold. A review of early research on animal psi.

Peoc'h, R. (1988a) Chicken imprinting and the tychoscope: an ANPSI experiment, *Journal of the Society for Psychical Research*, 55, 1–9.

Peoc'h, R. (1988b) Psychokinetic action of young chicks on an illuminated source, *Journal of Scientific Exploration*, 9, 223–9. Two key papers of René Peoc'h on PK by chicks.

Sheldrake, R. (2002) *Seven Experiments that Could Change the World*, 2nd edn, Rochester, NY: Park St. Press. A review of research on homing pigeons.

Sheldrake, R., Lawlor, C. and Turney, J. (1998) Perceptive pets: a survey in London, *Biology Forum*, 91, 57–74. Surveys of perceptive pets.

See also website: www.sheldrake.org Site including papers and experiments on animal psi and telepathy.

References

Beloff, J. (1993) *Parapsychology: A Concise History*, London: Athlone.

Duval, P. and Montredon, E. (1968) ESP experiments with mice, *Journal of Parapsychology*, 32, 153–66.

Randall, R. (1998) Animal psi revisited, *Paranormal Review*, 6, 12–15.

Schmidt, H. (1970) PK experiments with animals, *Journal of Parapsychology*, 36, 577–88.

Sheldrake, R. (1988) *The Presence of the Past*, London: Collins.

Sheldrake, R. (1999) Commentary on a paper by Wiseman, Smith and Milton on the 'psychic pet' phenomenon, *Journal of the Society for Psychical Research*, 63, 306–11.

Sheldrake, R. (2000) The psychic pet phenomenon, *Journal of the Society for Psychical Research*, 63, 126–7.

Sheldrake, R. and Smart, P. (1998) A dog that seems to know when his owner is returning: preliminary investigations, *Journal of the Society for Psychical Research*, 62, 220–32.

Sheldrake, R. and Smart, P. (2000a) A dog that seems to know when his owner is coming home: videotaped experiments and observations, *Journal of Scientific Exploration*, 14, 233–55.

Sheldrake, R. and Smart, P. (2000b) Testing a return-anticipating dog, Kane, *Anthrozoos*, 13, 203–12.

Wiseman, R., Smith, M. and Milton, J. (1998) Can animals detect when their owners are returning home? An experimental test of the 'psychic pet' phenomenon, *British Journal of Psychology*, 89, 453–62.

Wiseman, R., Smith, M. and Milton, J. (2000) The 'psychic pet' phenomenon: a reply to Rupert Sheldrake, *Journal of the Society for Psychical Research*, 64, 46–9.

Paranormal action

Chapter 10

Psychokinesis

Jane Henry

Psychokinesis (PK) (movement by the psyche) refers to 'paranormal' action, that is, the mind's ability to affect or move an object at a distance by intention alone.

Parapsychologists divide the phenomena into macro-PK, micro-PK, recurrent spontaneous PK and DMILS.

- Macro-PK is the ability to affect an object through mental intention where observation is sufficient to establish the effect, for example to affect the throw of a dice or deform the shape of a spoon.
- Recurrent spontaneous PK refers to naturally occurring PK, like poltergeist activity.
- Micro-PK refers to the ability to affect very small objects, such as random number generators (RNGs), where the effect is typically assessed statistically through significant deviations from chance.
- DMILS refers to direct mental interaction with living systems, such as raising or lowering heart rate by intention.

Examples of each of these varieties of PK follow. For a review of a wide range of PK phenomena see Schmeidler (1990).

Macro-PK

Macro-PK has a long history and covers a wide variety of events where mind appears to influence matter. Most spiritual traditions are associated with some form of psychokinesis, from healing the sick to apparent miracles like the biblical story of the parting of the Red Sea. Closer to home, gamblers have long believed they can affect dice or a roulette wheel by the power of intention.

In the mid-nineteenth century apports and materialisations were reported by spiritualists and physical mediums who claimed to be able to produce physical phenomena such as ectoplasm (Braude 1986). Such reports seem to have declined and are now very rare, though certain Indian gurus such as Sai Baba are attributed (by followers) with the ability to materialise. A controversial modern case including physical phenomena is discussed in Keen *et al.* (1999).

A few groups have attempted to create psychokinesis. For example a group in Toronto invented a 'ghost' named Philip and proceeded to conduct a series of seances with this fictitious character, in the hope of producing physical phenomena. Communication was achieved by raps on the table, one for yes and two for no. They managed to film various events including a table levitation (Owen and Sparrow 1976).

Recently only very few rare individuals have appeared to have any macro-PK ability. In the 1960s an American psychic, Ted Serios, demonstrated the apparent ability to project an image on photographic film through intention (Eisenbud 1977). Nina Kulagina, a Russian citizen, was an apparently outstanding exponent of macro-PK in recent times. She could reputedly move small objects on a table and was studied by a number of scientists (e.g. Vilenskaya 1995). An otherwise normal person, her heartbeat rose to 240 beats per minute and she lost up to three pounds during the concentrated bursts of energy needed to achieve these feats. She was checked to rule out magnetism or threads as an explanation (Broughton 1991, p. 144). Inspired by these feats, an American, Felice Parise, taught herself to move small objects, for example moving a compass needle 15 degrees under controlled conditions, an effect which she also found took a lot of effort (Watkins and Watkins 1973).

Individuals such as Uri Geller claim to be the focus for macro-PK events like bending spoons and fixing broken clocks. However, magicians can replicate many of these phenomena. Opinion as to whether Geller was doing any more than this is mixed. In the 1970s metal bending, for example the ability to bend the handle or cup of a spoon or fork by apparently stroking without force, attracted a lot of attention. Hasted (1981) took the more scientific approach of using strain gauges to measure the extent of metal deformation. A number of western children claimed to have this ability; unfortunately some were caught cheating. Few westerners now report macro-PK abilities, but there have been reports of Chinese children able to extract small objects from sealed bottles (Zhu Yi Yi 1995). The evidence to date suggests that if the ability to move objects exists, it is very rare.

Macro-PK is still highly controversial. It is an area where experimenters have to take particular care to guard against fraud (Wiseman 2001). Several cases of fraud have been reported. For example Randi (1986) describes a case where experimenters failed to detect the tricks used by a couple of young magicians to bend metal.

Early experiments

Most experimental PK work has aimed for statistically significant results rather than a transformed object. Rhine began the experimental investigation of psychokinesis using dice, aiming to see whether subjects could influence the side that fell face up by intention alone (Rhine 1944). Radin and Ferrari (1991) conducted a meta-analysis covering over 2,500 people's attempts to influence over 2.5 million dice throws since the 1930s. The meta-analysis showed a small but highly significant effect of about 51 per cent success with odds against chance of this happening of about a billion to one. See p. 53 for amplification.

Parapsychologists need to ensure that their results are not due to artefacts. One potential artefact presented by dice is that they often have numbers indicated by a depression in the dice. This makes the side with six on marginally lighter than the others and therefore slightly more likely to turn face up than the other numbers. In experimental and control conditions with such dice the hit rate has been shown to be higher for six than for five, which was higher than for the four die face. However before the effect was greater in the experimental condition and sixty-nine studies that controlled for this potential die face bias were highly significant (Radin and Ferrari 1991). It is unlikely that the results can be attributed to a small subset of experimenters as the results for the twenty-five experimenters contributing three or fewer experiments to the die database are also significant (Radin 1997, pp. 134–8). Nor are the results due to a few atypical studies, as recalculating the odds without the outliers again produced significant results. One remaining possibility is that the published experiments may be significant but unpublished experiments may not have been significant. To cancel out the positive significance there would have to have been nearly 18,000 unreported studies. There have not been enough parapsychologists in the world to conduct this many experiments, so most knowledgeable commentators accept that unreported studies cannot explain the positive effect in this series of experiments.

Recurrent spontaneous PK

Poltergeist cases have been reported on occasion for at least 500 years (Gauld and Cornell 1979). Typical features include objects moving for no apparent reason, sometimes breaking, and unexplained noises such as knocking. Some cases have involved electrical disturbance. Many cases appear to be short-lived. Roll (1977) found the average duration to be about five months for the nearly 100 cases he studied. Minor cases often have normal explanations, for example the plumbing giving rise to odd noises, and some cases involve fraud. Gauld and Cornell (1979) cite a case where the unexplained noises were found to be caused by rats rolling apples stored in the loft down the cavity wall and then making away with the apples! There remain a small number where very strange effects appear periodically over an extended period of time and the cause is not known.

Folklore suggests this is the work of unhappy 'spirits'. The focus for a number of the well-known cases appears to be disturbed teenagers, which has led some psychical researchers to wonder if disturbed people can project their 'energy' to affect the environment in ways we do not yet understand (e.g. Roll 1977). However, poltergeist activity is not exclusively associated with the young or the stressed (Rogo 1986). Hess (1989) suggests that the notion of an individual projecting energy is an Anglo-Saxon interpretation and that in countries where people believe in spirits poltergeist phenomena are assumed to entail a relationship between an individual and a spirit.

Lambert (1955) found that half of the fifty odd cases he studied were within a few miles of tidal water and that more cases were reported in winter. He wondered if hydraulic pressure caused by underground water movement could cause odd noises and objects to move. However, Cornell arranged some house-shaking experiments which seemed to suggest that property would be more likely to show serious structural damage before objects moved as they are reported to in poltergeist cases (Gauld and Cornell 1979).

Micro-PK

Most parapsychology PK investigation focuses on micro-PK experiments. The logic for initiating these experiments is that it might be easier to affect very small particles like electrons than solid objects, an idea suggested by psychologist John Beloff. Physicist Helmut Schmidt undertook various tests of people's ability to affect such micro-PK targets from the late 1960s on (e.g. Schmidt 1970). He used output generated randomly by a radioactive source; a detector counted the rate of emission of particles to determine a random target: in early experiments this was which of a series of lights would light up. This type of experiment presents the tricky problem of deciding whether the subject is using precognition to anticipate which light will come on or PK to affect the particle, counter and/or display output.

In this and many other experiments Schmidt has been a very successful PK experimenter producing a series of positive results. He has also run a series of significant RNG experiments where independent sceptical monitors determine which trials are experimental and which the control condition (Schmidt 1993). These later experiments appear to preclude fraud.

RNG experiments

Random number generator (RNG) or random event (REG) experiments have become the main way of testing for PK. Radioactive decay and electronic noise form the basis for true random number generators; an alternative is to use a complicated computer algorithm which generates a pseudo-random series. The RNG equipment is connected to a monitor which displays output from the random or pseudo-random source. The height, size or rate of the display is determined by the RNG and varies randomly about a mean. Experiments ask subjects to bias the display output. For example, subjects are presented with a computer screen and asked to increase the output shown on the display on one trial, decrease it on another and leave it alone in the control condition. The output may be displayed as a simple horizontal line. The task here would be to raise or lower the line or keep it as horizontal as possible. Alternatively the target might be a picture of snow with a varied rate of fall, or a sophisticated computer game. (Psi Invaders was modelled along the lines of Space Invaders for example. Here the chance of firing or the firing rate was partly or entirely controlled by random input.) These kinds of experiment offer an automated protocol, as the targets used in these experiments are random and determined automatically by machine and the results are recorded without human intervention. Electromagnetic shielding has also been used. Automating the experimental protocol in this way makes fraud very difficult indeed.

Nelson and Radin (1987) have conducted a meta-analysis of the RNG-PK experiments comprising some 832 experiments by 68 investigators including 258 control studies. The overall effect is small, at less than 51 per cent, where 50 per cent would be expected by chance, but it is highly significant as the odds against this happening by chance are of the order of over a trillion to one. Note that in both the dice and RNG control experiments (where subjects are not trying to affect the outcome of the RNG or die) the outcome was chance as expected. As is common in meta-analyses the RNG experiments were rated for the quality of the processes used, for example the use of control tests, automatic data recording and tamper-resistant RNG devices. In this RNG-PK series experimental quality does not appear to be related to the hit rate achieved (Radin and Nelson 1991, $r = 0.01$). Subsequently (from 1989 to 1996) Robert Jahn and colleagues at Princeton Engineering Anomalies Laboratory conducted over a thousand experiments with over 100 subjects (including the author) involving millions of trials. This series also produced a small effect size in line with that achieved in other meta-analyses for this type of experiment (Nelson *et al.* 1991). It seems that over the last fifty years the dice and RNG micro-PK experiments have produced a similar very small effect size. Most of the meta-analyses of these experiments have shown results that statistically were very unlikely indeed to be attributable to chance. Given how many experimenters and subjects were involved in the RNG work it had seemed that there might indeed be a small but reliable effect here. However, one more recent RNG meta-analysis comparing 300 experiments with around 100 controls found no difference between the effect sizes of the two groups (Steinkamp *et al.* 2002). (See Chapter 3, p. 54.)

Interestingly it has been suggested that the complexity or the type of machine has little or no effect on subjects' performance (Nelson *et al.* 1996).

Unbeknownst to the subject the experimenter may switch between machines generating the random numbers that determine the display, or change the sampling rate, with no apparent effect on performance. In contrast, intention may be a critical factor.

Both Schmidt and Jahn *et al.* found that RNG performance works at a considerable distance. For example in a quarter of Jahn *et al.*'s PEAR database the subjects were not physically present. Regardless of whether they were next door or thousands of miles away there was almost no difference in performance, that is, no decline with distance (Dunne and Jahn 1992).

Time displacement

Experiments have taken place in real time, using a precognitive protocol where the targets are selected after the subject has made their choice, and retrocognitively where targets were prerecorded but unknown to the participant or experimenter. Amazingly both precognitive and retrocognitive protocols have generated positive results in a similar manner to real-time experiments. Schmidt *et al.* (1986) provide a good illustration of a successful retrocognitive experiment where targets unknown to the participant were chosen at some time in the past.

Honorton and Ferrari's meta-analysis of 309 forced-choice precognition experiments between 1937 and 1987 involving 62 investigators and over 50,000 participants produced odds of 10^{25} to one against this occurring by chance. It would require a file drawer of over 14,000 unsuccessful unreported experiments to reverse these odds. Even when the 10 per cent of studies that produced the largest and smallest effects are excluded, the meta-analysis of the remaining 248 studies by 57 investigators achieved highly significant odds of around a billion to one (Honorton and Ferrari 1989). Study quality does not seem to have been a critical factor as the relationship between experimental quality by year and the average outcome by year was fairly flat (Radin 1997, p. 136).

Correlates

Nelson claims that the PEAR database positive result is not caused by a few psi-stars (Nelson *et al.* 1991). However, men performed better than women on average and close couples performed better than pairs with less of an emotional bond (Dunne 1995).

Work that has aimed to test whether it is possible to train in micro-PK skills suggests that goal focus seems to be a productive strategy, that is, you keep a clear idea of what you are trying to achieve but do not try to force it to happen. Being relaxed seems to help as does getting immediate feedback either during or after each trial or run.

In summary, the micro-PK meta-analyses appear to show a very small but fairly consistent effect that is not due to poor methodology, a limited number of participants or investigators or the absence of unreported studies.

Direct mental influence on living systems

Healers have long claimed to be able to improve the condition of physically ill people, and prayer is a common practice the world over (see Chapter 11 on healing). Some parapsychologists have attempted experiments designed to see if people can affect one another's physiology at a distance. Experiments aiming to affect a living system through intention are known to parapsychologists as DMILS (direct mental influence on living systems). In one early experiment Tart reported that a receiver reacted physiologically when their sender was given an electric shock (Tart 1963). Subsequent experiments have been kinder to their subjects!

Braud and Schlitz (1983) have conducted a series of experiments testing the power of intention to affect various physiological markers such as blood pressure or skin conductance. Typically a sender and a participant are placed in separate rooms some distance apart. The sender is asked to calm or arouse the participant at randomly determined times. There is also a control condition where no influence is attempted. The effect size in their skin conductance experiments and several replications is about 53 per cent. Braud and Schlitz's (1991) meta-analysis of around 650 DMILS sessions showed highly significant results with odds against this occurring by chance of over a million to one. (See p. 52 for an account of meta-analyses of work in this area.)

Field-consciousness

For some years followers of Maharishi Mahesh Yogi have been claiming that a group meditating together regularly could have a positive effect on their neighbourhood, as measured by reduced crime, drug abuse and conflict, for example. This claim has been met with fierce criticism by sociologists who point out that the social indicators used, including traffic accidents and war hostilities, are notoriously difficult to interpret even after obvious mediating variables like the weather and day of the week are taken into account (Dilbeck 1988, 1990).

Recently some parapsychologists have become interested in field-consciousness effects. Nelson (1996) noted a possible group consciousness effect on the weather. He found that on graduation day the weather at Princeton had been warmer than in surrounding towns for a number of years.

A few researchers have begun to test the possibility of a group and global consciousness effect on REGs. They predict a decrease in randomness where groups are focused on a common goal, that is, the REG output should be more ordered. There are now a number of linked computers situated at sites dotted around the globe producing data that can be examined for this purpose. Nelson has found a small effect with small focused groups. Nelson and Radin have found a small effect associated with a number of large-scale events where a large number of people are focused on a common event like New Year's Eve, the opening of the Olympics, the Academy Awards, prime-time TV or the death of Princess Diana. Bierman has found similar effects (Nelson 2001, Radin 2002). Not all events the experimenter(s) expected to produce a field effect of this kind have done so, the flooding in Nicaragua in 1998 being a case in point. However if the positive results continue to be replicated they seem to have implications for our understanding of the way the mind operates. Roger Nelson maintains a site with papers relating to this phenomenon at: http://noosphere.princeton.edu/papers/

There is also some evidence of a slight association between environmental factors such as geomagnetic fluctuations and the lunar cycle and psi performance (Persinger 1985, Radin, 1997, pp. 177–89).

Explanation

There are various speculations about what might cause PK but little firm evidence. The main theories interpret the effect as an artefact, anomaly, clever use of ESP or some yet to be understood PK capability.

Artefact

The main artefacts that might be thought to account for PK are fraud, error and unreported negative studies. As regards fraud, macro-PK parapsychologists need to be very careful that no trickery is involved. Early critiques of PK experiments suggested they were due to fraud or error; later criticisms centred around ways of tightening the experimental protocol which led to automated target selection and data recording together with sight, sound and sometimes electromagnetic shielding and the use of conservative statistical analyses. These controls make fraud and error an unlikely explanation.

The large numbers of PK trials employing various protocols with many different investigators in well-controlled conditions seem to have produced a positive PK effect in most meta-analyses to date, so by normal standards the effect would be considered an anomaly. The huge number of unreported studies needed to cancel out the many positive PK results makes it seem very unlikely indeed that unreported studies can account for the positive results reported in the RNG databases, for example. However the PK effect in the micro-PK studies is so very small that some people wonder if it could be some form of artefact.

ESP

Assuming there is a real 'PK' effect, it may be more a matter of ESP than PK. In certain cases participants may be able to use ESP to determine when to start the trial, on the assumption that they pick a time in RNG experiments when the random output will correlate with the output required in that particular trial. (See p. 58 for a discussion of the decision augmentation theory.)

Given the very different success rates of different investigators there is also the question of whose ESP or PK is operating. Is it the experimenter or the participant expecting a positive result that biases the output?

PK

Assuming the PK effect is real, there remains the problem of where in the chain the PK operates. Does the PK affect the random source, the counter, the display or the recording equipment?

Some physicists have argued that mental observation has the property of changing quantum mechanical events. This has led to a variety of quantum mechanical speculations about possible PK mechanisms such as the observational theories (see Rush 1986).

Conclusion

It appears there may be a small micro-PK effect, not accounted for by methodological inadequacies or a few investigators and participants. This includes effects on living systems. Macro-PK effects appear to be rare and such claims are still controversial. Recurrent spontaneous PK or poltergeist activity used to be attributed to spirits, but is now sometimes associated with a particular human, often an adolescent.

Recommended reading

Introductory

Radin, D. (1997) *The Conscious Universe: The Scientific Truth of Psychic Phenomena*, San Francisco: HarperCollins. Excellent account of parapsychological work on psychokinesis by a leading PK experimenter.

Advanced

Irwin, H.J. (2004) *An Introduction to Parapsychology*, 4th edn, Jefferson, NC: McFarland. Chapter on psychokinesis provides a good account of work on psychokinesis.

References

Braud, W.G. and Schlitz, M.J. (1983) Psychokinetic influence on electrodermal activity, *Journal of Parapsychology*, 47, 95–119.

Braud, W.G. and Schlitz, M.J. (1991) Consciousness interactions with remote biological systems: anomalous intentionality effects, *Subtle Energies*, 2, 1, 1–46.

Braude, S. (1986) *The Limits of Influence: Psychokinesis and the Philosophy of Science*, New York: Routledge and Kegan Paul.

Broughton, R. (1991) *Parapsychology: The Controversial Science*, London: Rider.

Dilbeck, M.C. (1990) Test of a field model of consciousness and social change: time series analyses of participation in the TM-Sidhi program and reduction of violent death in the US, *Social Indicators Research*, 22, 339–428.

Dilbeck, M.C., Banus, C.B., Polanzi, C. and Landrith III, G.S. (1988) Test of a field model of consciousness and social change: the transcendental meditation and TM-Sidhi program and decreased urban crime, *Journal of Mind and Behaviour*, 9, 4, 457–86.

Dunne, B.J. (1995) Gender differences in engineering anomalies experiments. Technical Note PEAR 95005, Princeton Engineering Anomalies Research, School of Engineering and Applied Science, Princeton University.

Dunne, B.J. and Jahn, R.G. (1992) Experiments in remote human machine interaction, *Journal of Scientific Exploration*, 6, 311–32.

Eisenbud, J. (1977) Paranormal photography. In B.B. Wolman (ed.) *Handbook of Parapsychology*, New York: Van Nostrand Reinhold.

Gauld, A. and Cornell, A.D. (1979) *Poltergeists*, London: Routledge and Kegan Paul.

Hasted, J. (1981) *The Metal Benders*, London: Routledge.

Hess, D.J. (1989) The poltergeist and cultural values. In L.A. Henkel and R. Berger (eds) *Research in Parapsychology 1988*, Metuchen, NJ: Scarecrow Press, 64–6, also 66–7.

Honorton, C. and Ferrari, D.C. (1989) Future telling: a meta-analysis of forced-choice precognition experiments, 1935–1987, *Journal of Parapsychology*, 53, 281–308.

Jahn, R.G. and Dunne, B.J. (1986) On the quantum mechanics of consciousness with application to anomalous phenomena, *Foundations of Physics*, 16, 721–72.

Jefferson, N.C., McFarland Keil, H.H.J., Herbert, B., Ullman, M. and Pratt, J.G. (1976) Directly observable PK effects, *Proceedings of the Society for Psychical Research*, 56, 197–235.

Keen, M., Ellison, A. and Fontana, D. (1999) The Scole Report, *Proceedings of the Society for Psychical Research*, 58, 220, Special Issue, 149–452.

Kreiger, D. (1986) *Therapeutic Touch: How to Use Your Hands to Help and Heal*, New York: Prentice Hall.

Lambert, G.W. (1955) Poltergeists: a physical theory, *Journal of the Society for Psychical Research*, 38, 49–71.

Nelson, R.D. (1996) Wishing for good weather: A natural experiment in group consciousness. Technical Note PEAR 96001.

Nelson, R. (2001) Correlation of global events with REG data: an internet based non-local anomalies experiment, *Journal of Parapsychology*, 65, 3, 247–71.

Nelson, R.D. and Radin, D.I. (1987) When immovable objections meet irresistible evidence, *Behavioural and Brain Sciences*, 10, 600–1. Princeton Engineering Anomalies Research, Princeton University.

Nelson, R.D., Dobyns, Y.H., Dunne, B.J. and Jahn, R.G. (1991) Analysis of variance of REG experiments: operator intentions, secondary parameters data base structure. Technical Note PEAR 91004, Princeton Engineering Anomalies.

Nelson, R.D., Bradish, G.J., Dobyns, Y.H., Dunne, B.J. and Jahn, R.G. (1996) Field REG anomalies in group situations, *Journal of Scientific Exploration*, 10, 11–42.

Owen, I. and Sparrow, M.H. (1976) *Conjuring Up Philip*, New York: Harper and Row.

Persinger, M. (1985) Geophysical variables and behaviour, intense paranormal experiences occur during days of quiet, global, geomagnetic activity, *Perceptual and Motor Skills*, 61, 320–2.

Radin, D. (1997) *The Conscious Universe: The Scientific Truth of Psychic Phenomena*, San Francisco: HarperCollins.

Radin, D. (2002) Evidence for relationships between random physical events and world news events, *Journal of Scientific Exploration* (in press).

Radin, D. and Ferrari, D.C. (1991) Effects of consciousness on the fall of dice, a meta-analysis, *Journal of Scientific Exploration*, 5, 61–84.

Radin, D. and Nelson, R.D. (1991) Evidence for consciousness-related anomalies in random physical systems, *Foundations of Physics*, 19, 1499–514.

Radin, D., Rebman, J.M. and Cross, M.P. (1996) Anomalous organization of random events by group consciousness: two exploratory experiments, *Journal of Scientific Exploration*, 10, 143–68.

Randi, J. (1986) The Project Alpha experiment, Part 1. In K. Frazier (ed.) *Science Confronts the Paranormal*, Buffalo, NY: Prometheus Books, 158–65.

Rhine, J.B. (1944) Mind over matter or the PK effect, *Journal of the American Society for Psychical Research*, 38, 185–201.

Rogo, D.S. (1986) *On the Track of the Poltergeist*, Englewood Cliffs, NJ: Prentice Hall.

Roll, W.G. (1977) Poltergeists. In B.B. Wolman (ed.) *Handbook of Parapsychology*, New York: Van Nostrand Reinhold, 382–413.

Rush, J.H. (1986) Physical and quasi-physical theories of psi. Chapter 11, in H. Edge *et al.* (eds) *Foundations of Parapsychology*, London: Routledge and Kegan Paul.

Schmeidler, G. (1990) PK: recent publications and an evaluation, *Advances in Parapsychology*, 6.

Schmidt, H. (1970) Mental influence on random events, *New Scientist and Science Journal*, 50, 757–8.

Schmidt, H. (1984) PK tests with a high-speed random number generator. In K.R. Rao (ed.) *The Basic Experiments in Parapsychology*, Jefferson, NC: McFarland.

Schmidt, H. (1993) New PK tests with an independent observer, *Journal of Parapsychology*, 57, 227–40. See also Observation of a kinetic effect under highly controlled conditions, 351–72.

Schmidt, H., Morris, R. and Rudolph, L. (1986) Channelling evidence for a PK effect to observers, *Journal of Parapsychology*, 50, 1–16.

Steinkamp, F., Boller, E. and Bosch, H. (2002) Experiments examining the possibility of human intentions interacting with random number generators: a preliminary meta-analysis, *Proceedings of the Parapsychological Association's 45th Annual Convention*, 256–72.

Tandy, V. (2000) Something in the cellar, *Journal of the Society for Psychical Research*, 66, 233–52.

Tart, C. (1963) Physiological correlates of psi cognition, *International Journal of Parapsychology*, 5, 375–86.

Vilenskaya, L. (1995) Physical mediumship in Russia. In A. Imich (ed.) *Incredible Tales of the Paranormal*, New York: Bramble Books.

Watkins, G.K. and Watkins, A.M. (1973) Apparent psychokinesis on static objects by a gifted subject: a laboratory demonstration. In W.G. Roll, R.L. Morris and J.D. Morris (eds) *Research in Parapsychology 1973*, Metuchen, NJ: Scarecrow Press, 132–4.

Wiseman, R. (2001) The psychology of psychic fraud. Chapter 4 in R. Roberts and D. Groome (eds) *Parapsychology*, New York: Arnold, 51–9.

Zhu YiYi (1995) Psychic phenomena in China. In A. Imich (ed.) *Incredible Tales of the Paranormal*, New York: Bramble Books.

Zilberman, M.S. (1995) Public numerical lotteries, an international parapsychological experiment covering a decade: a data analysis of French and Soviet numerical lotteries, *Journal of the Society for Psychical Research*, 60, 149–60.

Chapter 11

Healing

Daniel J. Benor

Psi healing (abbreviated as 'healing') is the systematic, intentional intervention by one or more persons to alter the condition of another living being or beings (person, animal, plant or other living system), by means of focused intention, hand contact, or 'passes', without apparently producing the influence through known, conventional physical or energetic means. This may involve the invocation of belief systems which include:

1 external agents such as God, Christ, other 'higher powers', spirits, universal or cosmic forces or energies
2 special healing energies or forces residing in the healer
3 psychokinesis
4 self-healing powers or energies latent in the healee.

Healing may be done by healers touching or passing their hands near the bodies of healees or may be projected by intent, meditation or prayer from a distance.

Healing has been described in ancient Egyptian and Greek texts and is found in every culture studied by modern social sciences. Healers generally claim they can improve the conditions of 80 per cent of people who seek their help. Virtually every known disease has been reported by healers to respond to their treatments. Unfortunately, most healers keep few if any records. Of those who do, it is rare indeed for them to have medical or technical training which would make their observations sufficiently precise to be of much scientific value.

There are many different varieties of healing, ranging from prayer healing through therapeutic touch to psychic surgery. LeShan (1974) found that the most common kinds of healers were: type 1 healers who see themselves as mentally uniting with the healee, generally in an altered state of consciousness; type 2 who see themselves as a channel for healing energy; and type 3 healers who see themselves as working with spirits. Excellent descriptions of healing may be found in Benor (2001a, 2001b), Krippner and Villoldo (1986), LeShan (1974), Meek (1977), Stelter (1976) and Krippner and Achterberg (2000).

During healing treatments, healees and healers commonly report heat, cold, tingling, vibrations and other sensations at the site of treatment. Though people may subjectively note heat when focusing on parts of their bodies, the sensations experienced with healing appear different from such self-induced sensations. They also vary from one person to another, and from one occasion to another. The sensations experienced during healing suggest to many that 'an exchange of energy' may be occurring (Benor 1984), usually attributed to a healing energy directly *from* or channelled from outside sources *through* the healer. It is also common for healees to report a generalised warmth, relaxation, release of anxieties and tensions, and general well-being during and following healing.

Research

Type 3 psychic healers in such countries as the Philippines and Brazil have been reported to perform surgery with their bare hands or with crude, unsterile instruments – with outstanding success, involving no pain, bleeding or infection. These have not been systematically investigated and are therefore not included in the following discussion.

Controlled studies

Research since the early 1960s (Benor 2001a, 2001b, Braud 1989, 1995, Solfvin 1984) has demonstrated highly significant effects of healing in controlled trials with enzymes, yeasts, bacteria, cell cultures *in vitro*, plants, animals and humans. For example, laboratory studies have shown that the growth of bacterial and fungal infections has been retarded (e.g. Nash 1982, Barry 1968), haemoglobin levels *in vivo* have been increased and hemolysis *in vitro* retarded (Kreiger 1975, Braud 1989). In a series of experiments Grad showed slowed goiter growth in rats fed an iodine-deprived diet and fed thiouracil to induce goiter (Grad 1977). In addition, water held by healers has demonstrated alterations under infra-red spectrophotometry, suggesting an alteration in hydrogen bonding (Grad 1965, Miller 1977, Patrovsky 1978, Schwartz *et al.* 1986).

A 1993 review of more than 150 published studies found over half were statistically significant, with over two-fifths showing effects significant at a probability of less than one in 100 (that the results could occur by chance) (Benor 1993). Most of the studies included were published in parapsychology journals. A dozen were doctoral or master's degree dissertations.

Table 11.1 Distant healing/prayer studies

Subject	*No. of studies*	*Significant results* $p < 0.01$	$p < 0.02–0.05$	*?*
AIDS	1		(+1)	
Cardiac intensive care	2	1	(+1)	
Pain, post-surgical	1	1		
Pain, anxiety, depression	1			
Hypertension	1			(?1)
Electrodermal activity	12	3	(+5)	
Physiological variables	1			
EDA		1		
finger blood volume (BVP)		1		
BP		1		
Warts	1			

(?) = possibly significant results but faulty reporting or design which prevented proper evaluation of the studies

Sources for Tables 11.1–11.4: Tables in D.J. Benor, *Healing Research*: Vol. IV, Medford, NJ: Wholistic Healing Publications, (in press). Copyright © Daniel J. Benor, MD.

Independent reviews of clinical healing studies by Solfvin (1984) and Schouten (1993) agree that the evidence is suggestive. Schouten points out methodological problems with some of the studies. Nevertheless, a substantial number of solid studies remain to suggest that healing is a potent intervention. A 2001 review of just under 200 controlled healing studies found two-thirds were significant (Benor 2001a, 2001b).

Tables 11.1–11.4 summarise the results from around 200 distant healing and controlled studies of healing with humans, animals and plants, over three-fifths of which report significant results. About two-fifths of these are significant at the 1 per cent level and a further fifth at the 5 per cent level (Benor 2001a, 2001b). The studies included in this review were assessed for attention to high technical standards of research, including blinds (in human studies), randomisation and statistical analyses of results, amongst other factors.

Prayer

One well-known controlled study on distant healing produced significant effects in patients with cardiac problems. Randolph Byrd, MD, arranged for prayer healing to be sent to 192 patients on a coronary care unit, while another 201 patients served as controls. This was done with a double-blind design, where neither the patients nor the treating or evaluating physicians knew which patients were sent the healing and which were not. The patients were randomly assigned to either of these groups, and no significant differences were noted between the groups on many variables. Highly

Table 11.2 Controlled studies of healing: non-human

Subject	*No. of studies*	*Significant results* $p<0.01$	$p<0.02–0.05$	*?*
Water	5	3		
Crystallisation	2			(?)
DNA	2		(+2)	
Enzymes	13	4	(+2)	(? +3)
Fungus/yeast	10	4	(+1)	(? +1)
Bacteria	10	2		(? +3)
Red blood cells	2	2		
Cancer cells	7	4		(? +2)
White blood cells	1	1		
Snail pacemaker cells	4	4		
Plants	26	10	(+5)	(? +2)
Motility				
flagellates	2			(? +1)
algae	2	1		
moth larvae	1	1		
Mice				
skin wounds	2	2		
retard goiter	2	2		
growth	2	2		
malaria	2		(+1)	
tumors decrease	3	1		(? +1)
increase	1			
anesthesia	14	9	(+5)	
Rats				
malaria	1		(+1)	
tumors	4	1	(+1)	
Hamsters				
amyloidosis	2		(+2)	

significant effects were found in the treated group, in which there were lower incidences of intubation/ventilation, use of antibiotics, cardiopulmonary arrest, congestive heart failure, pneumonia, and the use of diuretics. The study was published in the respected, conventional *Southern Medical Journal* (Byrd 1988). Harris's (1999) well-controlled follow-up also showed positive effects for the treatment group.

An excellent study by Sicher *et al.* (1998) matched twenty pairs of AIDS patient volunteers and in a double-blind trial used experienced healers to give half the group distant healing over a ten-week period. The control group received no healing from these healers. Both groups received standard medical treatments. After six months those sent healing had significantly fewer AIDS-related symptoms ($p=0.04$), lower severity of illnesses ($p=0.02$), made fewer visits to the doctor ($p=0.01$) and had fewer days in hospital ($p=0.04$).

Table 11.3 Controlled studies of healing: human

Subject	*No. of studies*	*Significant results* $p < 0.01$	$p < 0.02$–0.05	*?*
Allobiofeedback	15	3	(+4)	
pre-recorded	1			
Skin temperature	2	1		
Haemoglobin				
increase	4	4		
increase/decrease	1	1		
AIDS	2	2		
Immune functions	2		(+1)	
Hypertension	3	2		
Asthma/bronchitis	1			
Surgery	2	1	(+1)	
Muscle tension	2	2		
Muscle strength	1	1		
Myopia	1			(? +1)
Epilepsy	(1)			
Leukemia	(1)			
Tension headache	1	1		
Postoperative pain	3	2	(+1)	
Neck/back pain	1			(? +1)
Back	1			
Arthritis	2	2		
Arthritis/headache/back pain	1		(+1)	
Anxiety	15	5	(+5)	
Anxiety/depression	1	1		
Depression	3	2		
Grief	1			(+?)
Cancer				
wellbeing	1	1		
anticipatory nausea	1			(+?)
Alzheimer's				
disruptive behaviour	1		(+1)	
Self-esteem	1		(+1)	
Alcoholism	1		(+1)*	
Personal relationship	1			
Diagnosis	1 (+4)		(+1)	
Distant healing				
coronary care	2	1		
healing sensations	1	1		

* = opposite direction to predictions

Benor (2000) reviewed sixty-one reports of distant healing studies where healers sent an intent, wish or prayer to the healee. In some of these studies the healee was present and in others thousands of miles away. Distance did not appear to affect the outcome. Benor observes that to date there is no research to support the idea that healing through prayer is any more efficacious than healing attempted outside a religious context.

Table 11.4 Distant healing/controlled healing studies results summary

	Significant results	
	$p < 0.01$	$p < 0.02–0.05$
Number of significant experiments	94	46
Percentage significant	42%	21%

Meta-analyses

There have been a number of meta-analyses of healing which will now be discussed.

Abbot's (2000) meta-analysis covers fifty-nine randomised controlled studies (including ten dissertation abstracts and five pilot studies) of healing in humans up to the year 2000. Of twenty-two fully reported trials, ten suggested significant effects. There were eight studies rated as methodologically sound, of which five showed significant effects. Small sample sizes in the fifteen studies in the dissertations and pilot group may have contributed to the lack of significant effects in eleven of them. The inclusion of the dissertation abstracts and pilot studies weakens this analysis.

John Astin at the University of Maryland Medical School, Edzard Ernst, Chairman of the Department of Complementary Therapies at the University of Exeter in England, and Elaine Harkness reviewed twenty-three studies: five with prayer healing, eleven with non-contact Therapeutic Touch, and seven miscellaneous distant healing approaches. A positive effect was found in 57 per cent of these. The study is a bit peculiar in including non-contact Therapeutic Touch as distant healing, but within the study this category is analysed separately. Overall, for the sixteen trials with double-blinds, the average effect size was 0.40 ($p < 0.001$). For the ten Therapeutic Touch studies meeting their selection criteria, the average effect size was 0.63 ($p < 0.003$). For the prayer studies the effect size was 0.25 ($p < 0.009$). For the 'other' studies the average effect size was 0.38 ($p < 0.073$) (Astin *et al.* 2000). The authors conclude that 'the evidence thus far warrants further study' (an acknowledgement, in research reviewers' terminology, that the evidence has merit).

Braud and Schlitz's (1989) meta-analysis focused on electrodermal activity (EDA), a measure of skin resistance that reflects states of tension. Healers have been able to selectively lower and raise EDA, aided by feedback from a meter attached to the healee's skin. In a series of studies by William Braud and Marilyn Schlitz, there were 323 sessions with 4 experimenters, 62 influencers and 271 subjects. Of the 15 studies, 6 (40 per cent) produced significant results. Of the 323 sessions, 57 per cent were successful ($p = 0.000023$). That is, such results could have occurred by chance only twenty-three times in a million. Analysing nineteen experiments in which one person sought to influence another person's electrodermal activity (EDA), they found highly significant effects ($p < 0.0000007$) (Schlitz and Braud 1997). See also p. 52.

In a meta-analysis of Therapeutic Touch research, Winstead-Fry and Kijek (1999) found that out of twenty-nine dissertation and research studies that addressed questions of efficacy, nineteen showed at least partial support for the research hypothesis. The other ten rejected the hypotheses. Deficiencies in reporting details of the studies make it very difficult to compare them. A moderate combined effect size was found (0.39) in the thirteen studies that included means and standard deviations for treatment and control groups ($p < 0.001$).

Explanations

Placebo

Healing has generally been thought by conventional science to represent no more than wishful ritual to compensate for 'primitive' man's inability to master the forces of nature, or at best a placebo. The effects of placebo are certainly powerful. For example Honigfeld (1964) cites cases where a sugar pill gave 92 per cent of ulcer patients improvement and gave 62 per cent of diabetes patients sufficient control over their blood sugar levels. This explanation cannot account for the significant healing effects in double-blind trials. Spontaneous remission fails as an explanation on the same count.

Biological mechanism

Although the ultimate mechanism for the healer–healee intervention, as with other psi phenomena, is unknown, speculations about how healing might work follow. In biological organisms, especially humans, many explanations are often possible. Within the body healing might act through one or more of the following: altered hydrogen bonding in water (the body is 65 per cent water) (Grad 1965, Schwartz *et al.* 1986); enhanced action of enzymes (Smith 1972) and hormones (Grad 1977); elevations of haemoglobin levels (Krieger 1975); slowing of the growth of infecting organisms (Nash 1982); lowering blood pressure (Miller 1982); reducing pain (Redner *et al.* 1991) and anxiety (O'Laoire 1997), which may secondarily lead to a variety of beneficial effects on hormonal and immune systems; improving attitude, hope and spirituality.

Psychological harmony

Many healers believe that the physical effects of their treatments are of secondary importance to the alterations in awareness they bring about in the healee. The healers claim that illness is a product of disharmony and/or disease on physical, emotional, mental and/or spiritual levels. They feel that the manifestations of illness are meant to draw people's attention to the disharmonies in their lives and that the essential aspect of the healing is to enhance awareness of the causal stresses or attitudes which underlie the symptoms; to aid in finding better ways of coping with or accepting the problems; and to help people towards lessons which transcend the physical existence of a single lifetime. Healers may help people to die more peacefully, considering that this, too, is a healing. Increasing and enhancing awareness of transpersonal dimensions becomes a major component of many healers' interventions. This may be subsumed under religious activities or may involve a personal spirituality – an intuitive awareness of one's connectedness with nature, Gaia, Christ consciousness, and the All.

Role of energy

Healing seems to occur through intention and subtle energies. The subjective sensations during healing suggest an exchange of energies between healer and healee. For lack of identified healing energies, the term, 'subtle energies' is commonly used in healing. Conventional medicine continues to address the body primarily as matter. Healers have been saying for a long time that they are addressing the *energy body* when they do healings. Allopathic and energy medicine approaches may simply correspond to these two different aspects – matter and energy.

It is hard for conventional science and medicine to accept healing as a valid and potent treatment. However, modern science has gone through a similar process in assimilating the observations and theories of quantum physics. Some of the observations of quantum physics are *counter-intuitive* to conventional, Newtonian physics, and to 'everyday common sense'. In our everyday life we deal with measurable forces which produce measurable effects in material objects or chemicals. In quantum physics it has been shown that non-local effects may occur. Single electrons may bilocate when passing through two slits. The universe is so intricately interwoven that every element in it is ultimately influenced by every other element. An event may be considered as both occurring and not occurring – until an observer intervenes and determines which is the case. Much has been made of the similarities between modern physics and psi phenomena in books such as Capra's *The Tao of Physics*. The psychological and social processes in the assimilation of the new concepts of quantum physics took several decades of research before these observations, which run counter to our ordinary experiences of the world, were accepted. A similar process is apparent with psi healing.

There may be greater difficulty with the acceptance of healing, however, as this involves a shift in worldview with far more personal consequences than the abstract and highly theoretical shifts with quantum physics. Many people find it threatening to learn that another person might influence them through thoughts or intentions. Rather than examine and deal with their discomforts, they may prefer to reject the threatening concepts and to distance themselves from those who propose them. This is analogous to the ancient custom of killing the messenger who bears bad news. People who advocate a belief in healing may be discredited and may suffer discrimination.

Complementary relationship with allopathic medicine

The experience of integrating spiritual healing with conventional medicine in the United Kingdom (UK) is instructive. In the mid-1970s British healers formed a healing organisation which lobbied the government to allow healers to treat patients in National Health Service hospitals. With one governmental decision, 1,500 hospitals were opened to healers.

In the early 1980s, healers joined in organisations which standardised a code of conduct. The code of conduct was sent to various medical, nursing and midwifery associations for review and was given their approval.

Since 1988, the Doctor–Healer Network (DHN) has provided a forum for doctors, nurses and other conventional health care professionals to meet with healers, other complementary therapists and clergy to explore how healing can be integrated with conventional medical care. There are five DHN regional groups around the UK. There are general practitioners who have healers working in their offices, and some of the healers are paid under the National Health Service (NHS). Many more doctors are referring patients to healers at the healers' treatment rooms. Doctors have obtained postgraduate education allowance credits for learning to develop their healing gifts. Healers have worked regularly at hospital pain centres, cancer centres, a rheumatology ward and a cardiac rehabilitation centre. Clearly, the NHS, with its centralised, governmental management, facilitated this process.

Acceptability

The research data are crucial to doctors in considering whether they will have anything to do with healing. However, the research alone will not bring about change. In addition to convincing people at an intellectual level, it helps to be introduced to healing experientially.

On an individual basis, it is very difficult to change the view of health care professionals. Often individuals are afraid of peer censure, which can be brutal. Doctors, nurses and researchers may imperil their professional advancement, research grants and their jobs by advocating something which their employers, supervisors or peers do not accept. (In many ways this is akin to the treatment received by heretics who held beliefs which differed from those of their religious compatriots. (This has led some to suggest that *scientism* is the religion of the western world.)

It is understandable that people are slow to assimilate new observations and theories. It took me two years after observing an instantaneous healing before I was ready to explore the development of my own healing gifts.

Conclusion

The evidence from the many significant healing studies, combined with the absence of negative side effects of healing, suggests that spiritual healing can be an effective and safe treatment. Modern medicine remains sceptical. With further replication of the best controlled studies this position will be harder to sustain.

Recommended reading

Introductory

Solfvin, J. (1984) Mental healing. In S. Krippner (ed.) *Advances in Parapsychological Research 4*, Jefferson, NC: McFarland, 31–63. Overview of research into psychic healing.

Advanced

Benor, D.J. (2001a) *Spiritual Healing, Scientific Validation of a Healing Revolution*, Southfield, MI: Vision Publications. Light review of research on healing.

Benor, D.J. (2001b) *Spiritual Healing, Professional Supplement*, Southfield, MI: Vision Publications. Detailed review of research on healing.

Krippner, S. and Achterberg, J. (2000) Anomalous healing experiences. In E. Cardena, S.J. Lynn and S. Krippner (eds) *Varieties of Anomalous Experience*, Washington, DC: American Psychological Association, 353–96. Review of anomalous healing.

References

Abbot, N.C. (2000) Healing as a therapy for human disease: a systematic review, *Journal of Alternative and Complementary Medicine*, 6, 2, 159–69.

Astin, J.A., Harkness, E. and Ernst, E. (2000) The efficacy of 'distant healing': a systematic review of randomized trials, *Annals of Internal Medicine*, 132, 903–10. See also http://www.acponline.org/journals/annals/06jun00/astin.htm

Barry, J. (1968) General and comparative study of psychokinetic effect on a fungus culture, *Journal of Parapsychology*, 32, 237–43.

Benor, D.J. (1984) Fields and energies related to healing: a review of Soviet and Western studies, *Psi Research*, 3, 1, 8–15.

Benor, D.J. (1986) Research in psychic healing. In: B. Shapin and L. Coly (eds) *Current Trends in Psi Research*, New York: Parapsychology Foundation.

Benor, D.J. (1993) *Healing Research: Holistic Energy Medicine and Spirituality*, Munich: Helix Verlag GmbH.

Benor, D.J. (2000) Distant healing, *Subtle Energies and Energy Medicine*, 11, 3, 349–64.

Benor, D.J. (2001a) Healing Research, Volume I, Southfield, MI: Vision Publications.

Benor, D.J. (2001b) Healing Research, Volume II, Southfield, MI: Vision Publications.

Braud, W. (1989) Using living targets in psi research, *Parapsychology Review*, 20, 6, 1–4.

Braud, W. (1995) On the use of living target systems in distant mental influence research. In B. Shapin and L. Coly (eds) *Psi Research Methodology: A Re-examination*, New York: Parapsychology Foundation.

Braud, W. and Schlitz, M. (1989) A methodology for the objective study of transpersonal imagery, *Journal of Scientific Exploration*, 3, 1, 43–63.

Byrd, R. (1988) Positive therapeutic effects of intercessary prayer in a coronary care population, *Southern Medical Journal*, 81, 826–9.

Dossey, L. (1993) *Healing Words*, San Francisco: HarperSanFrancisco.

Grad, B. (1965) Some biological effects of the 'laying on of hands': a review of experiments with animals and plants, *Journal of the American Society for Psychical Research*, 59, 95–127.

Grad, B. (1977) Laboratory evidence of laying on of hands. In N.M. Regush (ed.) *Frontiers of Healing*, New York: Avon Books.

Harris, W.S. (1999) A randomized, controlled trial of the effects of remote intercessory prayer on outcomes in patients admitted to the coronary care unit, *Archives of Internal Medicine*, 159, 2273–8.

Honigfeld, G. (1964) Non-specific factors in treatments: review of placebo reactions and reactors, *Diseases of the Nervous System*, 25, 145–56.

Krieger, D. (1975) Therapeutic touch the imprimatur of nursing, *American Journal of Nursing*, 75, 784–7.

Krippner, S. and Villoldo, A. (1986) *The Realms of Healing*, rev. edn, Millbrae, CA: Celestial Arts (first published 1976).

LeShan, L. (1974) *Clairvoyant Realities*, Wellingborough: Turnstone.

Meek, G.W. (1977) *Healers and the Healing Process*, Wheaton, IL: Theosophical.

Miller, R.N. (1977) Methods of detecting and measuring healing energies. In J. White and S. Krippner (eds) *Future Science*, Garden City, NY: Anchor/Doubleday.

Miller, R.N. (1982) Study of remote mental healing, *Medical Hypotheses*, 8, 481–90.

Nash, C. (1982) Psychokinetic control of bacterial growth, *Journal of the Society for Psychical Research*, 51, 217–21.

O'Laoire, S. (1997) An experimental study of the effects of distant, intercessory prayer on self-esteem, anxiety, and depression, *Alternative Therapies*, 3, 6, 38–53.

Patrovsky, V. (1978) On the bioactivity of water, *International Journal of Paraphysics*, 12, 5 and 6, 130–2.

Redner, R., Briner, B. and Snellman, L. (1991) Effects of a bioenergy healing technique on chronic pain, *Subtle Energies*, 2, 3, 43–68.

Schlitz, M. and Braud, W. (1997) Distant intentionality and healing: assessing the evidence, *Alternative Therapies*, 3, 6, 62–73.

Schouten, S. (1993) Applied parapsychology studies of psychics and healers, *Journal of Scientific Exploration*, 7, 375–401.

Schwartz, S., De Mattei, R.J., Brame, Jr., E.G. and Spottiswoode, S.J.P. (1986) *Infrared Spectral Alteration in Water Proximate to the Palms of Therapeutic Practitioners*, Los Angeles: Mobius Society. Also in *Subtle Energies*.

Sicher, F., Targ, E., Moore, D. and Smith, H.S. (1998) A randomized double-blind study of the effects of distant healing in a population with advanced AIDS, *Western Journal of Medicine*, 169, 356–63.

Smith, J. (1972) Paranormal effects on enzyme activity, *Human Dimensions*, 1, 15–19.

Stelter, A. (1976) *Psi Healing*, New York: Bantam.

Winstead-Fry, P. and Kijek, J. (1999) An integrative review and meta-analysis of Therapeutic Touch research, *Alternative Therapies*, 5, 6, 59–67.

Chapter 12

Shamanism

Stanley Krippner

Shamans are socially designated practitioners who purport to deliberately alter their consciousness to obtain information or exert influence in ways useful to their social group, and in ways not ordinarily available to their peers (Krippner 2000). Dating back at least 30,000 years, shamans report experiences that parapsychologists would conceptualise as possible psi

Figure 12.1 María Sabina conducting a shamanistic ritual
Source: Stanley Krippner

phenomena – reported interactions between organisms and their environment (including other organisms) in which information and influence have taken place that cannot be explained through conventional science's understanding of sensory-motor channels. In other words, these reports are anomalous because they appear to preclude the constraints of time, space and energy.

Ever since shamans have reflected on their experiences, they have described reveries that appeared to transmit thoughts of another person, dreams in which they seemed to become aware of far-away events, rituals in which future happenings supposedly were predicted, and mental procedures that were said to produce direct effects on distant physical objects or living organisms (Rogo 1987). Are these occurrences instances of what parapsychologists now refer to as 'telepathy', 'clairvoyance', 'precognition', and 'psychokinesis'? Or are there conventional ways to explain these phenomena?

When shamans attempt to locate lost objects, they may be demonstrating clairvoyance. When they seek to communicate with someone at a distance, they could be manifesting telepathy. When they try to divine the future, they might be displaying precognition. When they attempt to heal someone at a distance, they could be practising psychokinesis. Purported psi phenomena are the most dramatic of the special powers that provide shamans with their authority, prestige and stature. Can these alleged capacities be demonstrated under psi-task conditions that would rule out such conventional explanations as logical inference, perceptual cues, subliminal perception, deception and coincidence? This is the challenge faced by parapsychology.

From a philosophical standpoint, presumptive parapsychological phenomena in shamanic practices differ from 'supernatural' or 'miraculous' phenomena. The latter, if they exist, stand *apart* from nature and may even *suspend* or contradict natural laws and principles. Parapsychologists assume that the phenomena they investigate are *lawful*, *natural*, and – at some point – will 'fit' into the scientific body of knowledge, either with or without a revision of the current scientific worldview.

Research findings

Weiant, in a paper delivered at an American Anthropological Association convention in 1960, reviewed some ethnographic accounts of possible parapsychological phenomena, remarking:

> I feel very strongly that every anthropologist, whether believer or unbeliever, should acquaint himself with the techniques of parapsychological research and make use of these, as well as any other means at his disposal, to establish what is real and what is illusion in the so-

> called paranormal. If it should turn out that the believers are right, there will certainly be exciting implications for parapsychology.
>
> (in Van de Castle 1977, p. 668).

The literature in scientific parapsychology presents a varied picture of research directions, ranging from second-hand reports and interviews, to informal observations, to controlled observations, to controlled experiments, as well as phenomenological accounts. In giving examples (and evaluations) of each category, a comprehensive review is not provided here; however, representative studies (almost all of them from the anthropological literature) have been cited that illustrate the problems and the prospects inherent to this field of study.

Interviews and second-hand reports

When Halifax (1979, pp. 134–5) interviewed the Mazatec shaman María Sabina in 1977, precognition was one topic they discussed. Sabina remarked,

> And you see our past and our future which are there together as a single thing already achieved, already happened. So I saw the entire life of my son Aurelio and his death and the face and the name of the man that was to kill him and the dagger with which he was going to kill him because everything had already been accomplished.

Carpenter and Krippner (1989) interviewed Rohanna Ler, an Indonesian shaman, who told them of her 'call' to heal. One of Ler's sons began to lose his sight and did not respond to conventional medical treatment. When the boy's eyes began to bleed, Ler was close to utter despair. Then she had a powerful dream in which an elderly man appeared and told her that it was her fate to become a healer. Her son was the first person she would heal; but if she turned down the call he would go blind and never recover his sight. The dream visitor gave Ler a stone; upon awakening she found a stone in her bed, placed it on her son's eyes, and he recovered completely. Subsequent dream visitors purportedly gave Ler a ring that she used as a 'power object' in her healing sessions.

Murphy (1964, p. 60) writes of a St Lawrence Island Eskimo informant who recalled a shaman producing sounds as though spirits were walking underneath and around the floor of his house, until 'the house seemed to shake and rattle as though it were made of tissue paper and everything seemed to be up in the air, flying about the room'. Another shaman was noted for his 'fox spirit' that purportedly could be seen running around the rim of the drum while the shaman conducted a ceremony. Murphy attributes these feats to conjuring, claiming that 'some shamans were more imaginative or better ventriloquists than others, while some were more dexterous at sleight of hand' (ibid). Murphy gives no specific explanations of the alleged techniques of legerdemain.

Critique

Interview material and second-hand reports can be valuable reflections on the life and beliefs of native people. However, interviewers need to be well trained so that they do not give inadvertent cues signalling to the interviewee what is 'expected' or what the interviewer 'wants to hear'. Many anthropological reports have been accepted as valid, but several decades later have fallen into disrepute as other investigators, conducting research in a more rigorous manner, have provided quite different descriptions and reports. On the other hand, an investigator who concludes that conjuring was at work needs to provide at least one plausible scenario for readers to consider. The Parapsychological Association has urged its members to consult with magicians when conducting research in which sleight of hand may surreptitiously have been utilised or, better yet, to add a magician to the investigative team.

Eyewitness observations

Eyewitness observations date back to Bogoras (1904–9) who made an intensive study of the Chuckchee Eskimos at the turn of the last century. He relates sitting in a tent as tribal members placed a walrus skin over the shaman's shoulders. As the shaman invoked the spirits, the walrus skin seemed to take on a life of its own. The portion draped over the shaman's back began elevating and shifting, although it never left the shaman's back. Bogoras grabbed the skin to discover how the trick was being done, but could not pull it off the shaman's back. Moreover, Bogoras claimed that he had been thrown about the tent by the skin's contortions, as the shaman sat quietly. Bogoras watched another shaman produce an incision into the skin of a client. Later, the shaman closed the opening and no trace of the incision remained.

A 1914 report by a Father Trilles concerned a Yabakou practitioner who told the priest he was about to have an out-of-the-body journey to a magicians' palaver in a distant village. The missionary expressed scepticism, and asked the practitioner to tell a student, who lived along the way, that he should come to see him at once, bringing shotgun cartridges. 'After gesticulation, words, chants, and having rubbed himself all over with a reddish liquid smelling like garlic, he fell into a lethargic sleep. His body was perfectly rigid.' The priest passed the night in the shaman's hut to be sure that there was no subterfuge. Three days later, the missionary's student arrived with the cartridges (Van de Castle 1974, pp. 276–7).

Erdoes (1972) relates attending a *yuwipi* ceremony in a converted railroad car with members of his family and about forty local Sioux residents. Once the kerosene lamp had been extinguished and the drumming commenced, Erdoes claims that tiny lights began to appear throughout the room, the shaman's rattles flew through the air, and Erdoes' electronic flash unit began flashing of its own accord (pp. 280–1).

Hallowell (1971) worked with the Salteaux Indians in Manitoba, Canada, and described a shamanic session held for a woman whose son had been missing for a week. Shortly after the ceremony began, the voice of a young man seemed to manifest through the shaman, explaining that he was in good health and giving the location where he was camping. Two days later, the son arrived home; he confirmed that during the night of the session he had been asleep at the very location indicated through the shaman (p. 68).

Adrian Boshier, an amateur South African anthropologist who refused to take medication for his epileptic seizures, found that these seizures attracted the attention of the local natives who saw them as 'signs' that he should become an apprentice for extensive training. Telling a parapsychological conference about his apprenticeship in 1973, Boshier (1974) reported that he had visited one shaman who 'threw the bones' and told him details about his past and future 'that were absolutely correct'.

Critique

These observations are provocative and suggest directions that future research can take. By themselves, they are barely evidential because the reader does not know how to assess their veracity. An observer requires a background not only in conjuring but also in critical analysis. Could the practitioner subtly be eliciting information from the observer that was later used in making a prediction or a statement about the observer's personal life? Nor does the reader know how many sessions observed by the writer produced material that was not accurate, how many dreams provided incorrect data, or how many clients of the shaman did not obtain useful details about their lives and problems. Hyman (1977) has demonstrated how a performer can give a 'cold reading' by using vague statements and sensory cues to construct a seemingly accurate description of a client. In many cases, the 'hits' so impress the client he or she forgets or ignores the 'misses'.

Controlled observations

Perhaps the first attempt to obtain controlled data on the anomalous abilities of shamans was initiated by Bogoras (1904–9), an ethnologist who had heard many reports about 'spirit voices' that whistle and speak during Chuckchee ceremonies in Siberia. Bogoras attributed these phenomena to ventriloquism; he decided to record a session and obtained permission to observe a shaman famous for his ability to evoke 'voices' from the spirits. Bogoras placed a recording funnel some distance from the shaman who sat in a stationary position during the demonstration, and who conducted the ceremony in almost total darkness. Several supposed spirit voices were heard. Soon Bogoras realised that the voices came from various points in the tent and not only from the area where the shaman was sitting. The distance effect was also apparent to people who heard the recording of the session, and Bogoras admitted that there was a marked difference between the voice of the shaman himself, who seemed to be speaking away from the funnel, and the spirit voices that seemed to be talking directly into the funnel. However, Bogoras never admitted that anything he had witnessed could have been anomalous; in his final report, published by the Museum of National History, he concluded that everything he observed was due to trickery, although he never explained how the voices could have been produced and manipulated.

Laubscher (1938), a South African psychiatrist, attempted to test the claims of Solomon Baba, a Tembu diviner. Unseen by anyone, Laubscher buried a small purse wrapped in brown paper, covered it with a flat stone, and placed a grey stone on the brown one. He then drove to the home of Baba who lived sixty miles away. Shortly after Laubscher's arrival, Baba began to dance. He then accurately described the purse, the wrapping paper, and the stones. On another occasion, Baba described the appearance of some missing cattle from a distant region, and even predicted the exact day of Laubscher's forthcoming trip to England although the specified date was several months after the time for which the original passage had been booked.

When Boshier (1974, p. 27) was working with a museum in Swaziland, he had an opportunity to test a local 'witchdoctor' named Ndaleni in the company of another native practitioner and Boshier's friend, a 'Miss Costello'. The 'target' item to be identified was the skin of a gemsbok, a South African antelope. Boshier recalls (paraphrased):

> Leaving her in my office with the other witchdoctor and Miss Costello, I went to a neighbouring building and took out the skin of a gemsbok. This I hid beneath a canvas sail on the back of my Landrover. Then I called her outside and told her I had hidden something that she must find. With the aid of the other witchdoctor, she knelt down and began to sing softly. Then, in a trance state, she informed me that I had hidden something across on the other side of that building over there. She told me that it had more than one colour, that it came from an animal, that it was raised up off the ground. Suddenly she got up, ran

around the building, out into the front where the Landrover stood and knelt down beside it. Again she began singing softly, and within five minutes of this she tore off one of her necklaces, and holding it in front of her like a divining rod, she walked around the Landrover, climbed into the back and took out the skin.

Critique

Boshier's study was impressive but flawed; because he knew the identity of the 'target' item, he may have passed non-verbal cues to Ndaleni who picked them up, consciously or unconsciously, perhaps employing similar techniques to the magician who locates a hidden object in a room through reading non-verbal cues. As for Laubscher's work, another person should have interviewed Solomon Baba. Laubscher knew the identity of the hidden object, and the reader of his report has no guarantee that Solomon Baba did not elicit clues from Laubscher during interactions that might have occurred before, during, or after the trance dance. Bogoras's account is presumptive in concluding that ventriloquism was at work and in not providing an explanatory mechanism for the differences that he and others purportedly observed on the recording.

Investigators who claim that fraud has occurred need to present a plausible scenario. They, too, should have a background in conjuring if they are to write knowledgeably about unusual phenomena. Chari (1960) has provided a guide to sleight-of-hand effects that one must be on guard for, basing his report on his investigations of fakirs in India, while Wiseman and Morris (1995) have compiled an excellent set of guidelines for testing psychic claimants.

Experimental studies

Rose (1956) conducted a series of telepathy and psychokinesis tests with Australian aborigines using specially designed cards and plastic dice, which were placed in a shaker and tossed on a table with the goal of having certain die faces appear uppermost. He obtained statistically significant results in several of his telepathy experiments; at above chance levels, subjects were able to guess the design on which Rose's wife was focusing, out of the subject's sight. Psychokinesis tests yielded chance results; Rose reported that the aborigines did not believe they could influence psychokinetic phenomena since that was a prerogative of the tribe's 'clever men' (i.e. shamans). Two of these 'clever men' were given telepathy tests but their scores were not significant.

Giesler (1986) conducted several studies, each carried out with a different group of Afro-Brazilian 'shamanic cultists'. In one study the subject was asked to describe the location where someone (an 'outbounder') had been taken – one which was determined after the shaman and the 'outbounder' had parted company. In another task, a glass of water, a white candle, and a spirit figure (taken from the Afro-Brazilian pantheon) were displayed and the subject was asked to guess the order in which the three objects appeared in a hidden list. The results were suggestive but not conclusive.

In Garhwal, India, Saklani (1988) screened a number of shamans who claimed to incorporate various deities (e.g. 'Muslim Pir', 'Goddess Dhari'). One shaman, Yashoda Devi, was selected for parapsychological studies. Tests in which Devi attempted to match 'token objects' with their owners yielded non-significant results as did an examination for psychokinetic effects on methanol. However, the height of plants from seeds was significantly greater in the group 'treated' by being held by Devi, while she chanted, than in the control group which had not been held by her. A significant effect in the absorption of saline solution 'treated' by the shaman was observed over control saline. The growth of seeds sown in the field and 'treated' by flasks of water previously held by Devi was somewhat more rapid on certain days of the study than that of control seeds given ordinary water. Saklani did not make it clear as to whether the person making the measurements was 'blind' to the 'treated' and control materials; even a fair-minded experimenter can inadvertently 'tilt' the results if he or she knows which group represents the experimental condition and which is the control.

Critique

Giesler's and Saklani's studies are among the few experimental parapsychological investigations to have been made of native practitioners who claim to have anomalous abilities. The results are neither compelling nor conclusive, but there were a few provocative results. In addition, their experimental designs, as well as their suggestions for improvements, might pave the way for future studies. Giesler (1984, p. 315), for example, has called for a 'multi-method' approach that would:

1 focus more attention on the psi-relevant contexts in native cultures;
2 combine ethnographic and experimental methodologies so that the strengths of one offset the weaknesses of the other;
3 incorporate a 'psi-in-process' method into the field research design.

Giesler proposed that, with this approach, the researcher may study ostensible psi processes and their relationship with other variables in the contexts of shamanic rituals and practices such as divination, trance mediumship, and healing. This would allow for control of the conditions of a psi task, and the results could be evaluated with a minimum of interference or disturbance of the psi-related activity.

Phenomenological accounts

For the shaman, there are no rigid boundaries between 'waking life' and 'dream life'; both are regarded as 'real' but full admission to the latter 'reality' usually depends on training and discipline. Malidoma Patrice Somé (1994, p. 233), an African Dagara shaman, remarks, 'Nothing can be imagined that is not already there in the inner or outer worlds'. Somé's autobiography is a phenomenological account of his preparation, initiation, and apprenticeship, often marked by presumptive psi phenomena. For example, Somé (1994, p. 244) recalls that at a crucial period in his initiation, he was told to enter a cave. He recalled (paraphrased):

> I went that way, jumping from rock to rock until I reached the entrance to the magical cave. The floor was sandy and dusty; I noticed with surprise that the walls were perfectly carved out of red granite. My fire went out. I closed my eyes in an effort to blot out images of what would happen if I had to back out. When I opened them again, I could see a light a little distance ahead of me. It grew bigger and bigger, and soon I realised that I had reached the other side of the mountain. Writing about what came next is an extremely difficult task. I saw a tree that distinguished itself from the others by its unusual size. Under the roots of the tree was a bluish-violet stone that glowed as I looked at it. It had a very bright centre whose light increased and decreased, making the stone seem as if it were breathing. My hand had taken on a violet colour as if the irradiation of the stone were infectious. The violet was so powerful that I could clearly see it shining through the back of the hand stuck on top of it. Soon I felt as if I were in the middle of a huge violet egg that had no shell. Inside this egg there was a whole world, and I was in it. In that moment of awareness, I had an epiphany, that the light we encounter on the road to death is where we belong. I could remember the entire experience I had just lived through, but it bore the aftertaste of a fantastic dream. Actually, I felt more like myself than I had ever felt before. Suddenly, out of nowhere, I saw a girl and found myself asking her for directions. She said, pointing west, 'You see those mountains over there? Go to the one in the middle, and cross to the other side of it. There is a cave there. That is your way home'. I found the cave the girl had told me about and ran in. It became dark as soon as I reached its interior. I could see the stony ceiling two or three feet above me. I had crossed back through the mountain almost instantaneously. Something bit me inside my hand. It was the blue stone, my only proof that what had happened had been real.

Critique

A phenomenological account is not evidential because it lacks the controls necessary to rule out prevarication, memory distortion, self-deception, and the like. However, there are very few accounts as graphic and as detailed as that offered by Somé. Obtaining a shaman's 'inner' view of a potentially parapsychological experience is a unique opportunity that should be encouraged by future investigators.

Implications

'Magic' is a term used to describe a body of applied technology used to influence domains a society believes are incalculable, uncertain, or unaccountable (Malinowski 1954, pp. 139–40); if 'magic' represents 'natural' principles (e.g. conjuring, attribution, anomalous occurrences that – in principle – are lawful), it is amenable to parapsychological investigation (Winkelman 1982). As the term is usually employed, human beings perform 'magic' while so-called 'supernatural' agencies (e.g. spirits, deities) perform 'miracles'. 'Magical' practices and phenomena would be amenable to scientific study because they follow 'natural laws'.

Explanations for the phenomena

In his anthropological survey of unusual experiences among tribal people, Jensen (1963, p. 230) remarks, 'there can be no doubt that man actually possesses such abilities', and leaves it open as to whether these capacities are parapsychological or not. There are any number of alternative explanations such as suggestion, imagination, exaggerated reporting, or a temporary extension of one's sensory and motor skills under unusual circumstances (e.g. physical and emotional arousal, ingestion of mind-altering substances, high levels of motivation). Nonetheless, the literature demonstrates that anomalous phenomena can be linked to shamanic calling, shamanic training, and shamanic practice.

It is likely that many if not most accounts of shamans' anomalous behaviours and experiences have ordinary explanations. One's reputation becomes enhanced as tales are told and retold over the years, becoming embellished in the process. In addition, coincidence can be magnified by practitioners who point out the significance of an unexpected rainstorm, the sudden appearance of a 'power animal', or an event that seems to conform with someone's dream of the previous night. It also must be recalled that in the shamanic worldview, one's imagination and dreams are as 'real' as public events, and those who listen to a shaman's stories might not be able to separate the two.

In addition, shamans were the first magicians as well as the first healers. They realised the value of drama, of shock, and of surprise in mobilising a client's self-healing capacities, and provided these elements through theatrical means. Murphy (1964), in her work among Eskimo shamans on Canada's St Lawrence Island, discovered that instruction in ventriloquism and legerdemain were part of shamanic training. Reichbart (1978) suggests that deliberate sleight-of-hand can be used by shamans to create a psychological environment conducive to the manifestation of genuine parapsychological phenomena.

In the meantime, the psychoneurology of shamanism may yield insights into the operation of psi phenomena. Winkelman (2000) has proposed a 'neurophenomenological framework' that would explain the world-wide distribution of shamanic characteristics and the role played by alterations of consciousness in shamanic practice (p. 75). Researchers in 'neurotheology' have used brain imaging techniques to study spiritual adepts, noting shifts in brain activity that accompany reports of such unitive experiences as 'oneness with the universe' (Newberg *et al.* 2001, pp. 115–16). Persinger (1993) has utilised electric stimulation to produce reports of unitive experiences from volunteers. All of these approaches would be especially appropriate for shamans who claim to have regularly occurring anomalous experiences.

Kelly and Locke (1982) suspect that parapsychological investigations in shamanic settings will become more fruitful to the degree that investigators succeed in penetrating sympathetically and in detail the interior of individual settings. A promising example was the work of Boshier among shamans in southern Africa, but his untimely death cut short these contributions. However, Van de Castle (1974, p. 281) was able to break through some of the customary reserve of Cuna Indian practitioners in Panama by bringing along a British sensitive who was so successful in demonstrating his skills in diagnosis and healing that villagers began requesting his services.

Conclusion

In regard to the scientific status of parapsychology, Irwin (1999, p. 319) has taken a position that is frequently heard among contemporary parapsychologists:

> In the final analysis, what fairly can be said of parapsychology? As far as spontaneous cases are concerned it seems likely that there are numerous instances of self-deception, delusion, and even fraud. Some of the empirical literature likewise might be attributable to shoddy experimental procedures and to fraudulent manipulation of data. Be this as it may, there is sound phenomenological evidence of

> parapsychological experiences and possibly even experimental evidence of anomalous events too, and behavioral scientists ethically are obliged to encourage the investigation of these phenomena rather than dismissing them out of hand. If all of the phenomena do prove to be explicable within conventional principles of mainstream psychology surely that is something worth knowing, especially in relation to counseling practice; and if just one of the phenomena should be found to demand a revision or an expansion of contemporary psychological principles, how enriched behavioral science would be.

The study of shamanism by parapsychologists and other scientists affords a unique opportunity to meet these goals. This opportunity has been bypassed for many decades, but the current interest in shamanism affords a chance for parapsychologists, with their unique training and perspective, to join the investigation.

Recommended reading

Introductory

Cowan, T. (1993) *Fire in the Head: Shamanism and the Celtic Spirit*, San Francisco: HarperSanFrancisco. William Butler Yeats refers to the 'fire in the head' that characterises visionary experiences; Cowan explores this theme in a lyrical cross-cultural exploration of shamanism and Celtic poets and storytellers.

De Rios, M.D. (1992) *Amazon Healer: The Life and Times of an Urban Shaman*, Bridport, Dorset: Prism. In this account of an Amazonian shaman, de Rios places don Hilde's alleged parapsychological phenomena at the centre of her discussion, rather than ignoring or debunking them, as is too often the case.

Harner, M. (1990) *The Way of the Shaman* (rev. edn), San Francisco: Harper & Row. In this description of 'core shamanism', Harner introduces his readers to exercises they can attempt themselves, and provides an elegant rationale for maintaining this vital tradition of 'personal learning'.

Krippner, S. and Welch, P. (1992) *Spiritual Dimensions of Healing: From Native Shamanism to Contemporary Health Care*, New York: Irvington. Krippner and Welch provide first-person accounts and describe the alleged parapsychological capacities of North American shamans and other spiritual practitioners they interviewed.

Larsen, S.L. (1988) *The Shaman's Doorway: Opening Imagination to Power and Myth*, Barrytown, NY: Station Hill Press (original work published 1976). Larsen not only provides an excellent introduction to shamanic mythology, but provides ways in which this tradition is relevant in contemporary psychotherapeutic, educational and healing practices.

Plotkin, M.J. (1993) *Tales of a Shaman's Apprentice: An Ethnobotanist Searches for New Medicines in the Amazon Rain Forest*, New York: Viking Penguin. This is an ethnobotanical account of nine visits to the tropical Amazonian forests; Plotkin describes the use of plants in healing rituals, for altering consciousness, and for ecological awareness.

Advanced

Eliade, M. (1972) *Shamanism: Archaic Techniques of Ecstasy*, trans. W.R. Trask, Princeton: Princeton University Press (original work published 1951). This classic text identifies shamanism not only as a phenomenon of Siberia (where the word originated) but also as a world-wide 'technique of ecstasy'.

Kalweit, H. (1992) *Shamans, Healers, and Medicine Men*, trans. M.H. Kohn, Boston: Shambhala. This perceptive account of shamanic healing has a parapsychological subtext, namely that the human mind cannot be confined to ordinary space and time.

Narby, J. and Huxley, F. (eds) (2001) *Shamans through Time: 500 Years on the Path of Knowledge*, New York: Jeremy P. Tarcher/Putnam. This compendium traces western accounts of shamanism across the centuries, demonstrating the shift from demonic explanations of their feats (including possibly parapsychological phenomena) to those based on the allegations that shamans are charlatans, psychotics, and – more recently – men and women of wisdom and sagacity.

Ripinsky-Naxon, M. (1993) *The Nature of Shamanism: Substance and Function of a Religious Metaphor*, Albany, NY: State University of New York Press. This account of shamanism serves as a corrective to Eliade's claim that the use of mind-altering substances represents a degeneration of shamanic practice; Ripinsky-Naxon demonstrates that it was there at the beginning.

Winkelman, M.J. (2000) *Shamanism: The Neural Ecology of Consciousness and Healing*, Westport, CT: Bergin and Garvey. Taking the position that the nature of shamanic constructs is ubiquitous, Winkelman proposes a 'neurophenomenological framework' to explain the phenomenon. Not only do shamanic states of consciousness 'integrate' brain functions, but certain mind-altering plants serve as 'psychointegrators' that assist this process.

References

Bogoras, V. (1904–9) *The Chuckchee: The Jessup North Pacific Expedition*, New York: American Museum of Natural History.

Boshier, A. (1974) African apprenticeship. In A. Angoff and D. Barth (eds) *Parapsychology and Anthropology*, New York: Parapsychology Foundation, 273–84.

Carpenter, B. and Krippner, S. (1989) Spice island shaman: a Torajan healer in Sulawesi, *Shaman's Drum*, Fall, 47–52.

Chari, C.T.K. (1960) Parapsychological studies and literature in India, *International Journal of Parapsychology*, 2, 24–36.

Devereux, P. (1993) *Shamanism and the Mystery Lines*, St Paul, MN: Llewellyn.

Drury, N. (1982) *The Shaman and the Magician: Journeys between the Worlds*, London: Routledge and Kegan Paul.

Duerr, H.O. (1985) *Dreamtime: Concerning the Boundary between Wilderness and*

Civilization, trans. F. Goodman, London: Basil Blackwell (original work published 1962).

Erdoes, R. (1972) *Lame Deer, Seeker of Visions*, New York: Simon & Schuster.

Giesler, P.V. (1984) Parapsychological anthropology: I: Multi-method approaches to the study of psi in the field setting, *Journal of the American Society of Psychical Research*, 78, 289–330.

Giesler, P.V. (1986) GESP testing of shamanic cultists: three studies and an evaluation of dramatic upsets during testing, *Journal of Parapsychology*, 50, 123–53.

Halifax, J. (1979) *Shamanic Voices*, New York: E.P. Dutton.

Hallowell, A.I. (1971) *The Role of Conjuring in Salteaux Society*, New York: Octagon Books.

Heinze, R.I. (1991) *Shamans of the Twentieth Century*, New York: Irvington.

Hyman, R. (1977) 'Cold reading': how to convince strangers that you know all about them, *Skeptical Inquirer*, 2, 18–37.

Irwin, H.J. (1999) *An Introduction to Parapsychology*, 3rd edn, Jefferson, NC: McFarland.

Jensen, A.E. (1963) *Myth and Cult among Primitive People*, Chicago: University of Chicago Press.

Kelly, E.F. and Locke, R.G. (1982) Pre-literature societies, *Parapsychology Review*, May–June, 1–7.

Krippner, S. (2000) The epistemology and technologies of shamanic states of consciousness, *Journal of Consciousness Studies*, 7, 93–118.

Laubscher, B. (1938) *Sex, Custom and Psychopathology: A Study of South African Pagan Natives*, New York: McBride.

Long, J.K. (ed.) (1977) *Extrasensory Ecology: Parapsychology and Anthropology*, Metuchen, NJ: Scarecrow Press.

Malinowski, M. (1954) *Magic, Science and Religion, and Other Essays*, Garden City, NY: Anchor Books.

Murphy, J.M. (1964) Psychotherapeutic aspects of shamanism on St. Lawrence Island, Alaska. In A. Kiev (ed.) *Magic, Faith, and Healing*, New York: Free Press, 53–83.

Narby, J. (1998) *The Cosmic Serpent: DNA and the Origins of Knowledge*, New York: Jeremy P. Tarcher/Putnam.

Newberg, A., D'Aquili, E. and Rause, V. (2001) *Why God Won't Go Away: Brain Science and the Biology of Belief*, New York: Ballantine.

Persinger, M.A. (1993) Vectorial cerebral hemisphericity as differential sources for the sensed presence, mystical experiences and religious conversions, *Perceptual and Motor Skills*, 76, 915–30.

Reichbart, R. (1978) Magic and psi: some speculations on their relationship, *Journal of the American Society for Psychical Research*, 72, 153–75.

Rogers, S.R. (1982) *The Shaman: His Symbols and His Healing Power*, Springfield, IL: Charles C Thomas.

Rogo, D.S. (1987) Shamanism, ESP, and the paranormal. In S. Nicholson (ed.) *Shamanism: An Expanded View of Reality*, Wheaton, IL: Theosophical Publishing House, 133–44.

Rose, R. (1956) *Living Magic: The Realities Underlying the Psychical Practices and Beliefs of Australian Aborigines*, Chicago: Rand McNally.

Saklani, A. (1988) Preliminary tests for psi-ability in shamans of Garhwal Himalaya, *Journal of the Society for Psychical Research*, 55, 60–70.

Scott, G.G. (2002) *The Complete Idiot's Guide to Shamanism*, New York: Alpha Books.

Some, M.P. (1994) *Of Water and the Spirit: Ritual, Magic, and Initiation in the Life of an African Shaman*, NewYork: Tarcher/Putnam.

Van de Castle, R.L. (1974) Anthropology and psychic research. In J. White and E.D. Mitchell (eds) *Psychic Exploration: A Challenge for Science*, New York: G.P. Putnam's Sons, 269–87.

Van de Castle, R.L. (1977) Parapsychology and anthropology. In B.B. Wolman (ed.) *Handbook of Parapsychology*, New York: Van Nostrand Reinhold, 667–86.

Winkelman, M.J. (1982) Magic: a theoretical assessment, *Current Anthropology*, 23, 37–66.

Winkelman, M.J. (1992) *Shamans, Priests and Witches: A Cross-Cultural Study of Magico-Religious Practitioners*, Tempe, AZ: Arizona State University.

Winkelman, M.J. (2000) *Shamanism: The Neural Ecology of Consciousness and Healing*, Westport, CT: Bergin and Garvey.

Wiseman, R. and Morris, R.L. (1995) *Guidelines for Testing Psychic Claimants*, Amherst, NY: Prometheus Books.

Anomalous experience

Chapter 13

Coincidence

Jane Henry

A coincidence occurs when two or more (apparently causally unrelated) events are connected in the mind of the observer. Such events are usually noticed when they seem odd, surprising or out of the ordinary. Coincidences typically concern simultaneous events but very improbable events are sometimes also considered as surprising coincidences if somewhat more distant in time. The term synchronicity is applied when a surprising concurrence of events is considered meaningful to the observer.

Common coincidence experiences include thinking of someone and then they call, turning on the radio and finding it is playing the song you are singing, or picking up the telephone to ring someone as they are about to ring you. More dramatic examples include finding a long-lost object in an improbable place or noting a dream that comes true. Inglis (1990) cites a case of someone getting up late after two alarms failed to go off, and catching a later train than usual as a consequence, only to find that the earlier one had crashed. Deschamps' famous example concerns plum pudding, which he came across just three times in his life. He was given his first taste as a schoolboy. Ten years later he saw some in a restaurant and was asked if he would mind sharing it with a Monseiur de Fontigibu. Years later he attended a dinner at which plum pudding was served, and amused himself with the thought that M. de Fontigibu would no doubt join them, and indeed as the pudding was served M. de Fontigibu was announced (Flammarion 1900).

Coincidence experiences are often taken to be personally meaningful and significant; Jung coined the term synchronicity for such events, though the idea that coincidences might have personal import is not new. Jung (1972) traced the concept of synchronicity to the Chinese concept of Tao (being in flow with life) and related it to the medieval doctrine of correspondentia found in the occult philosophies of Agrippa and Paracelsus (where all things are seen as in sympathy and interrelated).

Table 13.1 Coincidence classifications

Johnson (1899)	Chance, Causation, Design
Koestler (1972)	Cluster, Library angel, Deux ex machina, Joker
Inglis (1990)	Chance, Seriality, Synchronicity, Subliminal
Henry (1991)	Improbable cluster, Symbolically significant, Useful

Types of coincidence experiences

The term coincidence can be used to embrace psychic, mystical and other anomalous experiences, terms that are traditionally more loaded. It also has the advantage of eliciting accounts of everyday anomalies that are normally excluded when psychic or spiritual accounts are invited.

Various attempts have been made to classify coincidence experiences, the best known of which are shown in Table 13.1. These schemes have drawn attention to the role of chance, clusters of coincidences, their meaning, usefulness and improbable nature.

Here we will consider coincidence experiences in three broad categories: improbable clusters, the symbolically significant and useful coincidences (Henry 1991). Each will be discussed in turn.

Improbable clusters

Kammerer (1919) drew attention to coincidences that get our attention because of their apparent improbability. Some people feel that a particular number seems to feature in their life more than would be expected by chance. These coincidences need have no personal significance. For example, you get on the number nine bus to go to a theatre where you are allocated seat and ticket number nine, and the like. Kammerer felt that coincidences tended to occur in series and that such clusters of experience could only be explained by a new law of seriality.

Symbolically significant coincidences

Jung (1972) drew attention to the type of coincidence where the symbolic meaning to the individual is the significant aspect, most famously in his scarab beetle story. In the midst of a session in which a patient was relating the story of a dream about a golden scarab, Jung heard a scratching and opened the window to allow in a flying scarabaeid beetle (the nearest thing to a golden scarab in Europe). Being well read, Jung also recognised the beetle as a symbol of rebirth. He goes on to relate how this incident proved to be the turning point for this particular patient.

With Pauli, Jung formulated the idea of an acausal connecting principle which would allow for meaningful coincidences that could not be explained by chance, so-called synchronicities. Despite its popular appeal, several philosophers find this notion wanting; Beloff (1977) and Flew (1953) offer critiques.

Useful coincidences

Koestler (1972) focused attention on useful coincidences that lead to direct benefit: for instance, the so-called library angel, where one searches for a reference high and low, only to give up and have the book fall on your head at the right page, or be given to you by a friend.

Empirical work

Accounts

Over the years a number of people have addressed the question of coincidence experiences (e.g. Johnson 1899, Jung 1972, Koestler 1972, Vaughan 1979, Peat 1987, Diaconis and Mosteller 1989, Inglis 1990, Henry 1993). Most of the empirical work in this area has involved the collection of coincidence anecdotes. A large collection of cases can be found in Alice Johnson's 60,000-word treatise in the SPR Proceedings of 1899. Diaconis has amassed 200 files of American coincidences. A modern English collection, somewhat biased towards the arrestingly dramatic, is provided by Inglis (1990). Falk (1989) has shown that people tend to rate their own coincidence experiences as more surprising than other people's.

Surveys

A large but non-representative British survey suggests that coincidence experiences are more common than paranormal or spiritual experiences (Henry 1993). A smaller American survey found a similarly high incidence of coincidence experiences (Brown and Sheldrake 2001). The coincidence experiences reported in Henry's study were usually perceived to be personally meaningful. This may be a case of Weill's notion of positive paranoia – minds set to find personal meaning in everyday events in the world.

The most commonly experienced coincidences were association experiences, for example where a name comes to mind and you then see somebody with that name. Henry also found that cluster experiences – where one gets a run of the same number, for example – were quite common, as were small world experiences, for example being seated next to your delivery boy on a flight to Africa. Large minorities also cited ESP-type experiences, and incidents where problems were solved seemingly with the help of an unseen hand, such as an apparent guardian angel, or prayers were answered. Others related to the recovery of lost property. Women reported these experiences more often than men (Henry 1993).

Experiments

People are known to be poor at estimating the probability of events correctly and some experimenters have wondered if this is why meaning is sometimes attributed to a coincidence experience when it does not seem warranted. One line of work aims to show that sheep (psi believers) are worse at probability judgements – estimating the likelihood of an event – than goats (non-believers) (e.g. Blackmore 1992); the inference being that sheep incline to overestimate the improbability of certain events. Tasks include estimating the probability of coin-tossing outcomes or shared birthdays. Some experiments have supported this thesis (e.g. Blackmore and Troscianko 1985), though not all (Blackmore 1997). One study by Richards (1990) found no correlation between the ability to estimate probability and the frequency of reporting psychic experiences.

An often reported coincidence is a sense that a friend is about to call just before they do. Sheldrake has suggested an experiment to test telephone coincidences experimentally. Essentially four people are nominated as potential callers, who and when they call is determined randomly, the participant writes down who they think is calling when the phone rings, and calls are recorded (Brown and Sheldrake 2001). The same principle can be applied in an e-mail study. Sheldrake has had success with both types of experiment (see sheldrake.org).

Explanations

Most coincidences are readily explained as chance events. Much of the personal significance attributed to coincidences is easy for psychologists to explain away as misattribution of one kind or another. Nevertheless, given the striking nature of certain coincidences, it is understandable that in folklore and certain spiritual beliefs there is a long-standing view that some other principle operates in the world which brings about significant coincidences. Psychologists tend to view this notion as a form of 'magical thinking' and draw attention to statistical and psychological factors that might explain the perceived connection. Lay theories for coincidences include intuition, psi, destiny, affinity and intervention (Henry 1991). Examples of statistical, psychological and transpersonal explanations for coincidence experiences follow.

Statistical

Foremost among the statistical explanations for coincidences is *the law of large numbers*. This reminds us that there are a lot of people in the world so it is not surprising that strange coincidences happen to some of them some of the time. We would expect some fortunate souls to have won the lottery twice and a few less fortunate ones to have been struck by lightning several times, and they have. Similarly, while most people would find no correspondence between what they dream and what happens to them the next day, given the number of people in the world and the fact that we all dream every night it is not surprising that they sometimes match. Scott reckoned that if people dreamed that a friend was going to die once in their lifetime, given the number of people in Briton, one would expect someone to be correct every two weeks.

Humans are known to be *poor judges of probability* and hence likely to attribute significance to events that do not warrant it (Kahneman *et al.* 1982). Some events that appear improbable are not really so unlikely. One of the best-known examples of this phenomenon is the birthday problem. How many people would you expect there had to be at a party for there to be a fifty–fifty chance of two sharing a birth-date (i.e. day of the year)? The answer is twenty-three but most people assume it is much higher. Another is the gambler's fallacy. Gamblers often assume that if there has been a run of heads, a tail is more likely; in fact on any given throw of a coin it is just as likely to come down heads as tails. Sceptics argue that those believing in the personal significance of coincidence experiences may be unfamiliar with probability theory and so incline to misattribution, seeing significance in patterns where none exists (Diaconis and Mosteller 1996). For a review of the role of statistics and probability in explaining meaningful coincidence, with further examples, see Diaconis and Mosteller (1989) and Blackmore (1992).

Psychological

There are a number of other psychological reasons why people might incline to attribute significance to coincidence experiences where none is due. First, perception is an active process – we do not take in images passively, but are actively involved in constructing them according to our *expectations* – so we have a tendency to see what we expect. The mind has a known tendency to look for meaning, seeing images in inkblots, for example, and perhaps attributing meaning where it is not necessarily warranted.

There are also a number of *cognitive biases* that might be expected to enhance the attention we pay to coincidences; one is that we pay more attention to the *dramatic* than the everyday (Kahneman *et al.* 1982) – for example, remembering the one time you switched on the radio and it was playing the same top ten hit you were humming, but forgetting the millions of times you have switched it on when it wasn't! In addition, certain *attentional biases* can give us an illusion of control of the situation. We are more inclined to notice evidence that confirms our view. Memories are notoriously unreliable. Experiments show we are *unreliable eyewitnesses* of events (Loftus 1996). Cryptamnesia or a hidden cause can account for apparent coincidences, for example dozing in front of the TV and thinking you have dreamt of an assassination but in fact having heard about it as you dozed off. Chapter 2, pp. 28–9, and Chapter 4, pp. 65–6, also provide illustrations of some of the ways in which psychological factors can affect our interpretation of situations.

Wilson and Barber (1983) have described a subgroup of the population whom they refer to as *fantasy prone* (3 per cent), who are characterised by their excellent control of subjective imagery, having had imaginary childhood friends, and being good hypnotic subjects. It has been suggested that this group might be expected to report psychic and coincidence experiences more frequently. It has also been suggested that those believing in the personal significance of coincidence experiences may be inclined to magical thinking (Zusne and Jones 1989) and attributing significance to such experiences where none is warranted (Diaconis and Mosteller 1996). Watt (1991) offers a review of psychological processes relevant to coincidence experiences.

Transpersonal

While accepting that psychological factors play a part in the significance people grant to coincidence experiences, folklore tends to find explanations for 'synchronicities' that rely entirely upon chance, misperception and misattribution inadequate. Popular lay theories often incorporate a transpersonal explanation which may appeal to one of several different lines of argument centred around non-sensory information transfer, intervention from outside, intended physical manifestation or some form of sympathetic attraction.

The *information transfer* idea underlies Kammerer's law of affinity and Jung's acausal connecting principle one idea is that the experient psychically tunes into and picks up information from the collective unconscious (Jung 1972), a psi field or the common ground of mind and matter (Bohm 1981).

Those subscribing to the *intervention* hypothesis assume that something beyond this world is intervening in or affecting life events. Some people assume that this intervention is by personal beings such as spirits, including ancestral spirits in countries like Japan and Bali. Alternatively, God-like figures, such as Jesus, or gurus are attributed with the ability to bring about events that affect our life. An alternative view sees the intervention as more impersonal. People who believe in destiny and fate can interpret surprising coincidences as support for this view. In the Indian subcontinent and new age circles it is common to subscribe to the idea of Karma, where your actions produce a reaction in the cosmos which comes back to affect you. In this light certain coincidences may be seen as 'meant'.

Another perspective asserts that we create our own reality with our thoughts and that people can *manifest* desired coincidences in their life through intention – anything from finding a parking space to meeting their life partner.

Early cosmologists such as Hippocrates subscribed to the view that all things in the world were connected and that hidden affinities would cause *sympathetic* elements to seek each other out. Variants on this theme have continued to appeal to some people ever since.

Conclusion

While coincidence experiences may often be ascribed to chance, many people view certain coincidences as personally significant. Psychologists show how we can easily attribute unwarranted meaning to coincidence experiences, for example by underestimating the likelihood of the occurrence of the event. They also draw attention to cognitive weaknesses of perception and memory that incline them to question the accuracy of coincidence accounts. Nevertheless, throughout history many people have found their coincidence experiences so extraordinary, personally significant or useful that a significant proportion of the population are more inclined to draw on some yet to be understood acausal principle or outside agency to account for them.

Recommended reading

Introductory

Inglis, B. (1990) *Coincidence*, London: Hutchinson. Describes many coincidence experiences and discusses possible interpretations.

Advanced

Diaconis, P. and Mosteller, F. (1989) Methods for studying coincidences, *Journal of the American Statistical Association*, 84, 48, 853–61. Details common probability errors.

Watt, C. (1991) Psychology and coincidences, *European Journal of Parapsychology*, 8, 66–84. Describes psychological reasons why we may attribute meaning to coincidences where this is not warranted.

References

Beloff, J. (1977) Psi phenomena: causal versus acausal interpretation, *Journal of the Society for Psychical Research*, 49, September, 573–82.

Blackmore, S. (1992) Psychic experiences: psychic illusion, *Skeptical Inquirer*, 16, 4, 367–76.

Blackmore, S. (1997) Probability misjudgments and belief in the paranormal: a newspaper survey? *British Journal of Psychology*, 88, 683–9.

Blackmore, S. and Troscianko, T. (1985) Belief in the paranormal: probability judgements, illusory control, and the 'chance baseline shift', *British Journal of Psychology*, 76, 459–86.

Bohm, D. (1981) *Wholeness and the Implicate Order*, London: Routledge.

Brown, D.J. and Sheldrake, R. (2001) The anticipation of phone-calls, a survey in California, *Journal of Parapsychology*, 65, 145–56.

Diaconis, P. and Mosteller, F. (1996) Coincidences. In G. Stein (ed.) *The Encyclopedia of the Paranormal*, Amherst, NY: Prometheus.

Falk, R. (1989) Judgement of coincidences: mine versus yours, *American Journal of Psychology*, 102, 288–99.

Flammarion, C. (1900) *The Unknown*, London: Harper and Brothers.

Flew, A. (1953) Coincidence and synchronicity, *Journal of the Society for Psychical Research*, 37, November, 198–201.

Grattan-Guinness, I. (1983) Coincidences as spontaneous psychical phenomena, *Journal of the Society for Psychical Research*, 52, 793, 59–71.

Henry, J. (1991) Coincidence and synchronicity. Paper presented to SPR conference.

Henry, J. (1993) A survey of coincidence experiences, *Journal of the Society for Psychical Research*, 59, 831, 97–108.

Johnson, A. (1899) Coincidences, *Proceedings of the Society for Psychical Research*, XIV, 186–330.

Jung, C. (1972) *Synchronicity: An Acausal Connecting Principle*, London: Routledge and Kegan Paul.

Kammerer, P. (1919) *Das Gesetz der Serie* (*The Law of Series: A Doctrine of Repetitions in Events in Life and Society*), Stuttgart and Berlin: Deutsches Verlag-Anstalt.

Kahneman, D., Slovic, P. and Tversky, A. (1982) *Judgement under Uncertainty*, Cambridge: Cambridge University Press.

Koestler, A. (1972) *The Roots of Coincidence*, London: Hutchinson.

Loftus, E. (1996) *Eyewitness Testimony*, Cambridge, MA: Harvard University Press.

Peat, D.F. (1987) *Synchronicity*, New York: Bantam.

Richards, D. (1990) Paper presented to Society for Scientific Exploration Conference, San Francisco.

Vaughan, A. (1979) *Incredible Coincidences*, New York: Lippincott.

Williams, F. (1989) A phenomenological analysis of reported synchronistic experiences of adolescents. Unpublished Ph.D. thesis, Saybrook Institute, San Francisco.

Wilson, S.C. and Barber, T.X. (1983) The fantasy-prone personality. In A.A. Sheikh (ed.) *Imagery: Current Research, Theory and Application*, New York: Wiley, 340–87.

Zusne, L. and Jones, W.H. (1989) *Anomalistic Psychology: A Study of Magical Thinking*, 2nd edn, Hillsdale, NJ: Lawrence Erlbaum.

Chapter 14

Apparitions and encounters

Andrew MacKenzie and Jane Henry

An apparition entails a perceptual experience in which a person or animal (deceased or living) appears to be present though they are not (at least physically). The ghost of folklore is seen as an apparition of a dead person who may 'haunt' the same place repeatedly. Apparition and ghost experiences are common to most cultures.

Types

Most spontaneously occurring apparitions are of people, who may be dead, dying or alive at the time their apparitions are sensed. People also report apparitions of, or encounters with, other beings such as spirits, angels and aliens. Some apparitions are associated with other more impersonal phenomena such as mists or lights. Here apparitional experiences are considered under four categories:

1 Hauntings and apparitions of the dead
2 Apparitions of the dying and those undergoing a crisis
3 Apparitions of the living
4 Encounters with spirits, aliens and other beings

The last category includes reports of striking visions, such as those of the Virgin Mary, historical reports of visitations by demons and more recent reports of visitations by apparent aliens.

Apparitions of the dead

About two-thirds of apparitional experiences are of the dead; although a lower proportion has been reported in a younger sample (Palmer 1979, p. 228). Perhaps they knew fewer dead people!

Ghosts

The 'churchyard ghost' of fiction is usually described as a white, wispy, semi-transparent figure, seen at night. In real life, in experiences reported by reliable witnesses, an apparition is often mistaken for a living person, being three-dimensional, often showing awareness of the living, and sometimes able to speak a few words, and is sometimes reflected in mirrors. The figure may be in view for up to half an hour, although appearances are often for a minute or less. Although the figure is seemingly solid we would not be able to grasp it, and, if cornered, it would disappear or pass through a wall or door. An apparition may be seen in daylight, indoors or outside, and when seen in darkness may be slightly luminous.

Hauntings

A well authenticated case of haunting is that of the Cheltenham Ghost, published by the SPR in 1892 and updated in MacKenzie (1988). The ghost, that of a tall woman in black with a handkerchief held to her face as if weeping, haunted a house in Cheltenham now known as St Anne's but then as Donore, between 1882 and 1889. MacKenzie estimates that the figure was seen by seventeen people and heard by more than twenty. The figure was believed to be the apparition of Mrs Imogen Swinhoe, the second wife of Henry Swinhoe, the first owner of the house, which was built in 1860. A description of the haunting was supplied by a daughter of the house, Rosina Despard (later Dr Despard, MD), from notes in a diary. The figure, seen in daylight as well as at night, indoors and in the garden, was often mistaken for that of a living person but was less distinct in later appearances. Most of the evidence came from the Despard family and their staff, some of whom were interviewed by Frederic Myers, but there is an independent report by a solicitor who saw the apparition as a child. The apparition of a woman resembling the one described above was seen in 1958 and 1961 in Cotswold Lodge, now demolished, on the opposite side of St Anne's in Pittville Circus Road, and also in 1970, this time outside St Anne's, by a passing motorist. A more recent report of a sighting of the apparition came from a musician and a woman friend who together saw the figure behind St Anne's in July 1985. The musician saw the figure again when, this time alone, he was driving in Pittville Circus Road at night on 29 August of that year. It is unusual for reliable reports of the resumption of a haunting to be received 100 years later.

Collective cases

Apparitions are sometimes seen collectively, although all present may not share in the experience. Why this should be so is still open to debate. Tyrrell

(1943) found 130 collective cases. In the *Census of Hallucinations* Sidgwick *et al.* (1894) found that collective cases formed about 8 per cent of the total. Palmer (1979, p. 228) found that 12 per cent of cases were collective.

Apparitions of the dying

Crisis

'Crisis' cases, in which an apparition of a person is seen around the time of their death or involvement in an accident or near-death situation, were reported in the 1892 *Census of Hallucinations* (Sidgwick *et al.* 1894) and have continued to be reported up to the present day. Sometimes the apparition is seen some time after the death when conditions are favourable for the image to emerge, such as during a period of rest. It is necessary to draw an arbitrary line defining what constitutes coincidence with death. Gurney (1886) drew the line at up to twelve hours before or after death.

Sometimes, however, there is evidence of the appearance of an apparition at the exact time of death. One of the more convincing cases concerns Lieut. David E. McConnel, who was killed in a flying accident on 7 November 1918. That morning McConnel, aged 18, was asked by his Commanding Officer at Scampton, Lincolnshire, to fly a Camel aircraft to Tadcaster, sixty miles away. At 11.30 a.m. McConnel took leave of his roommate, Lieut. Larkin, saying he expected to be back in time for tea. At Tadcaster aerodrome, in dense fog, McConnel apparently lost control of his plane, 'nose dived', and crashed with the engine full on. A girl who saw the crash ran to the spot and found McConnel dead. The violence of the impact seems to have stopped the pilot's watch, which registered 3.25 p.m.

Lieut. Larkin was reading and smoking in his room when he heard someone walking up the passage. The door opened with the usual noise and clatter which McConnel always made and Larkin heard his greeting 'Hello, boy'. He half turned round in his chair and saw McConnel standing in the doorway, half in and half out of the room, holding the doorknob in his hand. He was wearing his full flying clothes including his naval cap, an unusual item of apparel. The two young men exchanged a few words. McConnel said 'Well, cheerio', closed the door and went out. Larkin did not have a watch, but was certain the time was between a quarter past and half past three because shortly afterwards a Lieut. Garner-Smith came into the room to enquire whether McConnel was back because they planned to go to Lincoln that evening. Larkin replied 'He is back. He was in this room a few minutes ago.' Garner-Smith then went off to search unsuccessfully for McConnel. Larkin discovered the news of McConnel's death when he overheard a group of officers discussing the crash in the Albion Hotel, Lincoln, that evening. Mrs Sidgwick (1892), commenting on the case, said 'it will be observed that we know the apparition to have been seen within a few moments of the death, but whether it occurred before or at the actual moment [is not known]. If it preceded the death, McConnel, dreaming in a fainting condition, may have imagined his expedition successfully accomplished and himself returned to his quarters.'

It will be noted that the apparition of McConnel spoke. This is an unusual feature of apparitions seen after death. Most are mute. Rosine Despard, for example, never succeeded in engaging the figure of the tall woman in black seen frequently at St Anne's, Cheltenham, in conversation.

A question frequently asked is 'How can you prove someone has seen a ghost?' One answer may be supplied by cases in which someone sees a person he or she assumes to be living and afterwards discovers that at the time the person concerned was dead. An example was provided by Mrs Cynthia Aspinall, who in 1967 was living in Dulwich, south-east London. Returning from a month's holiday in Suffolk she was dismayed to see a friend, Harry Evans, standing outside his home without an overcoat and looking wretchedly ill. She advised him to go indoors but he took no notice of her. On reaching her home Mrs Aspinall described to her husband the circumstances in which she had seen Mr Evans (he confirmed this), and a few days later at a coffee morning she spoke to Mr Evans's sister Kitty about a holiday spot in Scotland that would suit them both. When Kitty Evans broke down in tears Mrs Aspinall was told by a friend (also confirmed) that Harry Evans had died about a month earlier (MacKenzie 1987).

Apparitions of the living

Folklore and fiction lead us to expect apparitions of the dead, yet about 30 per cent of apparitions are of the living. An example of an apparition of the living comes from the novelist Olivia Manning. In the summer of 1945 she was in bed with her husband on the upper floor of a flat in Alexandria. She woke at 3 a.m. to see in the brilliant moonlight the figure of a journalist she knew well leaning against the door and staring at them. She woke her husband, who also saw the figure (he confirmed this). The journalist was, in fact, alive in Cairo at the time, but died during an operation a few years later (MacKenzie 1987).

Experimental cases

There are also a few case reports where people have consciously tried to project themselves to a particular person at a distant place. An example of an 'experimental' case where someone saw the 'ghost' of the living person trying to contact them is given at the start of Chapter 17. Essentially, a Mr Sinclair had had to leave his sick wife, and in the evening consciously tried to project himself to her to determine her condition. He felt he achieved this and was relieved to find that his wife was much better than when he had left her. The interest in the case is that the wife corroborates that she saw him at her bedside at the same time, a fact that worried her enough for her to try to contact the husband's office (Myers 1903, vol. 1, p. 697).

Encounter experiences

Through the ages people have reported all manner of other-worldly encounters including experiences of angels, fairies, demons, aliens, spirits and Gods. Many scientists assume these encounters are a product of the imagination, a fantasy for the dissociated mind, and a way to exteriorise unconscious thoughts that are perhaps particularly common in the fantasy-prone (Nickell 1995).

Some of those who have such experiences interpret them as literal encounters with a being from another world. *Cultural beliefs* seem to play a major role in determining much of what is experienced. In the Middle Ages people assumed they encountered demons, nowadays an alien seems the more likely interpretation. In the Christian west people have reported visions of the Virgin Mary, in India Krishna is the more probable visitor. Positive experiences of this kind may be accompanied by light and a sense of well-being.

Currently, experiences of UFOs and alien abductions are common. UFOs (unidentified flying objects) often take the form of moving lights. Some of these reports are clearly the result of people *mistaking aircraft*, satellites, weather balloons and the like. Derr has shown a correlation between the location of reports of UFO lights and *geophysical anomalies* (Devereux and Brooksmith 1997). Persinger (1990) suggests that apparitional phenomena might result from geomagnetic effects associated with the fault lines which he believes, on the basis of laboratory work, can trigger the temporal lobe to produce sensations that can be interpreted as an anomalous experience.

Since the 1950s when the first story of an alien encounter was publicised, reports of alien encounters and abductions have become increasingly common. Many of these accounts are elicited through hypnosis. Psychological studies show clearly how easy it is to get others to believe *false memories* to be true and to lead a subject to invent a story (Loftus 1993). Testimony elicited through hypnotic regression is suspect for this reason. Testimony is also suspect because typically what people say they experienced accords with the image of an alien encounter publicised in their country, for example being abducted by small greys in the USA and meeting tall more benign aliens in Scandinavia (Apelle *et al.* 2000 elaborate).

It has also been suggested that alien abduction experiences may be memories from partially *anaesthetised* patients undergoing day surgery. The increase in day surgery parallels the increase in reported alien abduction experiences. (Day surgery accounted for over half of all surgery in the USA in 1990.) It is argued that there are parallels between the experience of day surgery and reported abduction experiences. For example, the tranquillisers administered dilate pupils so that lights appear brighter; woman often report gynaecological investigations during abduction experiences and these are common outpatient procedures; patients recover with others in the recovery room and those claiming to have been abducted often note that other abductees were present (Wilson 1992).

Research

There are three main approaches to research on apparitions: collections of accounts of such experiences, surveys of the frequency of this kind of experience, and fieldwork in haunted houses. A fourth rare approach attempts to create an apparition.

Accounts

Most of the research in this area comprises collections of anecdotal cases. One of the more extensive works in the area is the *Census of Hallucinations* undertaken by the SPR towards the end of the nineteenth century. Of 17,000 people questioned, 9.9 per cent had had a sensory hallucination (Sidgwick *et al.* 1894). The early labours of the founders of psychical research produced a great storehouse of case material which can be studied in Myers's posthumous masterpiece *Human Personality and its Survival of Bodily Death* (1903) and in Gurney's (1886) *Phantasms of the Living*. The more interesting cases are often those where corroboration of the account has been obtained.

Surveys

Random surveys of the general population in the USA and Europe have suggested that something like a third of the population believe they have had 'contact with the dead'. According to Green and McCreery's (1975) survey of apparitional experiences most apparitions appear within about three metres of the person sensing them and are not known to them. The experience generally happens indoors in a place familiar to the experient, often when people are mentally inactive, for example lying down in about two-fifths of cases and walking in another fifth. The experience itself is generally brief, lasting less than a minute, but lasts over five minutes in a fifth of cases. Apparitions are normally experienced visually, this being the case in about four-fifths of cases (Green and McCreery 1975, p. 143). Perhaps a third have an auditory element.

A minority of apparitions are experienced as a sense of a presence that is felt, rather than seen. This may be such a strong feeling that the identity of a person, usually deceased, is known. Haraldsson *et al.*'s (1977) representative Icelandic survey of people's experiences of apparitions of the dead found that 16 per cent concerned a sense of presence compared to 42 per cent having visual experiences. Green and McCreery (1975) found that 8 per cent of their sample reported a sense of presence. An American sociological study of Chinese experiences of ghosts and ESP found that 3 per cent reported a presence experience (Emmons 1982). Emmons comments, 'Sometimes people just know that there is a ghost there and perhaps never experience anything sensory. It's as if an ESP message were received and waiting in the wings but had not yet popped out into the sensory stage.'

Emmons (1982) reports a case of a 22-year-old Chinese woman:

> Two years ago six or seven of us girls went to the new territories [in Hong Kong] for a picnic. We all felt there was an extra person with us. I felt that the person, a female was very friendly. We weren't afraid of her. Some of my friends saw a shadowy figure, very tall and thin, just a shape. When we went into a restaurant we gave her an extra place setting. At the table we couldn't see her, but when we were outside some could. Nobody knew who it might have been.

Reese, a Welsh general practitioner, interviewed 227 widows and widowers to determine the extent to which they had had hallucinations or illusions of their dead spouse (Rees 1971). Such hallucinations often lasted many years and were most common in the first ten years of widowhood. The proportions of men and women having these experiences were similar.

Fieldwork

Various intrepid investigators, including many amateur investigators, spend nights in reputedly haunted houses which are usually reported to have one or more ghostly apparitions. Nowadays investigators take temperature readings, run sound, video and infra-red cameras and take other measurements in an attempt to record any anomalous phenomena. Although there are numerous reports of recurrent sightings of ghosts and other apparitions, relatively few person-like apparitions have been caught on camera. Some investigators get small globes of light, which some claim are an artefact, such as reflection from the lens.

Recently there have been several attempts at mass investigations, where many participants are invited to a reputedly haunted site and asked to note their beliefs and experiences at the site. Wiseman *et al.* (2002) conducted a large-scale investigation of this sort at Hampton Court. Wiseman asked the hundreds of people there to fill in questionnaires indicating what they felt and to note anomalies on a map. Believers reported more unusual phenomena at the site than disbelievers, and those told activity had increased recently reported more phenomena than those told it had diminished. A number of people noted odd cold spots in the same places. The investigators' temperature recording equipment also detected odd temperature anomalies in these places, that is, parts of a room being colder than elsewhere. One inference that could be made here is that the cold spots disturb some people and that they associate them with a priori expectations of ghosts. There was also some suggestion of a relationship between the location at which participants reported experiences and local magnetic fields (Wiseman *et al.* 2002).

Experiment

There are a small number of informal experiments aimed at, or resulting in, ghost-like experiences, one of which is described above. The account of a group who decided to conjure up a spirit named Philip is described in Owen and Sparrow (1976; see also p. 126).

In the laboratory Persinger (Persinger *et al.* 2000) has applied magnetic fields to the temporal lobe to see if he can induce anomalous experiences. He can induce a sense of presence experimentally in this way in some subjects. These studies and anecdotal accounts of related experiences seemingly brought about by low frequency waves, described below, suggest that at least some apparitional experiences may be due to anomalous electromagnetic effects on the brain.

Explanations

Current interpretations of apparitions range from hallucinations and sleep paralysis, through some other psychological and possibly psi-mediated experience, to notions of spirits or some yet to be understood unusual objective phenomena. The hardest apparitions to explain by normal means are crisis apparitions where information about the death of a person appears to have been transmitted correctly by the apparition, and collective cases where more than one person sees the same apparition.

McCue (2002) offers an overview of theories of hauntings. Natural interpretations range from misinterpretation of normal sounds, to the effects of subterranean water (Lambert 1955), seismic effects, electromagnetic effects on the brain (Persinger and Cameron 1986) and the effects of standing waves (Tandy 2000). Theories positing the involvement of a discarnate agency suggest that ghosts are either spirits of some kind or telepathic communications engendered by spirits.

Hallucination

Apparitions can be thought of as nothing more than hallucinations and the bulk of cases probably are just that. For example, odd lights and sounds and apprehension combine with imagination and *expectation* to produce a fleeting ghost, especially where one is expected. The mind has a tendency to try to make sense of ambiguous data, perhaps seeing a ghost in a dark and poorly lit place where none is really there. One objection to the hallucination hypothesis has been that it does not seem to explain collective cases, where several people have the same apparitional experience.

However certain physical phenomena seem to induce 'ghost-like' hallucinations in some people. Persinger *et al.*'s (2000) study of the effect of complex magnetic fields on the temporal lobe of a susceptible individual shows that such phenomena can induce a clear sense of presence. Tandy and Lawrence (1998) report a case where a naturally occurring 19 Hz low frequency standing wave (produced by an extractor fan) induced phenomena suggestive of a ghost, including a sense of presence, a grey apparition and a sense of depression. Perhaps microwave towers can have similar effects on some people.

Sleep paralysis

Some cases may be exacerbated by sleep paralysis, a fairly common but not well publicised condition, where the body is paralysed but the mind is active, likely to be accompanied by hypnagogic imagery. Sceptics have suggested that apparitions entail hypnagogic imagery (Alcock 1981, p. 83). Cheyne *et al.*'s (1999, p. 319) model of sleep paralysis suggests three effects suggestive of apparitional and encounter experiences. Their 'Intruder' entails 'a sense of presence, fear, auditory and visual hallucinations' thought 'to originate in a hypervigilant state originating in the midbrain'. 'Incubus' entails 'pressure on the chest, breathing difficulties and pain' attributed 'to effects of motor neuron hyperpolarization on perception of respiration'. These both suggest the experience of an 'other'. 'Unusual bodily experiences' like 'floating, flying sensations, out-of-body sense and feelings of bliss' they relate to 'physically impossible experiences generated by conflicts between endogenous and exogenous activation related to body position and orientation and movement'.

Psychological

A physical theory of apparitions does not seem appropriate as apparitions do not leave footprints in the snow or open closed doors. Hence many people favour a psychological interpretation. Many researchers who have studied apparitions agree that such experiences have a psychological component; for example, Tyrrell (1943) thought an apparition 'is in reality a psychological phenomenon, the explanation of which must be sought in the processes of sense perception'.

It has also been argued that some extra-sensorily perceived information is translated by the brain into a psychologically produced hallucination of an apparition appropriate to the person's culture and beliefs (Myers 1903). Tyrrell (1943) believed that apparitions were telepathic in origin. He suggested that collective apparitions resulted from the mingling of unconscious minds to produce an apparitional drama, not unlike a dream.

Objective phenomena

It is an open question whether psychological interpretations are sufficient to explain cases where an apparition has some resemblance to a 'real' object. Some apparitional reports claim they cast shadows, are reflected in mirrors and show other properties suggesting they exist physically. This leads others familiar with the field to favour the consideration that apparitions are some sort of objective phenomenon but of an unknown nature. Harry Price considered the possibility that some apparitions might be 'real' objects – spatial though not physical – and that one function ESP powers might have is to make us aware of such 'real' objects.

Braude (1986 p. 214) argues that in

> collective cases we find certain features that appear to favour an objective explanation. For instance, in some cases the reaction of animals to *locations* where apparitions are ostensibly seen or sensed suggests a genuine perturbation of a region of physical space, and not merely the existence of a telepathic stimulus to which animals or humans may have been susceptible, and to which they would have had to respond to in a similar fashion.

Also in collective cases, people have reported apparitions from differing and appropriate perspectives (Gauld 1982, p. 249). Gauld (1979) recommends treating apparitions as a class of perceivable objective things, and suggests that we regard telepathic explanations of apparitions as attempts to explain them away (quoted from Braude 1986, p. 191).

A popular lay theory is that a ghost may represent some kind of replay of an emotional imprint on a place. This idea seems to accord with, say, an experience of an ancient battle appearing before you, but does not fit with apparitions that do different things on different occasions in the same place and those that appear to communicate with the person perceiving them.

Spirits

Folklore often interprets apparitions and ghosts as spirits of the departed. The idea of apparitions as spirits does not account for apparitions of the living quite so easily, unless one subscribes to the view that a 'soul' can be in more than one place. Gauld (1982) argues that apparitions provide little support for the notion of survival of death (see Chapter 18 on survival).

Conclusion

Apparitional and encounter experiences have been reported for centuries and include collective cases, where more than one person sees the same apparition, and crisis apparitions, where, on some occasions, people appear to glean correct information about the death of a relative they would not otherwise have known. We still have little idea what apparitions or encounters are. Experimental work suggests that some apparitional experiences and the sense of another being present may result from the effects of naturally occurring electromagnetic anomalies on the brain. The weight of opinion of those who have studied apparitions favours the idea that the experience has a psychological component rather than being a purely objective phenomenon. Many of the apparitions experienced by just one person are probably hallucinations; it is harder to account for the well-attested crisis and collective apparitions and encounters.

Recommended reading

Introductory

Gauld, A. (1982) *Mediumship and Survival*, London: Heinemann. An excellent book containing chapters on apparitions, and a theory of apparitions.

Gauld, A. and Cornell, A.D. (1979) *Poltergeists*, London: Routledge. A useful section on hauntings.

MacKenzie, A. (1982) *Hauntings and Apparitions*, London: Heinemann. Studies of some classic cases such as the hauntings at Cheltenham and Versailles.

Tyrrell, G.N.M. (1943) *Apparitions*, London: The Society for Psychical Research. Republished with an introduction by Professor H.H. Price, 1953, reprinted 1973. A classic text and good starting point.

Advanced

Apelle, S., Lynn, S.J. and Newman, L. (2000) Alien abduction experiences. In E. Cardena, S.J. Lynn and S. Krippner (eds) *Varieties of Anomalous Experiences*, Washington, DC: American Psychological Association, 253–82. Review of research on alien abductions.

Bennett, E. (1939) *Apparitions and Haunted Houses*, London: Faber. A collection of 103 cases.

Braude, S.E. (1986) *The Limits of Influence*, London: Routledge. Four chapters on apparitions.

Green, C. and McCreery, C. (1975) *Apparitions*, London: Hamish Hamilton. Also published by the Institute of Psychophysical Research, Oxford. A useful classification of cases.

Myers, F.W.H. (1903) *Human Personality and its Survival of Bodily Death*, London: Longmans Green and Co. A classic in print.

References

Alcock, J. (1981) *Parapsychology: Science or Magic? A Psychological Perspective*, Elmsford, NY: Pergamon Press.

Broad, C. (1962) *Lectures on Psychical Research*, London: Routledge and Kegan Paul.

Cheyne, J.A., Ruefer, S.D. and Newby-Clark, I.R. (1999) Hypnagogic and hypnapompic hallucinations during sleep paralysis: neurological and cultural constructions of the night-mare, *Consciousness and Cognition*, 8, 319–37.

Devereux, P. and Brookesmith, P. (1997) *UFOs and Ufology: The First 50 Years*, London: Blandford.

Emmons, C.F. (1982) *Chinese Ghosts and ESP*, London: Metuchen.

Gauld, A. (1979) Discarnate survival. In B.B. Wolman (ed.) *Handbook of Parapsychology*, New York: Van Nostrand Rheinhold, 577–630.

Gurney, E., Myers, F.W.H. and Podmore, F. (1886) *Phantasms of the Living*, London: Trubner.

Haraldsson, E., Gudmundsdottir, A., Ragnarsson, A., Loftsson, J. and Jonsson, S. (1977) National survey of psychical experiences and attitudes towards the paranormal in Iceland. In J.D. Morris, W.G. Roll, R.L. Roll and R.L. Morris (eds) *Research in Parapsychology 1976*, Metuchen, NJ: Scarecrow Press, 182–6.

Hart, H. (1956) Six theories about apparitions, *Proceedings of the Society for Psychical Research*, 50, 156, 153–239.

Lambert, G.W. (1955) Poltergeists: a physical theory, *Journal of the Society for Psychical Research*, 38, 49–71.

Loftus, E.F. (1993) The reality of repressed memories, *American Psychologist*, 48, 518–37.

McCue, P.A. (2002) Theories of haunting: a critical overview, *Journal of the Society for Psychical Research*, 66, 1, 1–21.

MacKenzie, A. (1971) *Apparitions and Ghosts*, London: Arthur Barker.

MacKenzie, A. (1987) *The Seen and the Unseen*, London: Heinemann.

MacKenzie, A. (1988) Continuation of the record of a Haunted House, *Journal of the Society for Psychical Research*, 5, 810.

Morton, R.C. (1892) Record of a haunted house: the Cheltenham ghost, *Proceedings of the Society for Psychical Research*, 8, 311–32.

Myers, F.W.H., Gurney E. and Podmore, F. (1886) *Phantasms of the Living*, 2 vols. London: SPR and Trubner and Co. Abridged edition by Mrs Sidgwick published in 1918, London: Kegan Paul and Trubner and Co.

Nickell, J. (1995) *Entities: Angels, Spirits, Demons and other Alien Beings*, Amherst, NY: Prometheus.

Owen, I.M. and Sparrow, M.H. (1976) *Conjuring up Philip*, New York: Harper and Row.

Palmer, J. (1979) A community mail survey of psychic experiences, *Journal of the American Society for Psychical Research*, 69, 333–9.

Persinger, M.A. (1999) Near-death experiences and ectasy: a product of the organization of the human brain. Chapter 5 in S. Della Salla (ed.) *Mind Myths*, London: Wiley.

Persinger, M.A. and Cameron, R.A. (1986) Are earth-faults at fault in some poltergeist cases? *Journal of the American Society for Psychical Research*, 80, 49–73.

Persinger, M.A., Tiller, S.G. and Koen, S.A. (2000) Experimental stimulation of a haunt experience and elicitation of paroxysmal electroencephalographic activity by transcerebral complex magnetic fields: induction of a synthetic ghost? *Perceptual and Motor Skills*, 90, 659–74.

Reese, W.D. (1971) Hallucinations of widowhood, *British Medical Journal*, 2 October.

Salter, W.H. (1938) *Ghosts and Apparitions*, London: Bell. See also Salter's *Zoar*, London, 1961.

Sidgwick, H., Johnson, A., Myers, F.W.H., Podmore, F. and Sidgwick, E.M. (1894) Report on the Census of Hallucinations, *Proceedings of the Society for Psychical Research*, 10, 25–422.

Tandy, V. and Lawrence, T. (1998) The ghost in the machine, *Journal of the Society for Psychical Research*, 62, 85, 360–4.

Tandy, V. (2000) Something in the cellar, *Journal of the Society for Psychical Research*, 66, 233–52.

Thalbourne, M. (1982) *Glossary of Terms Used in Parapsychology*, London: Heinemann.

Wilson, J. (1992) Are memories of alien abductions recollections of surgical experiences? *Journal of Scientific Exploration*, 6, 3, 291–4.

Wiseman, R., Watt, C., Greening, E., Stevens, P. and O'Keefe, C. (2002) An investigation into the alleged haunting of Hampton Court Palace: psychological variables and magnetic fields, *Journal of Parapsychology*, 66, 387–408.

Chapter 15

Out-of-body experiences

Susan Blackmore

An out-of-body experience (or OBE) is an experience in which a person seems to see the world from a location outside of the physical body. In other words, when you have an OBE you feel as though you have left the body and are able to see, feel, and move around without it. Note that this definition treats the OBE as an *experience* only. So if you *feel* as though you are out of your body then you are – by definition – having an OBE, whether or not anything has actually left the body. As Palmer (1978) pointed out: 'The OBE is neither potentially nor actually a psychic phenomenon. It is an experience or mental state, like a dream or any other altered state of consciousness. It may be associated with psi, but it is not a psychic phenomenon itself.' This broad definition allows researchers to study the experience without committing themselves to any particular theory of the OBE.

Surveys

Surveys show that about 15 to 20 per cent of the population have had an OBE at some time during their life (Blackmore 1982, 1996). Most of these people only have one, or a very few OBEs, although a few have many. Some people find the experience frightening but others value the pleasant sensations and visions, and some even learn to induce the experience at will.

Spontaneous OBEs most often occur during resting, just before sleep or when meditating. However, OBEs can occur at almost any time and occasionally the person carries on with what they were doing (such as walking, driving or even speaking) apparently without interruption. Common factors that provoke OBEs include relaxation, loss or disruption of body image, and reduced sensory input. Most spontaneous OBEs are very brief, lasting only a few seconds. Some begin with the experience of travelling down a dark tunnel, often with a bright white or golden light at the end. Others begin with rushing or whirring noises, odd vibrations or simply a brief period of blackout. Returning is usually gradual but occasionally there is a sensation of shock or disorientation (Muldoon and Carrington 1929, Alvarado and Zingrone 1997).

People who have OBEs (OBErs) often feel as though they can travel anywhere and see anything they wish. According to various occult traditions they have another body or double, sometimes referred to as the 'astral body'. This is usually something like a replica of the physical body, though less distinct. Sometimes it is ghostly or transparent and described as whitish or pale grey. In rare cases the double is connected to the physical body by a silver cord. Experiences with a second body have been called 'parasomatic' by Green (1968) and are contrasted with the more common 'asomatic' experiences in which the person feels as though they are just disembodied awareness or a point of consciousness. Occasionally people feel as though they are more like a bubble, a spot of light or a patch of mist.

Vision and hearing are said to be more powerful and clearer than normal. Some people even get the impression that they could see all around at once or hear anything anywhere if they wished to: a sense of limitlessness. OBEs are like dreams in some ways – for example, the scenery and lighting can be very strange, and the ordinary physical constraints of the physical world do not seem to apply. However, unlike ordinary dreams, OBEs feel very real, consciousness is clear, and the experience is usually remembered very vividly afterwards. In some ways OBEs are more like lucid dreams, that is, dreams in which you know *during the dream* that you are dreaming. OBEs sometimes merge into mystical experiences and they form a central part of the near-death experience (NDE). After an OBE, people say that their attitudes and beliefs are changed, usually in positive ways. A psychiatric analysis of hundreds of cases of OBEs showed that for many people their fear of death was reduced and their belief in survival increased (Gabbard and Twemlow 1984).

OBErs frequently interpret their experiences as psychic, paranormal or mystical. They sometimes claim that they could see not only their own bodies, but distant scenes, although the experimental evidence to support these claims is weak. More rarely they also claim to be able to influence distant events, although the frustration of being *unable* to influence things is more common. For example, OBErs sometimes try to touch people they see, only to find that the people do not notice them at all; or they try to switch on a light or move an object, only to discover that their hand goes right through it.

The occurrence of OBEs is not related to age, sex, educational level or religion (Green 1968, Gabbard and Twemlow 1984). However, OBErs score higher on measures of hypnotisability and absorption – that is, they can more easily become absorbed in films, books or fantasies (Irwin 1985). OBErs are also more likely to believe in the paranormal, to have various kinds of psychic experiences and to report frequent dream recall and lucid dreams.

Many popular techniques are available for inducing the experience, most of which use imagery and relaxation as key components (Blackmore 1982, Rogo 1983). Experimental techniques have also been developed using special sounds and visual displays, as well as imagery exercises and relaxation. From the early days of psychical research, hypnosis has been used to induce OBEs or 'travelling clairvoyance' (see Blackmore 1982, Alvarado 1992). Drugs have been known to produce OBEs, especially the psychedelics LSD, psilocybin, DMT and mescaline, and the dissociative anaesthetic ketamine which often induces feelings of body separation, floating and even dying. However, there is no known drug that can reliably induce an OBE.

There is no evidence to suggest that people who have OBEs are mentally ill in any way. Gabbard and Twemlow (1984) in their study of over 300 OBErs found that they were generally well adjusted with low levels of alcohol and drug abuse and no sign of psychotic thinking. Several other studies have failed to find any differences in various measures of psychopathology between people who do and do not have OBEs. Some people who have OBEs fear that they are ill or even going mad. They can often be helped simply by giving them information about how common OBEs are and the circumstances under which they are most likely to happen. Others fear that they will go out of their body and not be able to get back. This fear does not seem well founded. In both the occult and scientific literature it is said that if the physical body is touched or attention demanded in some way, the experience will end. Indeed it is generally hard to induce OBEs and it takes much practice to keep them going for long periods.

Experiments

Experiments on OBEs have mostly been of three types. Attempts to detect the double during OBEs began early in the twentieth century. Photographs were taken of projected doubles and attempts made to weigh the soul as it left the body of people dying of tuberculosis, but the studies were not well controlled and the effects disappeared when better methods were developed (for a review see Blackmore 1982). Recent studies have used magnetometers, thermistors, ultra-violet and infra-red detectors, as well as humans and animals. There has been limited success with animals but so far no reliable detector of an out-of-body presence has been discovered (Morris *et al.* 1978).

Many experiments have tried to detect paranormal vision or hearing during OBEs; that is, whether people can really see and hear what is going on at a distance. In early experiments mediums were asked to exteriorise their double and to smell scents or view the actions of people at a distance, but usually the medium herself could have seen what was going on. More recently, target letters, numbers or objects have been concealed from view in the laboratory and people who can have OBEs at will were asked to try to see them (for a review see Alvarado 1982). In a well-known experiment one subject correctly saw a five-digit number, but this success has never been repeated, and most other experiments have had equivocal results. There are many claims from case studies that people really can see at a distance during OBEs but the experimental evidence does not substantiate them.

The third type of experiment has involved physiological monitoring of OBErs. No unique physiological state seems to be involved. In the few studies done, the subject was found to be in a very relaxed waking state or in a state resembling that on the very edge of sleep. It is certainly clear that OBErs were not in REM (rapid eye movement), or dreaming, sleep. Therefore OBEs cannot be considered to be a kind of dream.

Explanations

There are three main theories which attempt to explain the OBE.

Leaving the body

First is the idea that something leaves the body. Most people who have an OBE find the experience so compelling and realistic that they jump to the obvious conclusion that 'they' have left their physical body. Many further conclude that this 'something' does not depend on the body and can therefore continue after physical death, although this does not necessarily follow since the physical body was alive at the time.

The idea that we have a double can be traced back to ancient Egypt and to Greek philosophy, and can be found in folklore and mythology from many cultures. It is also a part of many religious doctrines. A popular modern version, based in the teachings of Theosophy, is that of astral projection. It is suggested that we all have several bodies, of which the first three are the physical, the etheric and the astral. The astral is said to be able to separate from the physical and move about on the astral plane without it. In life the two bodies are connected by the silver cord but at death this is broken, freeing the consciousness.

There are numerous problems with this, and with all similar theories. It cannot specify what the astral body consists of, in what sense it is conscious or how this consciousness is related to the obvious sensory and memory functions of the brain, how it perceives the world without using any sensory apparatus and without being detected, and why the astral world appears the way it does. Also, studies have found that astral doubles are far from common and the silver cord extremely rare.

ESP

A second kind of theory is that OBEs are imagination plus ESP. In principle this might account for the claims of paranormal perception during OBEs without involving all the problems of other worlds and other bodies. However, this is the weakest possible kind of theory since imagination is such a broad term, and ESP is not well understood. In addition it is not easy to see how this theory could be tested, which makes it useless as a scientific theory.

Psychological theories

The final type of theory is that the OBE is a purely psychological phenomenon, involving no self, soul, spirit or astral body that leaves. Several theories of this kind have been proposed. They do not necessarily preclude the possibility of ESP but they make no special provision for it.

Psychoanalytic interpretations treat the OBE as a dramatisation of the fear of death, an uncoupling of the bodily ego from the mental ego, regression of the ego, or a reliving of the trauma of birth. Jung himself saw OBEs as part of the process of individuation and others have used his ideas of archetypes in trying to understand the OBE (see Alvarado 1992 for a review). In 1978, Palmer suggested that a loss of, or change in, the body image threatened the self-image and the OBE then occurred, through unconscious mechanisms, as one of several possible ways of re-establishing personal identity. The ego then strives to re-establish the normal body image and when this succeeds the OBE ends. Palmer added that some people could gain ego control over the process and so learn to have OBEs at will, providing access to deep unconscious material and latent psychic abilities. This theory relies heavily on psychoanalytic concepts which have not stood up well to psychological research, mostly being found to be either untestable or false.

A popular idea is to liken the OBE to birth. Superficially there may be similarities between the tunnel and the birth canal, or the silver cord and the umbilicus. However, the birth canal would look nothing like a tunnel to a foetus being pushed through it, the light would more likely be red with blood than bright white or yellow, and silver cords are, in any case, very rare. Memory from childhood is also extremely limited and unlike adult memory. Birth theories predict that people born by Caesarean section should not have either tunnel experiences or OBEs but in one study comparing people born normally with those born by Caesarean the same proportion of each group had had tunnel experiences and the Caesareans reported more OBEs.

Irwin (1985) suggested that the OBE begins with a disruption of the normal body sense leading to somaesthetic sensations of floating or flying.

This is then translated, by synaesthesia, into a complete experience of leaving the body, with visual, tactile, auditory and other senses all being transformed. The process requires attention to, or absorption in, the new experience and loss of contact with somatic sensations. This would explain not only the conditions under which the OBE occurs, but also the tendency for OBErs to score higher in tests of absorption.

Blackmore (1984) suggested a theory based on a change in perceptual perspective. We normally feel as though 'we' are behind the eyes looking out, but this viewpoint requires good sensory input to maintain it. OBEs occur when this normal self-image breaks down and the brain attempts to reconstruct it from memory and imagination. Memory images are often built in a bird's eye view (you remember scenes as though looking down from above). If such a memory image takes over as the current 'model of reality' an OBE occurs. Sounds might be incorporated relatively easily into the bird's eye view, but anything that is likely to rebuild the normal body image, such as movement or a touch on the body, will end the OBE. On this theory the OBE is entirely imagined but because the new viewpoint has taken over completely the experience feels totally realistic.

These psychological theories account for the conditions under which OBEs occur and explain why the OB world is rather like the world of imagination, with transparent walls, and the ability to move around at will and to see in all directions. They also explain why apparently correct details are often mixed with false ones since the brain has simply put together the best information it has. A close connection between OBEs and the body image is suggested by two studies using direct brain stimulation. In the 1930s the pioneer of electrical brain stimulation, Wilder Penfield, operated on epileptics when there was no other treatment available and stimulated the surface of the brain. On one occasion, when stimulating the temporal lobe, his patient cried out 'Oh God! I am leaving my body.' Over half a century later, and with much greater precision, a team of neurosurgeons in Geneva, Switzerland, achieved the same result with another epileptic patient. When a weak current was passed through an electrode on the right angular gyrus, she reported sinking into the bed or falling from a height. With increased current she said 'I see myself lying in bed, from above, but I only see my legs and lower trunk.' They were able to induce the same effect twice more, as well as various other body image distortions. They concluded that the OBE occurred because somatosensory and vestibular information were not properly integrated into a normal body image (Blanke *et al.* 2002).

When psychological theories of the OBE were first proposed, it was predicted that people with vivid imagery would be more likely to have OBEs. This was not found but since then OBErs have been shown to be better at spatial imagery, and at switching viewpoints in imagery, and to have superior dream control skills and a greater tendency to dream in bird's eye view.

Conclusion

Theories like these can potentially explain all the phenomenology of the OBE without recourse to any other bodies or alternative realities. However, claims of paranormal events during OBEs continue to be made and, while they are not incompatible with the psychological theories, they provide a challenge to any purely materialist theory of human nature. Only further research will find out whether these claims are valid or not.

Recommended reading

Introductory

Blackmore, S.J. (1982) *Beyond the Body*, London: Heinemann. Overview of cases, theories and scientific research.

Crookall, R. (1961) *The Study and Practice of Astral Projection*, London: Aquarian Press. A classic description from an occultist's point of view.

Fox, O. (1962) *Astral Projection*, New York: University Books. Firsthand descriptions of extraordinary experiences.

Muldoon, S. and Carrington, H. (1929) *The Projection of the Astral Body*, London: Rider & Co. Classic account, full of descriptions of experiences and the authors' own theories.

Advanced

Alvarado, C.S. (2000) Out-of-body experiences. Chapter 6 in E. Cardena, S.J. Lynn and S. Krippner (eds) *Varieties of Anomalous Experience*, Washington, DC: American Psychological Association. Extended review of work on out-of-body experiences.

Gabbard, G.O. and Twemlow, S.W. (1984) *With the Eyes of the Mind*, New York: Praeger. A study of cases with psychoanalytic interpretations.

Irwin, H.J. (1985) *Flight of Mind: A Psychological Study of the Out-of-Body Experience*, Metuchen, NJ: Scarecrow Press. A scientific and psychological overview of research and theories.

Rogo, D.S. (ed.) (1978) *Mind beyond the Body: The Mystery of ESP Projection*, Harmondsworth: Penguin. A compilation of chapters by various experts, including some scientists.

References

Alvarado, C.S. (1982) ESP during out-of-body experiences: a review of experimental studies, *Journal of Parapsychology*, 46, 209–30.

Alvarado, C.S. (1992) The psychological approach to out-of-body experiences: a review of early and modern developments, *Journal of Psychology*, 126, 237–50.

Alvarado, C.S. and Zingrone, N.L. (1997) Out-of-body experiences and sensations of 'shocks' to the body, *Journal of the Society for Psychical Research*, 61, 304–13.

Blackmore, S.J. (1984) A psychological theory of the OBE, *Journal of Parapsychology*, 48, 201–18.

Blackmore, S.J. (1996) Out-of-body experiences. In *Encyclopedia of the Paranormal*, ed. G. Stein, Buffalo, NY: Prometheus, 471–83.

Blanke, O., Ortigue, S., Landis, T. and Seeck, M. (2002) Stimulating illusory own-body perceptions, *Nature*, 419, 269–70.

Green, C.E. (1968) *Out-of-the-body Experiences*, London: Hamish Hamilton.

Morris, R.L., Harary, S.B., Janis, J., Hartwell, J. and Roll, W.G. (1978) Studies of communication during out-of-body experiences, *Journal of the American Society for Psychical Research*, 72, 1–22.

Palmer, J. (1978) The out-of-body experience: a psychological theory, *Parapsychology Review*, 9, 19–22.

Rogo, D.S. (1983) *Leaving the Body: A Practical Guide to Astral Projection*, Englewood Cliffs, NJ: Prentice Hall.

Chapter 16

Near-death experiences

Susan Blackmore

Near-death experiences (or NDEs) were popularised by the publication of Raymond Moody's *Life After Life* in 1975. Based on accounts of numerous survivors of cardiac arrest and other life-threatening situations, he put together a basic description which included such elements as peace and joy, passing through a dark tunnel with a bright light at the end, viewing the events from above (an out-of-body experience or OBE), the life review and panoramic memory, and the meeting with a 'being of light' who sometimes acted as judge. In a few cases people met some kind of barrier beyond which they could not go, or they had to make a choice between carrying on into the light and returning to life – and pain or suffering. In many cases the experiences were difficult to talk about but they often left the people changed for the better – reportedly less materialistic and with reduced fear of death.

These claims promoted the popular view that this must be evidence for life after death, but many scientists and doctors rejected the experiences as, at best, drug-induced hallucinations or, at worst, pure invention. Twenty-five years, and much research, later, it is clear that neither extreme is correct.

Explanations

The claim that the experiences are evidence for survival after death is untenable. Even though the boundary between life and death is pushed back by improved techniques, it is always possible to argue that the person did not actually die and the experiences were part of life and not death. Of course, if there is life after death, these experiences may give a clue as to what it is like, but they can never constitute proof that there is.

The opposing extreme is also untenable since further research has shown that the experiences are clearly not entirely invented, nor a product of drugs or medical interventions. Moody simply collected cases as they came along, but Ring (1980) studied 101 randomly selected survivors and confirmed that about 60 per cent reported peace, one-third out-of-body experiences, a quarter entered the darkness (or tunnel) and a few reported the later experiences such as life reviews and borders. The experiences seemed to have a definite pattern, even though not all of them included all the same features.

NDEs also appear to be widespread through many ages and cultures. Long before Moody, there had been similar descriptions of death-bed experiences (when the patients did go on to die) in the psychical research literature. Dying patients often described wonderful visions to those sitting at their bedside – including heavenly scenes, bright light, and friends or relatives who had already died coming to help them (Barrett 1926, Osis and Haraldsson 1977). There are isolated reports in the medical literature, and both historical and contemporary accounts from many other cultures (for a review see Blackmore 1993). They all tend to include the key features of tunnels, lights and OBEs, as well as visions of another world. Children also report similar, though sometimes simpler, experiences (Morse 1990).

Now that NDEs are so well known, and have become a common topic for TV shows and magazines, some modern stories are likely to be inventions, exaggerations or distortions. However, the older accounts include striking similarities and it seems unlikely that so many people in different ages and cultures would have invented them. The most interesting question then becomes why the features are so often the same.

Common theories attribute near-death experiences to the following:

1 expectation
2 drugs administered by doctors or patients
3 chemicals released by the brain under stress
4 anoxia or hypercarbia
5 temporal lobe activation
6 life after death

Each theory will be discussed in turn.

Expectation

Expectation certainly affects NDEs, in two ways. First, NDEs often happen to people who think they are dying, when in fact there is no serious clinical emergency. In other words, you do not have to be physically near death to have an NDE (Gabbard *et al.* 1981, Owens *et al.* 1990). Indeed, some aspects of the NDE, such as the out-of-body experience (OBE), can occur at any time and to perfectly healthy people (see Chapter 15 on OBEs). There are some differences between the NDEs of those who are and are not close to death but they are small compared to the similarities.

Second, the content of the NDE may vary with expectations about death. For example, Christians tend to see Jesus in the light, and Hindus see the messengers of Yamraj coming to take them away – and may refuse to go (Osis and Haraldsson 1977). However, the general pattern seems to be similar across cultures, suggesting that religious expectations are not responsible for the entire experience, or for most of its common features. If they were we might expect more pearly gates and fewer tunnels. We might also expect suicide attempters to have more hellish experiences and in fact they do not. Their NDEs are much like others' and tend to reduce future attempts at suicide (Greyson and Stevenson 1980, Ring and Franklin 1981, Rosen 1975).

All this suggests that, although expectation may change the details of NDEs, it cannot be used to explain their occurrence entirely, or even to account for the similarities across ages and cultures.

Drugs

Drugs given to dying patients cannot account for the experiences. Many classic cases have been reported from drug-free patients and from people who were falling from mountains (Noyes and Kletti 1972) or undergoing other accidents where no drugs were involved. More specifically, research shows that patients given anaesthetics or pain killers have fewer, or more muted and less detailed, NDEs than others (Ring 1980, Greyson and Stevenson 1980).

Endorphins

When under stress the brain releases many chemicals that act to reduce pain, or to help the person cope with the stress. These include endorphins (the brain's own morphine-like drugs), glutamate and chemicals similar to the drug ketamine.

Carr (1982) first suggested that endorphins could account for the NDE. Endorphins are released under stress, including both actual physical trauma and extreme fear – such as the fear of dying. They can block pain and induce feelings of well-being, acceptance and even intense pleasure, which might suggest they are responsible for the positive emotions in so many NDEs. There is much controversy over the occurrence of 'hellish' NDEs, with some researchers arguing that they are far more common than previously suspected (Atwater 1992, Greyson and Bush 1992). Occasionally NDEs change from pleasant to hellish. One 72-year-old cancer patient was administered naloxone and his pleasant NDE turned to horror and despair as the friendly creatures turned into the doctors treating him – suggesting that the naloxone (a morphine antagonist) had blocked the endorphins which were providing the pleasant feelings. This is circumstantial, though, and Morse (1990) has argued that endorphins are not responsible, suggesting that the neurotransmitter serotonin plays a more important role. Of eleven children who had survived critical illnesses including coma and cardiac arrest, seven reported NDEs, while twenty-nine age-matched controls, who had had similar treatments including the use of narcotics, did not report any NDEs. However, it is questionable whether the effects of narcotics administered during critical illness are comparable with those of endorphins.

Jansen (1997) has argued that endorphins are not potent hallucinogens and have a long-lasting effect that is quite unlike an NDE. However, the drug ketamine can induce states similar to NDEs. He therefore suggests that during NDEs the brain releases a flood of the neurotransmitter glutamate followed by ketamine-like chemicals which block the glutamate (NMDA) receptors in the brain, and produce the experiences. This theory has been criticised on the grounds that NDEs occur without any obvious stress or damage to the brain, and that ketamine experiences are not clear, vivid and memorable as NDEs are (Fenwick 1997).

Anoxia

The role of cerebral anoxia (or lack of oxygen in the brain) has been hotly debated. Some blame anoxia for all the features of the NDE, though this is implausible since so many NDEs clearly occur in the absence of anoxia (such as in people who only *think* they are going to die).

Anoxia causes a release of inhibition in the brain's cortex – that is, many cells are disinhibited and start firing more rapidly for some time. I have argued that this disinhibition may be responsible for the tunnel and light. Since the visual cortex is organised so that many cells are devoted to the centre of the visual field, and few to the periphery, random firing of cells will produce the effect of a bright light in the centre fading out towards darkness, in other words, a tunnel effect (Blackmore and Troscianko 1988). Endorphins and other internal effects can also lead to disinhibition. So I suggest that it is the disinhibition (not the anoxia itself) which is responsible for much of the NDE (Blackmore 1993).

It is also known that anoxia alone can cause odd experiences, such as the visions and out-of-body experiences reported by pilots trained in gravity-induced loss of consciousness (Whinnery 1990). There are also suggestions of NDE-like experiences in children suffering from reflex anoxic seizures, in which their heart stops and they become briefly unconscious (Blackmore 1998).

Others argue that the effects of anoxia are not like those of NDEs (for example, confusion rather than the clear thinking of a typical NDE), though this is complicated by the fact that different types and speeds of anoxia cause different effects. Sabom (1982) has made a case against anoxia being important and gives the example of an NDE in a patient with measured, normal blood gases, though it has been argued that his blood was taken from the femoral artery and that peripheral blood gases are not a reliable indicator of cortical blood gases.

Hypercarbia (increased carbon dioxide in the blood) is also thought to play a role in NDEs and has long been known to induce visions, lights, mystical experiences and OBEs.

Temporal lobe activation

The temporal lobe is also implicated in NDEs since it is sensitive to anoxia, and stimulating it artificially has long been known to induce hallucinations, memory flashbacks, body distortions and OBEs (Persinger 1999). The limbic system is also sensitive to anoxia and involved in the organisation of emotions and memory, suggesting a possible link with the life review that sometimes occurs during NDEs. An interesting effect of endorphins is that they increase the chance of seizures in the temporal lobe and limbic system and so they might produce the same effects as anoxia. One neuro-biological model of the NDE is based almost entirely on the notion of abnormal firing in the temporal lobe and associated parts of the brain (Saavedra-Aguilar and Gomez-Jeria 1989). Also, research looking for an 'NDE-prone personality' has led to the conclusion that those most likely to have NDEs may have more unstable temporal lobes (i.e. high temporal lobe lability) and show more 'temporal lobe signs' than others (Ring 1984), though it is not clear whether this is a cause or an effect of the NDE.

Life after death

A glimpse of life after death is probably the most popular way to interpret the NDE. Clearly none of the previous theories accounts entirely for all the experiences and many people argue that something beyond the brain is involved, such as a soul or spirit. Direct evidence for this is impossible to obtain. However, there are claims that during NDEs people have been able to hear conversations and see the actions of people around them and even observe things like the behaviour of needles on dials, which they could not possibly have known about in their comatose state (Sabom 1982). If such paranormal acquisition of information really occurs, it is evidence that any naturalistic account of NDEs must be insufficient.

The anecdotal nature of most of these claims, and the lack of independent corroboration, makes them hard to evaluate. In what is probably the most famous case, a woman called Maria saw a shoe on an inaccessible ledge of a hospital in Seattle and the social worker attending her eventually found this shoe exactly as Maria had described it (Clark 1984). However, the only account comes from the social worker and we do not have any corroboration from Maria or anyone else involved. There are also claims that the blind can see again during NDEs. At least one well-known case of an NDE in the blind was shown to have been a fiction (Blackmore 1993) but more recently Ring and Cooper (1997) studied experiences in thirty-one blind people, including some blind from birth. Some reported classic NDEs similar to those of sighted people, and a few claimed to have obtained visually-based knowledge that they could not have gained by any normal means. The researchers concluded that these people cannot see in the ordinary physical sense, but have attained what they call 'transcendental awareness'.

In general, sceptics tend to reject the evidence as inadequate, while proponents think it is conclusive. Perhaps it might be resolved by appropriate experiments, such as those using concealed targets in operating theatres and recovery rooms. Some are presently under way but no results have yet been published.

After having NDEs people frequently claim that their lives have been transformed. They seem to be less materialistic, less selfish, and more concerned with spiritual values than material ones (e.g. Morse 1992). A few claim to have gained paranormal powers. This transforming effect of NDEs is often attributed to a glimpse of heaven or a connection with the infinite. However, simply facing up to death can bring about a change in personal values and there is conflicting evidence about whether an NDE is necessary (Greyson 1990, Pope 1994, Groth-Marnat and Summers 1998). I have also argued that during the NDE the usual model of self breaks down and this brief experience of selflessness may bring about personal changes (Blackmore 1993). From some points of view it may not matter why these changes come about if they can help people in living their lives, and in facing their own death or the death of those they love.

Conclusion

At our current state of knowledge it probably remains a matter of personal preference whether to interpret the NDE as a glimpse of the life beyond or the product of the dying brain. Either way the NDE is clearly an interesting and potentially life-changing experience that can teach us much about living as well as dying.

Recommended reading

Introductory

Blackmore, S.J. (1993) *Dying to Live: Science and the Near-Death Experience*, London: Grafton. General overview, emphasis on naturalistic explanations and the 'dying brain' hypothesis.

Fenwick, P. and Fenwick, E. (1995) *The Truth in the Light*, London: Headline. An investigation of over 300 near-death experiences, with comparison of the theories.

Morse, M. (1990) *Closer to the Light*, London: Souvenir. Accounts of children's NDEs.

Advanced

Bailey, L.W. and Yates, J. (eds) (1996) *The Near-Death Experience: A Reader*, New York and London: Routledge. A collection of wide-ranging chapters by researchers and experiencers alike.

Greyson, B. (2000) Near-death experiences. Chapter 10 in E. Cardena, S.J. Lynn and S. Krippner (eds) *Varieties of Anomalous Experience*, Washington, DC: American Psychological Association. Authoritative review of research on NDEs.

Greyson, B. and Flynn, C.P. (eds) (1984) *The Near-Death Experience: Problems, Prospects, Perspectives*, Springfield, IL: Charles C. Thomas. Collection of useful articles by NDE researchers.

Persinger, M. (1999) Near-death experiences and ecstasy: a product of the organization of the human brain. Chapter 5 in S. Della Sala (ed.) *Mind Myths*, London: Wiley, 85–99. Explains the NDE experiences Persinger has generated by brain stimulation.

Ring, K. (1984) *Heading Towards Omega: In Search of the Meaning of the Near-Death Experience*, New York: Quill. Follow-up to one of the first scientific studies of NDEs.

References

Atwater, P.M.H. (1992) Is there a hell? Surprising observations about the near-death experience, *Journal of Near-Death Studies*, 10, 149–60.

Barrett, W. (1926) *Death-Bed Visions*, London: Methuen.

Blackmore, S.J. (1993) *Dying to Live: Science and the Near-Death Experience*, London: Grafton.

Blackmore, S.J. (1998) Experiences of anoxia: Do reflex anoxic seizures resemble near-death experiences? *Journal of Near Death Studies*, 17, 111–20.

Blackmore, S.J. and Troscianko, T. (1988) The physiology of the tunnel, *Journal of Near-Death Studies*, 8, 15–28.

Carr, D. (1982) Pathophysiology of stress-induced limbic lobe dysfunction: a hypothesis relevant to near-death experiences Anabiosis, *The Journal of Near-Death Studies*, 2, 75–89. Also reprinted in B. Greyson and C.P. Flynn (eds) (1984) *The Near-Death Experience: Problems, Prospects, Perspectives*, Springfield, IL: Charles C. Thomas, 125–39.

Clark, K. (1984) Clinical interventions with near-death experiencers. In B. Greyson and C.P. Flynn (eds) *The Near-Death Experience: Problems, Prospects, Perspectives*, Springfield, IL: Charles C. Thomas, 242–55.

Fenwick, P. (1997) Is the near-death experience only N-methyl-D-aspartate blocking? *Journal of Near-Death Studies*, 16, 43–53.

Gabbard, G.O., Twemlow, S.W. and Jones, F.C. (1981) Do 'near death experiences' only occur near death? *Journal of Nervous and Mental Disease*, 169, 374–7.

Greyson, B. (1990) Near-death encounters with and without near-death experiences: comparative NDE scale profiles, *Journal of Near-Death Studies*, 8, 151–61.

Greyson, B. and Bush, N.E. (1992) Distressing near-death experiences, *Psychiatry*, 55, 95–110.

Greyson, B. and Stevenson, I. (1980) The phenomenology of near-death experiences, *American Journal of Psychiatry*, 137, 1193–6.

Groth-Marnat, G. and Summers, R. (1998) Altered beliefs, attitudes, and behaviors following near-death experiences, *Journal of Humanistic Psychology*, 38, 110–25.

Jansen, K. (1997) The ketamine model of the near-death experience: a central role for the N-methyl-D-aspartate receptor, *Journal of Near-Death Studies*, 16, 5–26.

Moody, R.A. (1975) *Life After Life*, Atlanta, GA: Mockingbird.

Morse, M. (1992) *Transformed by the Light*, London: Piatkus.

Noyes, R. and Kletti, R. (1972) The experience of dying from falls, *Omega*, 3, 45–52.

Osis, K. and Haraldsson, E. (1977) *At the Hour of Death*, New York: Avon.

Owens, J.E., Cook, E.W. and Stevenson, I. (1990) Features of 'near-death experience' in relation to whether or not patients were near death, *The Lancet*, 336, 1175–7.

Pope, J. (1994) Near-death experiences and attitudes towards life, death and suicide, *Australian Parapsychological Review*, 19, 23–6.

Ring, K. (1980) *Life at Death: A Scientific Investigation of the Near-Death Experience*, New York: Coward, McCann and Geoghegan (and New York: Quill 1982).

Ring, K. and Cooper, S. (1997) Near-death and out-of-body experiences in the blind: a study of apparent eyeless vision, *Journal of Near-Death Studies*, 16, 101–47.

Ring, K. and Franklin, S. (1981) Do suicide survivors report near-death experiences? *Omega*, 12, 191–208.

Ring, K. and Lawrence, M. (1993) Further evidence for veridical perception during near-death experiences, *Journal of Near-Death Studies*, 11, 223–9.

Rosen, D.H. (1975) Suicide survivors, *Western Journal of Medicine*, 122, 289–94.

Saavedra-Aguilar, J.C. and Gomez-Jeria, J.S. (1989) A neurobiological model for near-death experiences, *Journal of Near-Death Studies*, 7, 205–22.

Sabom, M.B. (1982) *Recollections of Death*, London: Corgi.

Whinnery, J.E. (1990) Acceleration-induced loss of consciousness: a review of 500 episodes, *Archives of Neurology*, 47, 764–76.

Chapter 17

Imagery

Robin Taylor

Imagery can be defined as the production of perception (such as creating a visual image in one's mind's eye) without input from any of the sense organs. Most people associate imagery with visualisation (visual imagery) but it is important to note that imagery can occur in any sense modality, such as auditory, kinaesthetic or olfactory imagery. Psychic impressions appear as visions, in dreams, as an out-of-body experience, and as dismembered sounds and voices. For instance a psychic experience reported by Myers (1903):

> On the 5th of July, 1887, I left my home in Lakewood to go to New York to spend a few days. My wife was not feeling well when I left, and . . . at night, before I went to bed, I thought I would try to find out if possible her condition. I had undressed, and was sitting on the edge of my bed, when I covered my face with my hands and willed myself at Lakewood at home to see if I could see her. After a little, I seemed to be standing in her room before the bed, and saw her lying looking much better. I felt satisfied she was better . . . On Saturday I went home. When she saw me she remarked . . . 'I thought something had happened to you. I saw you standing in front of the bed the night (about 8:30 or before 9) you left, as plain as could be, and I have been worrying myself about you ever since. I sent to the office and to the depot daily to get some message from you.' . . . She had seen me when I was trying to see her and find out her condition. I thought at the time I was going to see her and make her see me.

The psi experience in this example manifested itself to both the husband and wife in visions of what apparently was the real state of the wife and the intentional state of the husband. We could argue that the psi information transferred between the couple was actually perceived through the brain in some deeper thought pattern (unconsciously perhaps) and translated through visual imagery into the visions that the couple saw of each other. The alternative is to suggest that the husband psychically changed the physical properties of the environment in front of his wife as she sat in her bed, so that she really did see something. The question for parapsychologists becomes, how is imagery actually linked to the psi process, and is it a key factor in psychic impressions, or a by-product?

Research

Spontaneous cases

The large number of reported psi experiences similar to the example above has prompted certain parapsychologists to comment that there appears to be a strong link between psi and imagery (Alvarado 1996). Reviews in the spontaneous case literature, such as those by Schouten (1979, 1981, 1983), conclude that the majority of psi experiences occur in the visual imagery mode. White (1964) has also pointed out that early gifted psychics relied heavily on mental imagery to perform a psychic task. The out-of-body experience (OBE) (Irwin 1981) is also associated with vivid visual imagery, as is the ability to detect auras (Alvarado and Zingrone 1994). However, the role of expectancy bias cannot be entirely ruled out in these latter cases. Respondents completing self-report questionnaires on imagery ability and some aspect of psi functioning that appears to centre around visual imagery (such as auras or OBEs) would not find it hard to guess that parapsychological researchers predict that there might be a positive correlation between the psi and imagery. Such expectancy effects are hard to exclude in self-report correlational research designs.

Experiments

The spontaneous case literature is quite striking in the abundance of imagery that occurs with the psi event. Also imagery-conducive situations such as hypnosis (Honorton 1977), dreaming (Van der Castle 1977) and the ganzfeld experiments (Bem and Honorton 1994) appear to facilitate psi functioning. Experimental parapsychologists have wondered whether people with higher imagery ability are more psychic.

To answer this question two broad lines of experimental research have been undertaken. The first is to assess experimentally a participant's imagery ability and to correlate this with their score on an experimental psi task; the second is to assess whether one can train up imagery ability and use this in experimental psi tasks successfully. A review of the role of imagery in psi experiments (George and Krippner 1984) presents a muddy picture as some studies show positive correlations, others negative correlations and a final group show no significant correlations. George and Krippner explain that trying to refine the instructional set to specifically apply imagery procedures did not appear to clarify the findings. The little work that has been done since appears to replicate the same ambiguity about the role of imagery ability. Gissurarson and Morris (1991) for instance found no evidence of a relationship between psi and self-reported imagery abilities, despite the acknowledgement that participants in his PK task tended to use imagery approaches. My research (Taylor 1993), on the other hand, appears to show that higher imagery ability is associated with higher psychokinesis (PK) scores.

Much of the research focusing on trying to train up imagery ability fails to show any advantage in imagery training effects (e.g. Morris and Hornaday 1981, Morris and Morrel 1985). George and Krippner (1984) have pointed out, though, that many of these studies did not in fact assess whether imagery ability had in fact improved. Braud (1983) in a pilot study found a positive correlation between an increase in imagery ability and an increase in psi ability. There is some suggestion that this result was replicated (Taylor 1993), though this is far from a clear replication.

Explanations

One interpretation of this finding argues that the results suggest there is no link between psi and imagery, hence no consistent relationship is found in the experiments to date. The apparent strong correspondence in the spontaneous case literature is due to some underlying cause in the real life situation which affects both psi and imagery. In this sense imagery would be regarded as an epiphenomenon to the psi event. For example, Wilson and Barber (1983) have described a fantasy-prone personality who scores relatively high on hypnotisability and absorption. Lynn and Roue (1988) found that the fantasy-prone score high on vividness of mental imagery. Barber and Wilson proposed that the fantasy-prone were more likely to 'experience' paranormal phenomena.

Measurement inadequacy

Alternatively others accept that there is a link between psi and imagery but posit that researchers have been using incorrect or unsophisticated procedures to study this relationship experimentally. One reason to favour this latter interpretation is that in the psychological literature the imagery debate continues with no clear resolution as to what exactly imagery is, how it operates and therefore how it can be measured (Pylyshyn 2002a, Thomas 2002). Some psychologists argue that imagery is no more than an epiphenomenon (Pylyshyn 2002a), while others claim that it is a very real cognitive process (Rollins 1989, Finke 1989, Kosslyn 1994) that can influence action (Marks 1999). Even for those psychologists who argue that imagery is a real ability, there is no consensus as to what would be an adequate test of it. Some researchers look at spatial relations tasks and take measurements of experimental subjects' ability to mentally manipulate objects to reveal answers posed to them by the experimenter, such as: which of objects B and C resembles object A in every aspect bar its orientation (Cooper and Shepherd 1973)?

Other researchers contest that self-report questionnaires are adequate and valid measures of imagery. Unfortunately scores on the spatial relations tasks and the questionnaires do not correlate significantly (Richardson 1983) and since it is claimed that the results from the different measures are robust it would seem that they are measuring different abilities.

Early parapsychology studies measuring imagery abilities in the main tended to concentrate on self-report questionnaires; the most frequently used has been the Betts Questionnaire of Mental Imagery (Betts 1909) or Sheehan's revised version of it (Sheehan 1967); however, Honorton (Honorton *et al.* 1974) questioned whether it really is measuring imagery. Later parapsychological studies have mainly used Marks's Vividness of Visual Imagery Questionnaire (Marks 1973). Hall *et al.*'s Movement Imagery Questionnaire is useful because it measures not only visual but also kinaesthetic imagery (Hall *et al.* 1985).

Obviously the prime concern is to ascertain what is a good measure of imagery before parapsychological imagery research can proceed in an intelligent manner. As in psychology, parapsychological experimental designs need to evolve in sophistication to minimise the possibility of artefactual correlation effects (Palmer and Lieberman 1975), or training effects being due to an experimental design artefact (Taylor 1993).

Two-stage model

Despite these conceptual and theoretical problems, parapsychologists have been struck by the spontaneous case literature cited above and the experimental literature replete with imagery that occurs with the psi event, such as: hypnosis (Honorton 1977), dreaming (Van der Castle 1977) and the ganzfeld experiments (Bem and Honorton 1994). Although the existing experimental literature has failed to empirically confirm this relationship between imagery and psi, this has not stopped some parapsychologists proposing theoretical models to explain this relationship.

The *two-stage model* developed by Tyrrell (1947) is relevant to ESP effects. It has been elaborated by Rhine (1978) and Irwin (1979), and postulates that psychic information is picked up unconsciously (stage I) and then mediated to the consciousness via various means (stage II), one of which may be through imagery (visual or otherwise). It is further hypothesised that this mediation is like any other normal process that transfers unconscious information to the conscious level and therefore it is subject to similar transformations. Hence we may receive psychic information but it

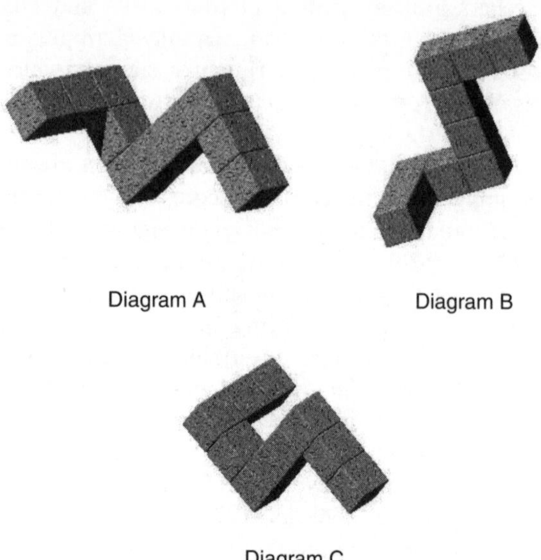

Figure 17.1 A spatial relations task to measure imagery ability. A psychology participant must say which of two diagrams (B or C) is the same object as the first diagram (A).
Adapted from Cooper and Shepherd (1984)

may manifest itself to us in imagery of an allegorical or symbolic nature which we do not instantly recognise as a psychic impression.

Lability hypothesis

Braud (1981) has proposed a model in which psi processes may interact through a labile system (something that changes state readily). Imagery is a method that a person can use to try to impose their intention on a labile system such as a random event generator. Conversely, imagery may be the labile system which can be influenced by the intention of another person (Braud and Jackson 1983) or by the stability of an inert object. Although there has not been much explicit experimental follow-up on the lability hypothesis, Braud still considers it to be viable and rates the associated imagery as an important enabler for consciousness to interact with the environment (Braud 1994).

Conclusion

Parapsychological experimental interest in the relationship between psi and imagery has waned, despite an apparently strong anecdotal and weak

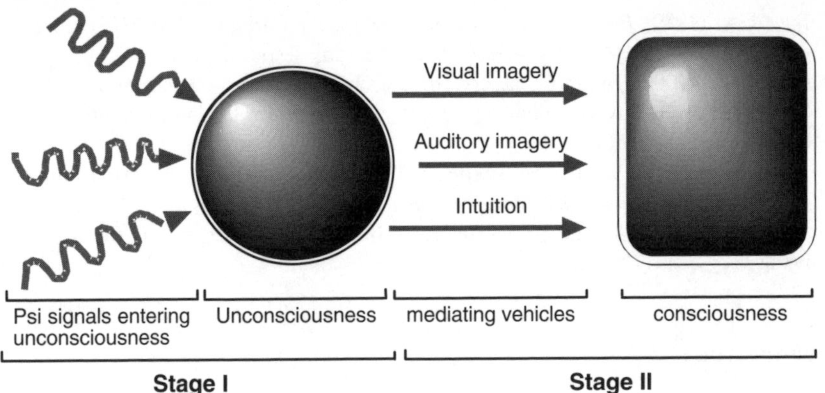

Figure 17.2 Two-stage model of acquiring and becoming conscious of psychic impressions

experimental link between psi and imagery. This may appear odd as parapsychological research appears to have subsumed imagery as part of the paradigm of parapsychological phenomena (see Sherwood 2000, 2001, Bentall 2000, or the ganzfeld literature). However, psychologists are unsure as to the precise nature of imagery (Pylyshyn 2002a) and how best to measure it. Research will be easier once the imagery research domain becomes better resolved.

Recommended reading

Introductory

George, L. and Krippner, S. (1984) Mental imagery and psi phenomena: a review. In S. Krippner (ed.) *Advances in Parapsychology 4*, Jefferson, NC: McFarland, 65–82. Still the best review of parapsychological experimental research that relates explicitly to the role of imagery.

Schouten, S.A. (1983) A different approach for analyzing spontaneous cases: with particular reference to the study of Louisa E. Rhine's case collection, *Journal of Parapsychology*, 47, 323–40. The last of three collections of spontaneous cases that Schouten analysed. Several of Schouten's excellent articles (see below) offer a good way to gain an understanding of the importance of imagery in the psi process.

Advanced

Bentall, R. (2000) Hallucinatory experiences. Ch. 3 in E. Cardena, S.J. Lynn and S. Krippner (eds) *Varieties of Anomalous Experience*, Washington, DC: American Psychological Association. Erudite account of hallucinatory images including their relationship to psi.

Finke, R.A. (1989) *Principals of Mental Imagery*, Cambridge, MA: MIT Press. A good guide to imagery in psychological research, despite its age.

Pylyshyn, Z. (2002) Mental imagery: in search of a theory, *Behavior and Brain Sciences*. A return to the 'imagery debate' with a good selection of commentaries by current luminaries.

Tyrrell, G.N.M. (1947) The 'Modus Operandi' of paranormal cognition, *Proceedings of the Society for Psychical Research*, 48, 65–120. The original account of the two-stage model of psi and the role of imagery has the merit of being very clearly written.

References

Alvarado, C.S. (1996) Exploring the features of spontaneous psychic experiences, *European Journal of Parapsychology*, 12, 61–74.

Alvarado, C.S. and Zingrone, N.L. (1994) Individual differences in aura vision: relationships to visual imagery and imaginative-fantasy experiences, *European Journal of Parapsychology*, 10, 1–30.

Bem, D.J. and Honorton, C. (1994) Does psi exist? Replicable evidence for an anomalous process of communication, *Psychological Bulletin*, 115, 4–18.

Betts, G.H. (1909) *The Distribution and Functions of Mental Imagery*, New York: Teachers College, Columbia University.

Braud, W. (1981) Lability and inertia in psychic functioning. In B. Shapin and L. Coly (eds) *Concepts and Theories of Parapsychology*, New York: Parapsychology Foundation.

Braud, W. (1983) Prolonged visualisation practice and psychokinesis: a pilot study. In W.G. Roll, J. Beloff and R.A. White (eds) *Research in Parapsychology 1982* Metuchen, NJ: Scarecrow Press, 187–98.

Braud, W.G. (1994) The role of mind in the physical world: a psychologist's view, *European Journal of Parapsychology*, 10, 66–77.

Braud, W. and Jackson, J. (1983) Psi influence upon mental imagery, *Parapsychology Review*, 14, 13–15.

Cooper, L.A. and Shepherd, R.N. (1973) Chronometric studies of the rotation of mental images. In W.G. Chase (ed.) *Visual Information Processing*, New York: Academic Press.

Cooper, L.A. and Shepherd, R.N. (1984) Turning Something over in the mind. *Scientific American*, 251, 6, 106–117.

Gissurarson, L.R. and Morris, R.L. (1991) Examination of six questionnaires as predictors of psychokinesis performance, *Journal of Parapsychology*, 55, 119–45.

Hall, C., Pongrac, J. and Buckholz, E. (1985) The measurement of imagery ability, *Human Movement Science*, 4, 107–18.

Honorton, C. (1977) Psi and internal attention states. In B.B. Wolman (ed.) *Handbook of Parapsychology*, New York: Van Nostrand Reinhold, 435–72.

Honorton, C., Tierney, L. and Torres, D. (1974) The role of mental imagery in psi-mediation, *Journal for the American Society for Psychical Research*, 68, 385–94.

Irwin, H.J. (1979) *Psi and the Mind: An Information Processing Approach*, Metuchen, NJ: Scarecrow Press.

Irwin, H. (1981) Some psychological dimensions of the out-of-body experience, *Parapsychology Review*, 12, 1–6.

Kosslyn, S.M. (1994) *Image and Brain: The Resolution of the Imagery Debate*, Cambridge, MA: MIT Press.

Lynn, S.J. and Roue, J.W. (1988) The fantasy-prone person: hypnosis, imagination and creativity, *Journal of Personality and Social Psychology*, 51, 404–8.

Marks, D.F. (1973) Visual imagery differences in the recall of pictures, *British Journal of Psychology*, 64, 17–24.

Marks, D.F. (1999) Concsiousness, mental imagery and action, *British Journal of Psychology*, 90, 4, 567–85.

Morris, R.L. and Hornaday, J. (1981) An attempt to employ mental practice to facilitate PK. In W.G. Roll and J. Beloff (eds) *Research in Parapsychology 1980* Metuchen, NJ: Scarecrow Press, 103–4.

Morris, R.L. and Morrel, N.M. (1985) Free response ESP training: a significant failure. In *Research in Parapsychology 1984*, Metuchen, NJ: Scarecrow Press, 51–4.

Myers, F.W.H. (1903) *Human Personality and its Survival of Bodily Death*, Vol. 1, New York: Longmans, Green and Co.

Palmer, J. and Lieberman, R. (1975) The influence of psychological set on ESP and out-of-body experiences, *Journal of the American Society for Psychical Research*, 69, 193, 213.

Pylyshyn, Z. (2002a) Mental imagery: in search of a theory, *Behavior and Brain Sciences*.

Pylyshyn, Z. (2002b) Stalking the elusive mental image screen: Pylyshyn's reply to commentators, *Behavior and Brain Sciences*.

Rhine, L.E. (1978) The psi process in spontaneous cases, *Journal of Parapsychology*, 42, 20–32.

Richardson, A. (1983) Imagery: definition and types. In A.A. Sheikh (ed.) *Imagery: Current Theory, Research and Application*, New York: Wiley.

Rollins, M. (1989) *Mental Imagery: On the Limits of Cognitive Science*, London: Yale University Press.

Rush, J.H. (1986) What is parapsychology? In H.L. Edge, R.L. Morris, J. Palmer and J.H. Rush (eds) *Foundations of Parapsychology*, Boston: Routledge & Kegan Paul, 1.

Schouten, S.A. (1979) Analysis of spontaneous cases as reported in 'Phantasms of the Living', *European Journal of Parapsychology*, 2, 408–55.

Schouten, S.A. (1981) Analysing spontaneous cases: a replication based on the 'Sannwald Collection', *European Journal of Parapsychology*, 4, 9–48.

Sheehan, P.W. (1967) A shortened form of Betts' questionnaire upon mental imagery, *Journal of Clinical Psychology*, 23, 386–9.

Sherwood, S.J. (2000) A comparison of the features of psychomanteum and hypnagogic/hypnopompic experiences, *International Journal of Parapsychology*, 11, 2, 97–121.

Sherwood, S.J. (2001) WWW survey of the content, sensory modalities, and interpretation of hypnagogic and hynopompic experiences, *Journal of Parapsychology*, 65, 4, 377–8.

Taylor, R.K. (1993) Training to use an imagery strategy for PK-RNG games. In N.L. Zingrone and M.J. Schlitz (eds) (1998) *Research in Parapsychology, 1993:*

Abstracts and Papers from the 36th Annual Convention of the Parapsychology Association, 1993 (pp. 91–95) Lanham, MD: Scarecrow Press, Inc.

Taylor, R. (1996) Training imagery skills for enhanced psychic functioning: two experiments with athletes, *European Journal of Parapsychology*, 12, 1–22.

Thomas, N.J.T. (2002) The false dichotomy of imagery, *Behavior and Brain Sciences.*

Van der Castle, R.L. (1977) Sleep and dreams. In B.B. Wolman (ed.) *Handbook of Parapsychology*, New York: Van Nostrand Reinhold, 473–99.

White, R.A. (1964) A comparison of old and new methods of response to targets in ESP experiments, *Journal of the American Society for Psychical Research*, 58, 21–56.

Wilson, S.C. and Barber, T.X. (1983) The fantasy-prone personality. In A.A. Sheikh (ed.) *Imagery: Current Research Theory and Application*, New York: Wiley, 340–90.

After-life associations

Chapter 18

Survival

Alan Gauld

There is an extensive literature on the ostensible evidence for survival of bodily death and it will only be possible to touch on a very small part of it. A much longer, but still very incomplete, list of references is given by Gauld (1977). Among general surveys of the material the following may be especially noted: Myers (1903 – the great early classic), Hart (1959), Salter (1961), Ducasse (1961), Beard (1966), Jacobson (1973), Gauld (1982), Lorimer (1984), Thouless (1984), Edge (1986), Almeder (1992), Coly and McMahon (1995), Paterson (1995), Roy (1996) and Griffin (1997) and Braude (2003).

It will be convenient to consider the more specialised literature under the two broad headings of ostensible evidence for survival and interpretations of that evidence.

Evidence for survival

An initial difficulty here is that it is by no means clear or agreed what does or could constitute evidence for survival. Some credulous persons accept almost any odd phenomenon, however trivial, as the work of 'the spirits', while others (to whom we shall come) hold, for various reasons, that no empirical findings whatsoever could constitute evidence for survival. Under these circumstances the simplest course will be briefly to mention those categories of phenomena that have most frequently been supposed to yield empirical evidence for survival, and afterwards touch on their possible interpretations. These phenomena may be taken under five headings.

Certain phenomena of mediumship

'Mediums' are individuals through whose agency or through whose organisms there are ostensibly received communications from deceased human beings or other supposed disembodied or remote entities. The phenomenon of mediumship has been reported in one form or another from a large proportion of the past and present societies of which we have records. Often they have become institutionalised, as in Siberian and North American shamanism, and western Spiritualism. In our own society mediums are customarily divided into 'mental' and 'physical'. In mental mediumship the communications are transmitted through automatic speaking, writing, etc., or through the medium's own ostensible 'clairvoyant' and/or 'clairaudient' awareness of the communicating entities. In physical mediumship the communications are transmitted through ostensibly paranormal happenings (raps, object movements, 'direct voice', 'materialisations', etc.) in the medium's own vicinity. It is to be noted that the mere occurrence of paranormal physical phenomena purportedly emanating from a certain deceased person would not by itself constitute evidence for survival, any more than would, say, the mere occurrence of automatic writing purportedly inspired by such a person. Evidence of survival (if any) comes from the content of the communications – the memories, personal characteristics, intellectual skills, etc., apparently displayed.

The most consistently remarkable mediumistic communications of which we have full records and detailed assessments are undoubtedly those which 'came through' two mental mediums, the American Mrs Leonora E. Piper (1859–1950), and the British Mrs Gladys Osborne Leonard (1882–1968). Both of these ladies were 'trance' mediums, that is, their normal personalities were apparently displaced by those of the communicating entities, and both were the subject of numerous papers in the *Proceedings of the SPR*. Mrs Leonard was particularly noted for her successful 'proxy' sittings, that is, sittings in which the sitter actually present hopes to obtain communications for an absent third party of whose concerns he knows little or nothing. General introductions to the Piper and Leonard material will be found in Salter (1950) and Gauld (1982). The longest general account of Mrs Piper is that in Holt (1915); the identities of certain of her leading sitters hitherto concealed by pseudonyms will be found in Kenny (1986). A popular but useful account of Mrs Leonard is Smith (1964).

Cross-correspondences

In a small number of cases of ostensible communication through mediums we have not just evidence of identity but apparent evidence that the communicator is pursuing a characteristic purpose independent of any that might be attributed to the medium or sitters (see Richmond 1938). The best-known cases of this kind are the 'cross-correspondences' manifested between 1901 and 1930 in the automatic writings of a number of automatists associated with the SPR. The principal automatists were Mrs M. de G. Verrall and her daughter Helen (later Mrs W.H. Salter), Mrs 'Willett' (Mrs W. Coombe-Tennant), Mrs 'Holland' (Mrs Fleming, the sister of Rudyard Kipling) and Mrs Piper. The plan behind the cross-correspondences ostensibly originated with three recently deceased founders of the SPR, F.W.H. Myers, Edmund Gurney and Henry Sidgwick. The idea was that different parts of a message should be communicated through different mediums in such a way that the contribution of each should remain meaningless and the whole only make sense when the parts were brought together. The cross-correspondence materials are voluminous and their proper interpretation is exceedingly difficult. For general introductions to them see Saltmarsh (1938) and Salter (1961).

Various endeavours have been made over the years to devise statistical methods for the assessment of mental mediumistic material. An interesting early attempt to apply such methods is that by Prince (1923) and an interesting recent one that by Robertson and Roy (2001).

Children who ostensibly remember previous lives

The best-known apparent evidence for reincarnation comes from certain much-publicised cases of supposed hypnotic regression into past lives. However, few of these cases stand up to serious scrutiny. By far the most remarkable evidence for reincarnation comes from the extensive and careful work of Professor Ian Stevenson, of the University of Virginia, and his collaborators, on the ostensible past-life recollections of very young children in a normal waking state. The cases concerned come mainly, but not exclusively, from cultures in which belief in reincarnation is widespread. The children involved commonly begin to exhibit their past-life recollections as soon as they can speak and when, as happens in an appreciable proportion of cases, these recollections are provisionally verified, a meeting with the previous family generally takes place. The time-interval between the death of the previous personality and the birth of the present one varies from culture to culture, but is commonly a matter of months or a few years. In a disproportionately high percentage of cases, the previous personality has died violently, and, in a small number of these cases, the present personality has been found to possess birthmarks or abnormalities mirroring the death-wounds of the previous personality. The distance between the home of the previous personality and the home of the present personality has varied from zero to hundreds of kilometres. Among the 3,000 or so cases in Stevenson's files are quite a few in which careful investigations have failed to reveal any normal lines of communication between the two families. Stevenson has published detailed reports of selected cases in a series of volumes starting with his *Twenty Cases Suggestive of Reincarnation* (1974). He has also written a more popular résumé of his work and conclusions (Stevenson 2001). For a comprehensive review and assessment see Matlock (1990); on birthmarks, etc. see Stevenson (1997). See also Chapter 19 on reincarnation.

Possession

Among Stevenson's cases of ostensible reincarnation are a handful in which the previous personality has not 'taken over' until quite a few years after the birth of the more recent personality, which it apparently displaces. Such cases constitute apparent examples of long-term or permanent possession (with which may be contrasted the transient 'possessions' to be found in examples of trance mediumship). The takeover is usually ushered in by a period of coma or apparent death. The individual concerned seemingly wakes up as someone else with a totally different set of memories. In some cases these ostensible memories have been verified in considerable detail and no lines of communication between the past and present families have come to light. Examples are the cases of Jasbir–Sobha Ram (Stevenson 1974, pp. 34–52) and of Sumitra–Shiva (Stevenson *et al.* 1989). A well-known older case with similar features is that of Lurancy Vennum–Mary Roff (Myers 1903, I, pp. 360–70). The Vennum–Roff case and the Sumitra–Shiva case are described in some detail in Almeder (1992).

Apparitions of the dead

Apparitions of deceased persons are by no means uncommon, but only a few can be regarded as constituting possible evidence for survival. Where the figure seen is of a person known to the percipient, and known by him to be dead, there is usually no adequate reason for supposing it anything other than an internally generated hallucination. For an apparition to constitute prima facie evidence for survival, it must visually or verbally convey to the percipient information previously unknown to him, but known to the deceased person in question. Best of all would be the conveying of information apparently calculated to promote the fulfilment of some desire characteristic of the deceased. Such cases are rare, and in most cases it is difficult to exclude the possibility that the information and purposes apparently displayed are those of the living percipient, mediated by an hallucination, rather than those of a *revenant*. On the problems of interpretation see Gauld (1982). Among collections including possibly relevant cases are those of Bennett (1939), Collins (1948) and MacKenzie (1982). See also Chapter 14 on apparitions.

OBEs and NDEs

Spontaneous out-of-body experiences (OBEs – experiences in which the world is apparently seen from a point of view outside the perceiver's body) are not uncommon. Although they may convince the experients that they possess a separable soul which could in principle survive the death of the body, it is far from clear that there are compelling reasons for regarding such experiences as anything other than unusual and complex hallucinations. In some cases an experient has ostensibly acquired information unavailable to him from the position of his physical body, but available from his apparent position during the OBE. But even in such cases the hallucinatory experience may be regarded simply as the vehicle through which knowledge acquired by ESP can express itself, just as it might have expressed itself through dreams, visions, hallucinations, etc. Similar considerations apply to near-death experiences (NDEs), which seem to be becoming more frequently reported as techniques of cardiac resuscitation improve. Physiological changes induced by a crisis situation may produce certain sorts of experiences (leaving the body, passing through a tunnel, approaching a golden realm, being sent back thence by an authority figure) which profoundly impress those who live to tell the tale, and sometimes their audiences too. But although the experiences have certain features which cross cultural boundaries, other features are manifestly culturally influenced (see, for example, Zaleski 1987), which suggests that we are dealing with hallucinations rather than with the perception of an other-worldly reality. However, these issues are the subject of on-going controversy and research. The topic of OBEs and NDEs is reviewed at some length by Almeder (1992). On OBEs see Green (1968) and Blackmore (1982) and Chapter 15; on NDEs see Ring (1980), Sabom (1982), Rogo (1989) and Fenwick and Fenwick (1995) and Chapter 16. Recent claims (Parnia *et al.* 2001, Van Lommel and Van Wees 2001) that NDEs may take place while subjects are deeply comatose or clinically dead await further investigation.

Interpretations

The interpretations put upon the ostensible evidence for survival tend to be heavily influenced by extraneous considerations. Some philosophers (e.g. Penelhum 1970, Flew 1987; cf. the bibliographical essay and some of the selections in Edwards 1992) have argued that the concept of survival of bodily death is incoherent because the notion of personal identity is inextricably tied to that of bodily continuity. Other philosophers and many neuroscientists would allege that the known dependence of mental functions on the brain renders survival of bodily death an impossibility. For reviews of these and kindred arguments see Edge (1986), Stokes (1993), Paterson (1995) and Rosenberg (1998).

Persons who thus reject the very possibility of survival have to find other explanations of the so-called evidence for survival. Some have dwelt on the scope in certain cases for fraud, cryptomnesia (hidden memory), misrecording, misperception, misinterpreting and wishful thinking. These factors, however, do not seem adequate to explain away all, or anything like all, of the better evidence. Others have sought to explain away much of the evidence for survival by proposing that in cases of verified mediumistic communications, apparently correct past-life memories, veridical post-mortem apparitions, etc., the medium, subject or percipient obtains the information concerned by ESP (telepathy or clairvoyance) directed upon still extant sources (persons who knew the deceased, records of his or her career). The trouble with this hypothesis is that it soon requires one to postulate ESP of a scope and complexity which no ESP experiments have ever fully demonstrated. Hence the ESP concerned has been nicknamed 'super-ESP'. The 'super-ESP hypothesis', and the correlated 'super-PK hypothesis', have generated a good deal of controversy (see, for example, Gauld 1982, Braude 1986). A classic early criticism of the evidence for survival and defence of a super-ESP position is Dodds (1934).

Among recent works generally favourable to a survivalist interpretation are those by Ducasse (1961), Stevenson (2001) and Almeder (1992).

Conclusion

If one looks at a good selection of the better-attested and most carefully investigated cases, of the kinds discussed above, it is by no means easy to dismiss them all in terms of the various standard counter-explanations – trickery, lying, illusion, delusion, wishful thinking, errors of memory, and so forth. But when it comes to finding other sorts of explanations (call them paranormal ones), many problems remain, for it is soon apparent that these other explanations are deeply entangled with one or more of a number of further and no less refractory problems, philosophical, empirical and scientific: philosophical problems about the criteria of personal identity over time and whether such identity can meaningfully be supposed to survive destruction of the body; empirical problems concerning the reality, scope and nature of ESP, or the dependence of memory on the intactness and proper functioning of the brain; scientific problems about the coherence of the alleged phenomena with fundamental scientific theories. Work on these issues is likely in the future to be as important for the interpretation of the evidence for survival as is the mere amassing of further examples of such evidence, interesting and important though that might be.

Recommended reading

Introductory

Gauld, A. (1982) *Mediumship and Survival*, London: Heinemann. Includes brief accounts of the evidence from apparitions, out-of-body and near-death experiences, cases of ostensible obsession and possession, and cases of ostensible past-life memories in children.

Advanced

Almeder, R. (1992) *Death and Personal Survival: The Evidence of Life After Death*, Lanham, MD: Littlefield Adams. The views of a philosopher particularly interested in the evidence for reincarnation.

Ducasse, C.J. (1961) *A Critical Examination of the Belief in a Life After Death*, Springfield, IL: C.C. Thomas. Lucid general survey by a distinguished philosopher.

Gauld, A. (1977) Discarnate survival. In B.B. Wolman (ed.) *Handbook of Parapsychology*, New York: Van Nostrand Reinhold. Contains an extensive bibliography.

Myers, F.W.H. (1903) *Human Personality and its Survival of Bodily Death*, 2 vols, London: Longmans, Green. Classic and comprehensive early source-book.

Salter, W.H. (1961) *Zoar, or the Evidence of Psychical Research Concerning Survival*, London: Sidgwick and Jackson. Particularly informative about the cross-correspondences and related matters.

Stevenson, I. (1997) *Where Reincarnation and Biology Interact*, Westport, CT: Praeger. Surveys birthmarks and other congenital defects as evidence in cases of ostensible reincarnation.

Stevenson, I. (2001) *Children Who Remember Previous Lives: A Question of Reincarnation*, rev. edn, Jefferson, NC: McFarland. A summary review of the author's work in this area.

References

Beard, P. (1966) *Survival of Death: For and Against*, London: Hodder and Stoughton.

Bennett, E. (1939) *Apparitions and Haunted Houses*, London: Faber and Faber.

Blackmore, S. (1982) *Beyond the Body: An Investigation of Out-of-the-Body Experiences*, London: Heinemann.

Braude, S. (1986) *The Limits of Influence*, London: Routledge and Kegan Paul.

Braude, S. (2003) *Immortal Remains: The Evidence for Life after Death*, Lanham, MD: Rowman and Littlefield.

Collins, B. Abdy (1948) *The Cheltenham Ghost*, London: Psychic Press.

Coly, L. and McMahon, J.D.S. (eds) (1995) *Parapsychology and Thanatology*, New York: Parapsychology Foundation.

Dodds, E.R. (1934) Why I do not believe in survival, *Proceedings of the Society for Psychical Research*, 42, 147–78.

Edge, H.L. (1986) Survival and other philosophical questions. In H.L. Edge *et al.* (eds) *Foundations of Parapsychology: Exploring the Boundaries of Human Capability*, London: Routledge and Kegan Paul.

Edwards, P. (ed.) (1992) *Immortality*, New York: Macmillan.

Fenwick, P. and Fenwick, E. (1995) *The Truth in the Light*, London: Headline.

Flew, A.G.N. (1987) *The Logic of Mortality*, Oxford: Oxford University Press.

Green, C.E. (1968) *Out-of-the-Body Experiences*, Oxford: Institute of Psychophysical Research.

Griffin, D.R. (1997) *Parapsychology, Philosophy and Spirituality: A Postmodern Explanation*, Albany: State University of New York Press.

Hart, H. (1959) *The Enigma of Survival*, Springfield, IL: C.C. Thomas.

Holt, H. (1915) *On the Cosmic Relations*, 2 vols, London: Williams and Norgate.

Jacobson, N. (1973) *Life without Death?* New York: Delacorte Press.

Kenny, M.G. (1986) *The Passion of Ansel Bourne: Multiple Personality in American Culture*, Washington, DC: Smithsonian Institution Press.

Lorimer, D. (1984) *Survival? Body, Mind and Death in the Light of Psychic Experience*, London: Routledge and Kegan Paul.

MacKenzie, A. (1982) *Hauntings and Apparitions*, London: Heinemann.

Matlock, J.G. (1990) Past life memory case studies. In S. Krippner (ed.) *Advances in Parapsychological Research 6*, Jefferson, NC: McFarland.

Parnia, S., Waller, D.G., Yeates, R. and Fenwick, P. (2001) A qualitative and quantitative study of the incidence, features and aetiology of near-death experiences in cardiac arrest survivors, *Resuscitation*, 48, 149–56.

Paterson, R.W.K. (1995) *Philosophy and the Belief in a Life after Death*, London: Macmillan.

Penelhum, T. (1970) *Survival and Disembodied Existence*, London: Routledge and Kegan Paul.

Prince, W.F. (1923) The mother of Doris, *Proceedings of the American Society for Psychical Research*, 17, 1–216.

Richmond, Z. (1938) *Evidence of Purpose*, London: Bell.

Ring, K. (1980) *Life at Death*, New York: Coward, McCann and Geoghegan.

Robertson, T.J. and Roy, A.E. (2001) A preliminary study of the acceptance by non-recipients of mediums' statements to recipients, *Journal of the Society for Psychical Research*, 65, 91–106.

Rogo, D. Scott (1989) *The Return from Silence: A Study of Near-Death Experiences*, Wellingborough: The Aquarian Press.

Rosenberg, J.F. (1998) *Thinking clearly about Death*, Indianapolis: Hackett.

Roy, A.E. (1996) *The Archives of the Mind*, Stanstead: SNU Publications.

Roy, A.E. and Robertson, T.J. (2001) A double-blind procedure for assessing the relevance of a medium's statements to a recipient, *Journal of the Society for Psychical Research*, 65, 161–74.

Sabom, M. (1982) *Recollections of Death*, New York: Harper and Row.

Salter, W.H. (1950) *Trance Mediumship: An Introductory Study of Mrs Piper and Mrs Leonard*, London: Society for Psychical Research.

Saltmarsh, H. (1938) *Evidence of Personal Survival from Cross Correspondences*, London: Bell.

Smith, S. (1964) *The Mediumship of Mrs Leonard*, New Hyde Park, NY: University Books.

Stevenson, I. (1974) *Twenty Cases Suggestive of Reincarnation*, 2nd edn, Charlottesville: University Press of Virginia.

Stevenson, I., Pasricha, S. and McLean-Rice, N. (1989) A case of the possession type in India with evidence of paranormal knowledge, *Journal of Scientific Exploration*, 3, 81–101.

Stokes, D. (1993) Mind, matter and death: cognitive neuroscience and the problem of survival, *Journal of the American Society for Psychical Research*, 87, 41–84.

Thouless, R.H. (1984) Do we survive bodily death? *Proceedings of the Society for Psychical Research*, 57, 1–52.

Van Lommel, P. and Van Wees, E.I. (2001) Near-death experiences in survivors of cardiac arrest, *The Lancet*, 358, 2039–45.

Zaleski, C. (1987) *Otherworld Journeys: Accounts of Near Death Experiences in Medieval and Modern Times*, New York: Oxford University Press.

Chapter 19

Reincarnation

Ian Stevenson

Reincarnation may be defined as the idea that a person consists of a material body and a non-material or mental component; the mental component can survive the death of the material body and later become associated with a new physical body.

Belief

The belief is held (with variations in details) by adherents of almost all major religions except Christianity and Islam. In addition, members of many Shi'ite Muslim groups believe in reincarnation, and between 20 and 30 per cent of persons in western countries who may be nominal Christians also believe in reincarnation. Although reincarnation is not a feature of orthodox Judaism, the branch of Hasidic Jews believe in it. Ethnologists have documented the belief among nearly all the traditional religions of ethnic groups in Africa, North and South America, and Australia/Oceania. The tribes of north-west North America continue to believe in reincarnation despite negative attitudes towards it on the part of Christian missionaries and churches. The nineteenth-century German philosopher Arthur Schopenhauer offered a definition of Europe as that part of the world where the inhabitants did *not* believe in reincarnation.

Evidence

A wide variety of phenomena has been adduced in support of the belief in reincarnation.

Hypnotic regression

Some sensitives claim to 'read' the previous lives of their clients, but what they say is nearly always banal, vague, and unverifiable. The same can be said of nearly all claims to regress persons with hypnosis to previous lives. In most reported instances of this procedure the 'previous personality' is a kind of historical novel: much is unverifiable and probably fiction, and what is verifiable is usually attributable to information from reading, radio, television, or other normal sources (Stevenson 1994). The claim that anyone can, with hypnosis, remember a previous life is unfortunately widespread and is deplorable. Too often, uneducated hypnotists prey on other uneducated persons. Nevertheless, systematic research with hypnotic regression deserves encouragement. Rarely, a case developed through hypnosis shows some unusual and important feature, such as responsive xenoglossy (Stevenson, 1974a).

Cases of young children

The best evidence supporting the belief in reincarnation comes from the cases of young children who, typically between the ages of 2 and 5, make statements about a previous life they claim to have lived before being born. Their statements are often accompanied by behaviour that is unusual for their family but appropriate for the life the child claims to remember. For example, a child of Sri Lanka said she remembered a life in which she had drowned in a flooded paddy field; she referred to a bus that had splashed water on her before she had drowned. These and other statements corresponded to the life and death of a girl in a nearby village who had drowned when, walking along a narrow elevated road, she had stepped back to avoid a passing bus and fallen into a flooded paddy field. Even before the subject could speak, she had shown a marked fear of being immersed in water and also a fear of buses. She also showed traits, such as a fondness for bread and sweet foods, that were unusual in her family and characteristic of the girl who had drowned (Stevenson 1977).

Cases of this kind can be found readily in many parts of the world, and more than 2,500 of them have been investigated, mainly in South Asia, western Asia, West Africa, and north-west North America. These are areas where nearly all the inhabitants (or members of certain tribes) believe in reincarnation. About 200 similar cases, however, have been investigated in western Europe, and among non-tribal people of the United States and Canada.

Four features of the cases occur with such regularity in all cultures that we may appropriately refer to them as 'universal features'. They are: the early age of speaking about the previous life (2 to 5); a forgetting of the imaged memories between the ages of 5 and 8; a high incidence of violent death in the claimed previous life; and mention of the mode of death by the subject. Other features vary widely in different cultures. For example, in about 26 per cent of the cases in Myanmar (formerly Burma) the child says it had a previous life as a member of the opposite sex (Stevenson 1983). Cases of the 'sex-change' type also occur frequently in Nigeria and Thailand; but only 3 per cent of cases in India have this feature, and it does not seem to occur at all among the cases of Lebanon and those of the tribes of north-west North America (Stevenson 1986). The belief about the possibility of sex change from one life to another correlates inexactly with the incidence of cases of the sex-change type. For example, the Druses of Lebanon and the tribes of north-west North America believe that sex change is impossible, which agrees, we might say, with the complete absence of this type of case among them. On the other hand, the Hindus of India and the Buddhists of Myanmar (Burma) believe equally in the possibility of sex change, and yet we have found a much lower percentage of such cases in India compared with Myanmar.

Physical and other correspondences

Some 35 per cent of the subjects have birthmarks and birth defects. In the majority of these cases the subject's marks or defects correspond to injuries or an illness experienced by the deceased person whose life the subject remembers; and medical documents have confirmed this correspondence in more than forty cases (Stevenson 1997a, 1997b). Pasricha (1998) has reported ten cases in India with birthmarks and birth defects; in most of the cases medical records verified the correspondence of the abnormalities to wounds on the concerned deceased persons.

Studies of the features of the cases separated by one or two generations have shown the features to be stable across time in India (Pasricha and Stevenson 1987) and Turkey (Keil and Stevenson 1999). Moreover, less formal reports before the period of systematic investigations began often recorded the same features as those observed in recent investigations (Fielding Hall 1898, Stevenson 1960, Sunderlal 1924).

Two pairs of monozygotic twins who remembered previous lives differed significantly both in physical features and in behaviour; the physical and behavioural differences accorded with features in the persons whose lives the twins remembered (Stevenson 1997a, 1997b, 1999). Such twin pairs have identical genes and closely similar environments; the different previous lives they remembered may explain the observed differences between the twins of such pairs. These biological components in the cases appear to be of great potential importance. They suggest a previously unrecognised factor in the causation of some birth defects and other bodily features.

In some cultures parents (or other adults) often identify a newborn baby as being a particular deceased person reborn on the basis of birthmarks or other indications, such as dreams (Stevenson 1966, 1974b, 1987). In relevant dreams a deceased person indicates an intention to reincarnate in a particular family; the dreamer is usually a married woman who later becomes the subject's mother. Such dreams occur often among the tribes of north-west North America, in Myanmar, and in Turkey; but, as far as we know, they never occur in Lebanon and only rarely in India and Sri Lanka.

Most children who are designated at birth or soon after as someone reincarnated later speak about the life of the concerned deceased person; but some children do not; they remain silent about the presumed previous life, although they may show behaviour similar to that of the deceased person they are said to have been in a previous life (Keil 1996). The silence of these children argues against the assumption, sometimes expressed, that a subject's parents influence him or her to accept the identity of a deceased person according to the parents' expectations.

Methods of investigation

Interviews with firsthand informants are the principal instruments of investigation. Investigators talk with the child subject if he or she will talk with them; in this, much depends on the skill of the investigator and that of the interpreter, if there is one. After the child, the parents and other siblings are the most important informants; sometimes grandparents, other family members and neighbours furnish useful information. On the side of the deceased person concerned, the surviving relatives of that person are the preferred informants.

A person corresponding with significant closeness to the details of the child's statements (a 'previous personality') is not found in every case. Indeed, such 'unsolved cases' are the majority in Sri Lanka and the USA (Cook *et al.* 1983).

Attempts are made to supplement oral testimony with written records whenever these are available. Hospital reports and post-mortem reports are especially important.

Interpretations

Investigating the cases of children who claim to remember previous lives is far from easy; but it is much easier to find and investigate them than it is to understand them.

Reincarnation

An important criticism of the cases is their much greater frequency in countries and cultures with a strong belief in reincarnation. In addition, in many cases the subject and the deceased person whose life the subject remembered have belonged to the same family or village. These facts could prepare parents to expect that a particular person would reincarnate in their family, and from this expectation they might attach undue importance to vague allusions a child might make; and they might even, by asking leading questions, guide the child to identify itself with the deceased person. This argument has merit for many cases, but becomes weak or valueless when applied to cases in which the two families have lived in quite separate communities and have had no contact with each other before the case developed. Many cases have this strength. Ten examples of this type of case were reported in Stevenson (1975), three in Stevenson and Samararatne (1988a, 1988b) and fifteen in Stevenson (1997a: see table 15-2, p. 1144). Mills has published four examples of this type of case (Mills 1989, Mills *et al.* 1994). Pasricha (1990) has published two examples. Haraldsson has published three examples (Haraldsson 1991, Mills *et al.* 1994).

Faulty memory

Another criticism suggests that even when the two families have not known each other before the case developed, they might – when they did meet – have mingled and confused their memories about what the child had said earlier. They might then – quite innocently – have credited the child with paranormal knowledge about a deceased person that he or she had not really demonstrated. A counter-argument to this criticism is provided by a small number of cases – unfortunately still only 1.5 per cent of all those investigated – in which someone made a written record of what the child said before the two families met. In these cases at least, errors of memory can be excluded. I have published reports of two cases of this group in Stevenson (1975) and another three examples in Stevenson and Samararatne (1988a, 1988b). Haraldsson has published two examples in Haraldsson (1991) and another example in Mills *et al.* (1994).

In many other cases, especially ones in which an investigator arrives soon after the families meet, it seems improbable that errors of memory can account for all the facts of the case. Moreover, a comparison of the cases with and without a written record of the child's statements made before the two families met showed that the overall number of statements was lower for the cases with a written record made after the families concerned had met; and there was no difference between the two groups in the number of correct statements the subject made (Schouten and Stevenson 1998). This result tells against the suggestion that informants tend to embellish and improve cases after the families concerned have met. Nevertheless, an important task for future research is that of finding more cases that can be investigated before the families concerned meet.

Extrasensory perception

Alternative interpretations besides reincarnation and faulty memory on the part of informants need to be considered in appraising individual cases. Some students of this subject have suggested that the children of cases with good evidence of paranormal knowledge may derive their information through extrasensory perception from living persons who knew the deceased person whose life the child claims to remember. This interpretation does not adequately explain the cases with birthmarks and birth defects; it requires immense capacities for paranormal cognition between the subject and living persons, for which we find no evidence; and it fails to account for the syndrome of unusual behaviours shown by many of the subjects – behaviours, such as phobias, appetites, and habits of dress, which correspond to known behaviour of the concerned deceased person or are conjecturable about him or her.

Still another interpretation is that of maternal impressions (Stevenson 1992). According to this concept, images in the mind of a pregnant woman may influence the form of an unborn baby. This explanation may apply to some cases of birthmarks and birth defects, but is not applicable to cases in which the pregnant woman knew nothing of the wounds on the person whose life the child later claimed to remember (Stevenson 1997a: see table 15-2, p. 1144). It also does not adequately explain the unusual behaviour, such as phobias, that so many of the children show.

Recent developments

During the past ten years several independent investigators have reported results broadly similar to those published in the 1960s to 1980s. In addition, two of the independent investigators have introduced new strategies of research, and these deserve mention.

Haraldsson has conducted psychological tests on thirty children of Sri Lanka who claimed to remember previous lives compared with thirty other children of the same age, sex and background (Haraldsson 1995, 1997). He found that the subjects, on average, had superior intelligence and better memories than their peers; they were not more suggestible than their peers. Their parents noted more behavioural problems in the subjects than the peers' parents noted in their children; this result is perhaps not surprising considering how often the subjects claim to have other parents elsewhere.

Keil (1996) has made a special study of those subjects (mentioned above) whose parents identify them, usually on the basis of dreams and birthmarks, as a particular person reborn. He has undertaken a longitudinal observation of such children during infancy, with repeated visits over several years. This may show the extent of the effect of parental expectations on the development of these children.

Conclusions

Children who claim to remember a previous life are a natural phenomenon the features of which have now been reported for more than a hundred years. Many cases show weaknesses in the accuracy of the testimony. Many may be childish fantasies. In other cases the deceased person about whose life the child spoke belonged to the child's family or community, and the child might have learned about this person by normal means. When we exclude all these cases, however, a substantial number of others remain in which the child made correct, often detailed statements about the life and death of a deceased person who lived in another community and belonged to a family completely unknown to that of the subject. In some of these cases written records made before the child's statements were verified exclude errors of memory on the part of informants.

Interpretations of the cases as due to paranormal cognition between the subjects and living persons who knew the concerned deceased person fail to account for all features of many cases. This is particularly true of cases in which the subjects have birthmarks and birth defects corresponding to wounds or other marks on the person whose life the subject claims to have lived.

The cases have much relevance to the mind/brain problem and to other unsolved problems of biology and medicine, such as physical and behavioural differences between monozygotic twins and the causes of some birth defects.

Notes

1 Reprints of most of the Stevenson journal articles cited are available at nominal cost from: Division of Personality Studies, University of Virginia, Box 800152, Health System, Charlottesville, Virginia 22908-0152, USA. Fax: 1 434-924-1712. E-mail: dops@virginia.edu. Stevenson 1997a and 1997b can be ordered from: http://info.greenwood.com or Greenwood Publishing Group, Inc., 88 Post Road West, P.O. Box 5007, Westport, CT 06881-5007, USA.

2 The Division of Personality Studies is grateful to the Nagamasa Azuma Fund, the Bernstein Brothers Foundation, and Mr Richard Adams for their support. Dawn Hunt and Patricia Estes improved this chapter with helpful suggestions.

Recommended reading

Introductory

Stevenson, I. (1974b) *Twenty Cases Suggestive of Reincarnation*, 2nd edn, Charlottesville: University Press of Virginia. (First published by the American Society for Psychical Research in 1966.) Contains detailed reports of twenty fairly typical cases from India, Sri Lanka, Brazil, Lebanon and Alaska, and offers details of the testimony concerning such cases.

Stevenson, I. and Samararatne, G. (1988a) Three new cases of the reincarnation type in Sri Lanka with written records made before verification, *Journal of Nervous and Mental Disease*, 176, 12, 741. Brief summaries of three of the rare cases for which we can exclude errors of memory on the part of informants for what the subject said before the two families met.

Advanced

Haraldsson, E. (1995) Personality and abilities of children claiming previous-life memories, *Journal of Nervous and Mental Disease*, 183, 7, 456–51. Comparison of psychological tests with children who remember previous lives and matched peers.

Stevenson, I. (1994) A case of the psychotherapist's fallacy: hypnotic regression to 'previous lives', *American Journal of Clinical Hypnosis*, 36, 3, 188–93. A critical review of claims to regress persons to previous lives with hypnosis.

Stevenson, I. (1997b) *Where Reincarnation and Biology Intersect*, Westport, CT: Praeger. Describes persons who had birthmarks or birth defects corresponding to wounds (sometimes other marks) on the persons whose lives they remembered. Contains colour figures of pertinent marks and defects.

Stevenson, I. (2001) *Children Who Remember Previous Lives: A Question of Reincarnation*, rev. edn, Jefferson, NC: McFarland (first published 1987). An overview of forty years of research on reincarnation cases. It includes summaries of fourteen fairly typical cases, including western ones, reviews the variants in the belief and case features in different cultures, methods of investigation and alternative interpretations.

Stevenson, I. and Samararatne, G. (1988b) Three new cases of the reincarnation type in Sri Lanka with written records made before verifications, *Journal of Scientific Exploration*, 2, 2, 217–38. Detailed reports of cases where reports were made prior to verification.

References

Cook, E.W., Pasricha, S.K., Samararatne, G., U Win Maung, and Stevenson, I. (1983) A review and analysis of 'unsolved' cases of the reincarnation type: II. Comparison of features of solved and unsolved cases, *Journal of the American Society for Psychical Research*, 77, 115–35.

Ducasse, C.J. (1961) *A Critical Examination of the Belief in a Life After Death*, Springfield, IL: Charles C. Thomas.

Fielding Hall, H. (1898) *The Soul of a People*, London: Macmillan.

Gauld, A. (1982) *Mediumship and Survival: A Century of Investigations*, London: Heinemann.

Haraldsson, E. (1991) Children claiming past-life memories: four cases in Sri Lanka, *Journal of Scientific Exploration*, 5, 233–61.

Haraldsson, E. (1997) A psychological comparison between ordinary children and those who claim previous-life memories, *Journal of Scientific Exploration*, 11, 3, 323–35.

Keil, J. (1996) Cases of the reincarnation type: an evaluation of some indirect evidence with examples of 'silent cases', *Journal of Scientific Exploration*, 10, 4, 467–85.

Keil, J. and Stevenson, I. (1999) Do cases of the reincarnation type show similar features over many years? A study of Turkish cases a generation apart, *Journal of Scientific Exploration*, 13, 2, 189–98.

Mills, A. (1989) A replication study: three cases of children in northern India who are said to remember a previous life, *Journal of Scientific Exploration*, 3, 133–84.

Mills, A., Haraldsson, E. and Keil, H.H.J. (1994) Replication studies of cases suggestive of reincarnation by three independent investigators, *Journal of the American Society for Psychical Research*, 88, 207–19.

Pasricha, S.K. (1990) *Claims of Reincarnation: An Empirical Study of Cases in India*, New Delhi: Harman Publishing House.

Pasricha, S.K. (1998) Cases of the reincarnation type in northern India with birthmarks and birth defects, *Journal of Scientific Exploration*, 12, 2, 259–93.

Pasricha, S.K. and Stevenson, I. (1987) Indian cases of the reincarnation type two generations apart, *Journal of the Society for Psychical Research*, 54, 239–46.

Schouten, S.A. and Stevenson, I. (1998) Does the socio-psychological hypothesis explain cases of the reincarnation type? *Journal of Nervous and Mental Disease*, 186, 8, 504–6.

Stevenson, I. (1960) The evidence for survival from claimed memories of former incarnations, *Journal of the American Society for Psychical Research*, 54, 1, 51–71, 95–117.

Stevenson, I. (1966) Cultural patterns in cases suggestive of reincarnation among the Tlingit Indians of southeastern Alaska, *Journal of the American Society for Psychical Research*, 60, 3, 229–43.

Stevenson, I. (1974a) *Xenoglossy: A Review and Report of a Case*, Charlottesville: University Press of Virginia.

Stevenson, I. (1975) *Cases of the Reincarnation Type (Vol. I): Ten Cases in India*, Charlottesville: University Press of Virginia.

Stevenson, I. (1977) *Cases of the Reincarnation Type (Vol. II): Ten Cases in Sri Lanka*, Charlottesville: University Press of Virginia.

Stevenson, I. (1983) *Cases of the Reincarnation Type (Vol. IV): Twelve Cases in Thailand and Burma*, Charlottesville: University Press of Virginia.

Stevenson, I. (1986) Characteristics of cases of the reincarnation type among the Igbo of Nigeria, *Journal of Asian and African Studies*, 21, 3–4, 204–16.

Stevenson, I. (1987) Children who remember previous lives, Charlottesville: University of Virginia Press.

Stevenson, I. (1992) A new look at maternal impressions: an analysis of 50 published cases and reports of two recent examples, *Journal of Scientific Exploration*, 6, 4, 353–73.

Stevenson, I. (1997a) *Reincarnation and Biology: A Contribution to the Etiology of Birthmarks and Birth Defects*, 2 vols, Westport, CT: Praeger.

Stevenson, I. (1999) Past lives of twins, *The Lancet*, 353, 17 April, 1359–60.

Stevenson, I. (2000) The phenomenon of claimed memories of previous lives: possible interpretations and importance, *Medical Hypotheses*, 54, 4, 652–9.

Sunderlal, R.B.S. (1924) Cas apparents de réminiscences de vies antérieures, *Revue Métapsychique*, 4, 302–7.

Chapter 20

Religion

Michael Perry

The same data (or alleged data) are approached very differently by parapsychology and religion, and in this chapter we shall focus mainly on the Christian religion, though with occasional glances elsewhere. A parapsychological approach tries to establish the facts of the matter and to see whether a satisfactory theoretical superstructure may be built on them. Religious statements tend to begin as metaphysical assertions based on revelation, however much they may subsequently be shown to be consistent with reason and with the data of the observed world. Parapsychology cannot answer metaphysical questions about the existence of God or what, if there is a God, his (or her, or its) purposes are in creating and peopling the universe. Some religious believers hold that the phenomena of parapsychology make it more likely than not that the universe has non-human, invisible inhabitants (angels, spirits, or demons); but, as a former Dean of St Paul's remarked, 'No one who understands what he is about would suppose that . . . God could be the conclusion of an investigation by scientific methods. . . . The most which we can expect from psychical research is some significant addition to the data' (Matthews 1940, p. 6). Admittedly, light may be shed on particular questions about Divine activity by devising suitable tests (for instance, see Benor 1993 and Dossey 1993, 1996, 1997 on the effectiveness of prayer). Many religions, however, are unhappy with that kind of approach, believing that it is tantamount to trying to put God to the test, which is an impiety.

Miracles

The foundation documents of many of the world's religions make many claims of paranormal happenings, but most religious personages around whom such accounts gather have discouraged too great an interest in the phenomena (referred to in Eastern religions as *siddhis*), regarding them as a distraction from genuine spirituality. For this reason, many contemporary holy men are not helpful towards parapsychological researchers.

The Bible contains 'an almost embarrassing abundance of parapsychological riches. Examples of telepathy, clairvoyance, precognition, mediumship, psychokinesis, and out-of-the-body experiences abound' (Bennett 1978, p. 113) – see, particularly, the accounts of the wonder-worker Elisha in the second book of Kings in the Old Testament, or of Jesus of Nazareth in the gospel stories of the Christian New Testament. For Christians, the miracle *par excellence* is the resurrection of Jesus of Nazareth, which at least one writer has interpreted as a series of crisis apparitions of the recently-departed (Perry 1959).

Accounts of paranormal healings, the multiplication of food, levitation and telepathy are commonplace in the biographies of some religious personages (for Christian examples, see Thurston 1952). St Joseph of Copertino (1603–63) is notorious for the accounts of his frequent levitations, usually when in a state of religious ecstasy (Eisenbud 1982). Nearer our own day, stories about the bilocatory powers of Padre Pio, canonised by the Pope in 2002, are innumerable (see Grosso 1982). The paranormal powers of the American clairvoyant and healer Edgar Cayce (1877–1945) became the basis of the Association for Religion and Enlightenment (Johnson 1998). The contemporary Indian holy man Sri Sathya Sai Baba claims to produce apports at will, often of quantities of grey ash but frequently watches or pieces of jewellery. The same is true of Swami Premananda. But there are serious doubts about Sai Baba and Premananda (see Haraldsson and Wiseman 1995 and Wiseman and Haraldsson 1995), and the same is even more true of the ancient accounts. Are they literally true? Or have natural phenomena been misinterpreted? Or is it all due to the fertile imagination of the hagiographer? Or to blatant fraud?

If we take miraculous happenings as examples of more general paranormal phenomena, we have already ceased to regard them as events which run contrary to natural law. This is not inconsistent with a view of miracles which sees them as revelatory events – unusual ones, which compel us to take note of them, and through which the believer may discern some supernatural influence on the world around him; but not necessarily events which involve the suspension of the laws of nature (see Perry 1986, Rogo 1982).

In the Roman Catholic Christian tradition, persons cannot be formally acknowledged as saints unless miracles (usually of a parapsychological nature) are reported around them (see White 1981, 1982). In the process of canonisation, it is the province of the *promotor fidei* (or, as he was popularly known, the 'Devil's Advocate') to examine alleged miracles with a sceptical mind. Prospero Lambertini (1675–1758) occupied this post before becoming Pope Benedict XIV (see Haynes 1970), and his monograph on the subject, 'De servorum Dei beatificatione et beatorum canonizatione', has earned him the soubriquet 'The Father of Christian Parapsychology'.

Religious attitudes

The very existence of a *promotor fidei* indicates that Christians ought to require a deal of convincing before accepting a religious interpretation of contemporary accounts of parapsychological happenings. There is some evidence (Thalbourne and Houtkooper 2002) of a positive correlation between religious attitude and paranormal belief. But the attitude of many Christians to the phenomena in question is one of deep suspicion, due in large part to such biblical strictures as are to be found in texts like Leviticus 19.31 ('Do not resort to ghosts and spirits or make yourselves unclean by seeking them out'), or Deuteronomy 19.9–14 ('These nations whose place you are taking listen to soothsayers and augurs, but the LORD your God does not permit you to do this'), or Isaiah 8.19–20 ('People will say to you, "Seek guidance from ghosts and familiar spirits . . ." , but what they say has no force'). They also instance the fate of King Saul. The night before the battle of Gilboa, he consulted a woman who claimed to be able to contact the dead prophet Samuel for advice. (She has become known as the 'Witch of En-Dor' from the chapter heading – but not the text – of the King James Bible at this point; but what she claimed to do was closer to mediumship than to witchcraft.) King Saul received cold comfort, and died in battle the next day (1 Samuel 28). His fate was blamed on the sin of consulting a ghost rather than the living God (1 Chronicles 10.13).

These prohibitions have been explained in ways which show that it is possible to use psychic gifts to God's glory (see Perry 1999a, 2003), but it remains true that, just as in Old Testament times the practitioners of the psychic were thought of as propagating a rival religion to that of the canonical authors, so in more modern times they have been regarded by many members of the Christian churches as propagators of non-Christian beliefs and therefore to be held at arm's length. Despite this, the organisations now known as the Churches' Fellowship for Spiritual and Psychical Studies (Bunce 1993) and Spiritual Frontiers Fellowship International were founded in England and the USA in 1953 and 1956 respectively. For a survey of twentieth-century official reports from various Christian churches on psychic phenomena and their practitioners, see Haddow (1980).

Some non-Christian or post-Christian belief systems take a more positive attitude towards psychic phenomena. Most Pagans and practitioners of Wicca (witchcraft) regard the phenomena as entirely natural, and to be used at will, provided no harm is done to others by their exercise. Some occultists positively encourage the development of willpower (often in an altered state of consciousness) in the belief that the focused will is capable of psychokinetic effects on friends and foes. And shamanistic religion (Eliade 1951 – though see Bowker 1997, p. 884) depends on initiates who have undertaken a mystic and psychic journey into another world and can give guidance to those who seek their help either in life, during illness or misfortune, or at the time of death. But the religion for which parapsychological phenomena are determinative is modern Spiritualism.

Spiritualism

Paranormal phenomena have been interpreted within a religious framework for as long as records go back in antiquity (Dodds 1971), but Spiritualism as a modern religion dates only from the mid-nineteenth century. It arose after the experiences of Andrew Jackson Davies ('The Seer of Poughkeepsie') and the phenomena centring on the young Fox sisters in Hydesville, New York in 1848. They interpreted poltergeist-type knockings as due to the agency of an entity whom they nicknamed 'Mr Splitfoot' and, by means of a code, they got it to answer questions which they put to it. Mental and physical mediumship soon became the rage in circles of all social classes and levels of intelligence in the USA, Britain and continental Europe.

Spiritualists believe the prima facie explanation of the phenomena, that is, that they can be methods of communicating with discarnate intelligences; but, as a religion, Spiritualism is no more monolithic than many another religious system. Beliefs range from those of the Spiritualists' National Union, which since 1987 has forbidden Christian symbols in any new chapel set up under its auspices, to the Greater World Christian Spiritualist Association, founded in the 1930s 'to proclaim the indivisibility of Christianity and Spiritualism' and to reinterpret the gospel story in a spiritualistic light (see Perry 1992, pp. 112–18).

The Christian churches have always mistrusted Spiritualism on theological grounds, and challenge its claim to spiritual authority. The 1920 Lambeth Conference of Anglican bishops from all over the world received a report (Lambeth 1948) that recognised Spiritualism as a protest against a materialistic ethos, but rejected it because it did not have the Christian belief in the divinity of Jesus at its heart. The report did, however, recognise that some people do have psychic gifts, and that it was legitimate for them to use them – though with cautious restraint. In 1936, the then Archbishop of Canterbury (Cosmo Gordon Lang) set up a committee to look into 'the subject of communications with discarnate spirits and the claims of Spiritualism'. It reported in 1939, but the bishops decided not to publish the document. Part was leaked to a Spiritualist newspaper in 1947, but the whole report was not made public until 1979 (the full text with historical essays and comment appears in Perry 1999b). Christian doctrine asserts that human beings survive the death of the body, but it is a matter for empirical research to determine whether the departed may communicate with those of us who remain on this earth, and whether particular lines of research do or do not provide good evidence for such communication. On the other hand, one cannot be a Spiritualist without believing that messages received from mediums can be (and often are) what they purport to be.

Several of the founders of the Society for Psychical Research (SPR) were Spiritualists, but the SPR was set up in a determined effort to follow the example of scientists such as Crookes, Galton and Wallace to use the scientific method to settle questions which had hitherto largely been decided on religious and metaphysical grounds. Christians have been happier investigating the alleged phenomena than using them as a basis for a religious faith. Thus the first volume of the SPR Proceedings carried an article by a country clergyman on thought-transference; the wife of the then Archbishop of Canterbury was amongst the SPR's first members; Bishop Boyd Carpenter of Ripon was its President in 1912; and W.R. Matthews, Dean of St Paul's, was one of several distinguished Christians to have delivered the SPR F.W.H. Myers Memorial Lecture (Matthews 1940).

Death and after

The near-death experience (see Chapter 16) poses many questions for religious believers. It may have lessons to teach us for our life in this world (Lorimer 1990). It may be a mystical experience (Fenwick and Fenwick 1995), or a legitimate glimpse into the world of the life to come (Rawlings 1979), or simply evidence for the last wild paroxysms of a brain close to collapse (Blackmore 1994). According to some commentators it may even be a Satanic delusion devilishly planned to lull humanity into believing that all will be well with it in the next life, whereas the gate that leads to that life is a very narrow one (Weldon and Levitt 1978). Susan Blackmore holds that all the aspects of the near-death experience are electro-neurologically explicable and that there is no such thing as the self, but only a subjectively created illusion which will reveal itself as nothingness when the brain's organisation breaks up at death. That is close to the Buddhist no-self (*anatta*) doctrine. Clearly, experience may be sacred, but its interpretation is fiercely disputed.

The same is true of mediumistic evidence for human survival of bodily death (see Chapter 18). Accurate statements could be the result of telepathy from the incarnate sitter, or messages from a discarnate spirit, or clairvoyance from a printed source – or, what they appear prima facie to be, messages from the alleged discarnate human communicator. Parapsychological and religious explanations overlap. In any case, the most that parapsychological research could prove would be that some people survived death for some period of time, and were able to communicate with persons remaining on this earth; but that all survive eternally – whether they communicate or not – is a matter of religious doctrine and unprovable.

Again, how do the data which appear to support the idea of reincarnation (see Chapter 19) appear to religious believers (Hick 1976, pp. 297–396; Wilson 1981, Pandarakalam 1999)? Some religions accept reincarnationist ideas more readily than others, though, for example, Buddhist and Hindu doctrines are far from identical (see Bowker 1997, pp. 803–4). It is a disputed point whether we all reincarnate – and *ad infinitum* – or whether only some humans need (or choose) to reincarnate, and whether reincarnation comes to an end when the spiritual purposes of a series of reincarnations have been achieved.

Many Christian interpreters of the data who do not believe in reincarnation either prefer to interpret them as examples of retrocognitive telepathy whereby the subject 'locks into' the remaining memories of a past figure, or else believe that they are communications from the surviving spirit of a previously incarnate person (who may have suffered wounds similar to birthmarks or birth defects in the person who believes himself to be a reincarnation of that previous character). Either of these scenarios avoids belief in the reincarnation of an individual personality into a new body.

It is clear that facts never come without interpretation. But that is not peculiar to religion. In orthodox science and in parapsychology, as well as in religion, the relation between faith, reason, and evidence is a subtle and complex one (Perry 1984, pp. 52–65) and the facts which parapsychology investigates can be interpreted within a religious or a materialistic paradigm according to the preconceptions of the interpreter. Even without bringing religion into it, this is an aspect of the subject which has bedevilled parapsychology from its earliest times. Again, experience is sacred, interpretation free.

Exorcism

Many people are troubled, either by discovering that they seem to have psychic gifts or that they (or the place where they live or work) seem to be receiving unwanted attentions of a psychic nature. They may seek the consolations of religion.

Partly as a result of a number of injudicious attempts in the mid-1970s at the exorcism of people supposedly possessed by evil spirits, a number of Christian churches began to make provision for helping people subject to psychic disturbances of various kinds – either uninvited (such as poltergeist disturbances, apparent place memories, or ostensible sightings of departed humans who seemed to want to contact them) or invited (as a result of experimentation with the ouija-board or occultist activities). The term 'exorcism' is beginning to be replaced by the concept of the 'deliverance ministry' (Petitpierre 1972, Mitton and Parker 1991, Perry 1996, Walker 1997) in which representatives of the Christian church aim to help those who find difficulty in coping with experiences which have a psychic or occult presenting symptom. Practitioners of this ministry do not always presuppose that the cases with which they deal are the work of a personal Devil or that they are the symptoms of humans possessed by evil spirits. They may – and more often are – the result of psychological or interpersonal tensions, or the activity of departed human beings who need pastoral care rather than banishment to Hell. Unfortunately, some Christians act hysterically when confronted with anything apparently of a parapsychological nature, and one therefore needs to choose one's counsellor with care unless one is to end up in a worse state than before.

The deliverance ministry in many churches is linked with the wider ministry of healing (Hacker 1998, Lawrence 1998, House of Bishops 2000), and parapsychological studies have been made (Benor 1993, Dossey 1993, 1996, 1997, Stannard 2000) on the effectiveness of prayer and the practice of 'spiritual healing' (see Chapter 11).

Psychic experience is not always dysfunctional. Religious or mystical experience is often accompanied by psychic phenomena, and *De Numine*, published by the Religious Experience Research Centre at the University of Wales, Lampeter, often prints articles of parapsychological interest. Mystical experience is characterised by feelings of unity with nature or the divinity; time appears to be transcended, although the experience is transient; and the whole experience is accompanied by emotions of ineffability. Peter and Elizabeth Fenwick (1995) believe that the near-death experience is a form of mystical experience.

Conclusion

Those of us whose interests lie in the borderlands between religion and parapsychology know that religious experience

> has a psychic dimension, and if we are to handle this area of life, we must keep current on the advances made in understanding it. Psychic phenomena and religious experience are not synonymous terms . . . but the facts and theories related to parapsychology aid in our understanding of religious phenomena.
>
> (Neff 1971, p. 170)

Recommended reading

Introductory

Perry, M. (2003) *Psychical and Spiritual: Parapsychology in Christian Faith and Life*, North Somercotes: CFPSS. Pleads for an understanding of the psychic faculty on the part of Christians, and critically reviews the evidence.

Tart, C.T. (ed.) (1997) *Body Mind Spirit: Exploring the Parapsychology of Spirituality*, Charlottesville, VA: Hampton Roads. A selection of articles by distinguished parapsychologists on the 'scientific evidence for the existence of spiritual dimensions'.

Advanced

Perry, M. (1984) *Psychic Studies: A Christian's View*, Wellingborough: Aquarian. Essays, lectures, and sermons on the implications of psychic experience for Christian thinking.

See also the journals: *The Christian Parapsychologist*, *De Numine*, and *The Journal of Religion and Psychical Research*. See appendix for publication details.

References

Bennett, B.M. Jr (1978) Vision and audition in biblical prophecy. In B. Shapin and L. Coly (eds) *Psi and States of Consciousness*, New York: Parapsychology Foundation, 103–23.

Benor, D.J. (1993) *Healing Research: Holistic Energy, Medicine, and Spirituality*, London: Helix.

Blackmore, S. (1994) *Dying to Live: Science and the Near-Death Experience*, London: Grafton.

Bowker, J. (ed.) (1997) *The Oxford Dictionary of World Religions*, Oxford and New York: Oxford University Press.

Bunce, B. (1993) *So Many Witnesses: the Story of the Churches' Fellowship for Psychical and Spiritual Studies*, North Somercotes: CFPSS.

Dodds, E.R. (1971) Supernormal phenomena in classical antiquity, *Proceedings of the Society for Psychical Research*, 55, 189–237.

Dossey, L. (1993) *Healing Words: The Power of Prayer and the Practice of Medicine*, London: HarperCollins.

Dossey, L. (1996) *Prayer is Good Medicine: How to Reap the Healing Benefits of Prayer*, New York: HarperSanFrancisco.

Dossey, L. (1997) *Be Careful What You Pray For: You Just Might Get It*, New York: HarperSanFrancisco.

Eisenbud, J. (1982) The flight that failed, *The Christian Parapsychologist*, 4, 211–17.

Eliade, M. (1951) *Le Chamanisme*, Paris (published 1964 as *Shamanism: Archaic Techniques of Ecstasy*, London: Routledge and Kegan Paul).

Felser, J.M. (1999) Parapsychology without religion, *Journal of the American Society for Psychical Research*, 93, 259–79.

Fenwick, P. and Fenwick, E. (1995) *The Truth in the Light: An Investigation of Over 300 Near-Death Experiences*, London: Hodder Headline.

Grosso, M. (1982) Padre Pio and the paranormal, *The Christian Parapsychologist*, 4, 218–26.

Hacker, G. (1998) *The Healing Stream: Catholic Insights into the Ministry of Healing*, London: Darton, Longman and Todd.

Haddow, A.H. (1980) The churches and psychical research: a review of some twentieth-century official documents, *The Christian Parapsychologist*, 3: 291–303.

Haraldsson, E. and Wiseman, R. (1995) Reactions to and an assessment of a videotape on Sathya Sai Baba, *Journal of the Society for Psychical Research*, 60, 203–13.

Haynes, R. (1970) *Philosopher King: The Humanist Pope Benedict XIV*, London: Weidenfeld and Nicolson.

Hick, J. (1976) *Death and Eternal Life*, London: Collins.

House of Bishops (2000) *A Time to Heal: A Report to the House of Bishops on the Healing Ministry*, London: Church House Publishing.

Johnson, K.P. (1998) *Edgar Cayce in Context: The Readings, Truth and Fiction*, Albany, NY: State University of New York Press.

Lambeth (1948) The Report of the Seventh Committee of the 1920 Lambeth Conference [on 'Spiritualism, Christian Science, and Theosophy'] in *The Lambeth Conferences 1867–1930*, London: SPCK.

Lawrence, L.R. (1998) *The Practice of Christian Healing: A Guide for Beginners*, London: SPCK.

Lorimer, D. (1990) *Whole in One: the Near-Death Experience and the Ethic of Interconnectedness*, London: Arkana.

Matthews, W.R. (1940) *Psychical Research and Theology*, London: Society for Psychical Research.

Mitton, M. and Parker, R. (1991) *Requiem Healing: A Christian Understanding of the Dead*, London: Darton, Longman and Todd.

Moore, E.G. (1977) *Believe it or Not: Christianity and Psychical Research*, London and Oxford: Mowbray.

Neff, R. (1971) *Psychic Phenomena and Religion*, Philadelphia, PA: Westminster Press.

Pandarakalam, J.P. (1999) Previous life memories, *The Christian Parapsychologist*, 13, 250–6.

Perry, M.C. (1959) *The Easter Enigma: An Essay on the Resurrection with Special Reference to the Data of Psychical Research*, London: Faber and Faber.

Perry, M.C. (1984) *Psychic Studies: A Christian's View*, Wellingborough: Aquarian Press.

Perry, M.C. (1986) *Miracles Then and Now*, North Somercotes: CFPSS.

Perry, M.C. (1992) *Gods Within: A Critical Guide to the New Age*, London: SPCK.

Perry, M.C. (ed., for the Christian Deliverance Study Group) (1996) *Deliverance: Psychic Disturbances and Occult Involvement*, 2nd edn, London: SPCK.

Perry, M.C. (1999a) Biblical prohibitions and Christian parapsychology, *The Christian Parapsychologist*, 13, 153–8.

Perry, M.C. (ed.) (1999b) *Spiritualism: The 1939 Report to the Archbishop of Canterbury*, North Somercotes: CFPSS.

Petitpierre, Dom R., OSB (ed., for a Commission convened by the Bishop of Exeter) (1972) *Exorcism*, London: SPCK.

Rawlings, M. (1979) *Beyond Death's Door*, London: Sheldon Press.

Rogo, D.S. (1982) *Miracles: A Parascientific Inquiry into Wondrous Phenomena*, New York: Dial Press.

Stannard, R. (2000) Experimenting with prayer, *The Christian Parapsychologist*, 14, 87–92.

Thalbourne, M. and Houtkooper, J.M. (2002) Religiosity/spirituality and belief in the paranormal, *Journal of the Society for Psychical Research*, 66, 113–15.

Thurston, Herbert S.J. (1952) *The Physical Phenomena of Mysticism*, London: Burns Oates.

Walker, D. (1997) *The Ministry of Deliverance*, London: Darton, Longman and Todd.

Weldon, J. and Levitt, Z. (1978) *Is There Life After Death?* Eastbourne: Kingsway.

White, R.A. (1981) Saintly psi: a study of spontaneous ESP in saints, *Journal of Religion and Psychical Research*, 4, 157–67.

White, R.A. (1982) ESP phenomena in the saints, *Parapsychology Review*, 13, 15–18.

Wilson, I. (1981) *Mind out of Time? Reincarnation Investigated*, London: Gollancz.

Wiseman, R. and Haraldsson, E. (1995) Investigating macro-PK in India: Swami Premananda, *Journal of the Society for Psychical Research*, 60, 193–202.

Appendices

Appendix 1

Glossary

Anoxia – oxygen deprivation to the brain

Apparition – a perceptual experience in which a person or animal (deceased or living) appears to be present though they are not (at least physically)

Bio-PK – psychokinesis on a living organism, e.g. lowering blood pressure, see also DMILS

Clairvoyance – non-sensory awareness of some scene or object, literally 'clear seeing'

Coincidence – the occurrence of two or more (apparently causally unrelated) events connected in the mind of the observer

Decision augmentation theory – an approach which views PK as a precognitive selection effect

DMILS – direct mental interaction with a living system, normally physiology, e.g. electrodermal activity

Double-blind – an experiment where neither the experimenter nor participants are aware who is receiving active or placebo treatments, or what the target is until after completion of the experiment

Effect size – a measure of the size of the performance

Electrodermal activity (EDA) – a measure of skin resistance that reflects states of tension

ESP – see extrasensory perception

Extrasensory perception (ESP) – where the mind acquires information without recourse to any apparent physical or known sensory means; also known as paranormal cognition. (ESP includes telepathy, clairvoyance, precognition and retrocognition)

File drawer – the number of unpublished negative studies (left in researchers' files)

Forced-choice – experiments where the number of targets is restricted, e.g. Zener cards

Free-choice – experiments where the target is not restricted and may be any picture or location, for example remote viewing

Ganzfeld – experimental procedure designed to reduce participants'

sensory input by having white noise played in their ears and restricting vision to a diffuse glow, thought to be conducive to introspective impressions and ESP

Ghost – normally an apparition of a dead person who may 'haunt' the same place repeatedly

Goats – people who do not believe in the existence of psychic phenomena

Healing – psychic healing is the systematic, intentional intervention by one or more persons to alter the condition of another living being or beings (person, animal, plant or other living system), by means of focused intention, hand contact, or 'passes', without apparently producing the influence through known, conventional physical or energetic means

Hypnagogic imagery – a particularly vivid form of imagery experienced when going to sleep

Hypnapompic imagery – a particularly vivid form of imagery experienced as one is waking up

Macro-PK – psychokinesis effects visible to the naked eye, e.g. 'spoon bending'

Medium – a person apparently able to communicate with and pass on information from a spirit

Meta-analysis – a statistical procedure for combining and analysing the significance of groups of experiments, e.g. a series of ganzfeld experiments

Micro-PK – psychokinesis only detectable by statistical analysis, e.g. in RNG experiments

Near-death experience (NDE) – an experience reported by survivors of cardiac arrest and other life-threatening situations often comprising several of the following elements: peace and joy, passing through a dark tunnel with a bright light at the end, viewing the events from above, a life review and panoramic memory, meeting with a 'being of light'

Out-of-body experience (OBE) – an experience in which a person seems to see the world from a location outside of the physical body and feels as if they are able to see, feel and move around without the body

Paranormal – an interaction with one's environment other than through currently understood sensory channels

Parapsychology – literally beyond psychology. The psychology of the paranormal, associated with the scientific study of psychic and paranormal experiences, in particular ESP and PK

PEAR – Princeton Engineering Anomalies Research

PK – see psychokinesis

Poltergeist – literally noisy spirit; term used to encompass recurrent spontaneous PK disturbances (typically in the form of sudden unexplained noises, moved objects, temperature changes and sometimes marks on individuals) usually associated with particular individual(s) in particular location(s)

Precognition – non-inferential awareness of some future state of affairs

Premonition – an experience of forewarning which appears to anticipate a future event and which could not reasonably have been inferred from information available before that later event

Psi – a non-sensory form of awareness; interactions between an organism and the environment involving information exchange or influence not presently understandable via known sensory-motor channels; covers ESP and PK, or any paranormal process. From the Greek letter indicating an unknown quantity in equations

Psychic – from the Greek 'psyche', refers to an individual with apparent psi ability

Psychic research – the study of psychic or paranormal experiences, especially phenomena found in the field such as spontaneous ESP and RSPK, as in hauntings or poltergeists for example. Now often superseded by the term parapsychology

Psychokinesis (PK) – literally mind movement; the influence of someone's thoughts on the physical world other than by motor action of the body, i.e. paranormal action (mind over matter)

REG – random event generator, a random or pseudo-random source linked to a display producing unpredictable output used in experiments

RNG – random number generator

Reincarnation – the idea that the soul or some mental part of the person survives death and can be associated with another physical body in another life

Remote viewing – experiments where subjects aim to describe a remote location by ESP

Retrocognition – non-inferential awareness of a past event

RSPK – recurrent spontaneous psychokinesis, e.g. poltergeists

Second sight – a special psychic ability believed to be an inborn natural faculty of mind, often thought to run in particular families

Shamans – socially designated practitioners who purport to deliberately alter their consciousness to obtain information or exert influence in ways useful to their social group, and not ordinarily available to their peers, often entailing altered trance-like states of consciousness involving contact with a 'spiritual realm'

Sheep – people who believe in the existence of psychic phenomena

SPR – Society for Psychical Research

Synchronicity – a surprising concurrence of events considered meaningful to the observer; a personally significant coincidence

Telepathy – literally remote speaking; non-sensory communication between separated individuals (mind to mind)

Zener cards – each card has one of the following symbols: a circle, a cross, wavy lines, a square or a star

Appendix 2

Websites, organisations and journals

Wyllys Poynton

Argentina

Revista Argentina De Psicologia Paranormal
Salta 2015 (cod 1137), Capital Federal, Buenos Aires, Argentina
Web: www.soho-ar.com
Publishes *Revista Argentina De Psicologia Paranormal*

Instituto de Parapsicologia
Zabala 1930, 1712 Castelar-Prov. de Buenos Aires
E-mail: kreiman@arnet.com.ar
Publishes *Cuadernos de Parapsicologia*

Australia

Australian Institute for Psychical Research
Department of Behavioural Sciences, University of Sydney, P.O. Box 170, Lidcombe, NSW 2141
Contact: Michael Hough
Publishes *AIPR Bulletin*

University of Adelaide
Department of Psychology, Adelaide SA 5005
Contact: Dr Michael Thalbourne

Department of Psychology
University of New England, Armidale, NSW
Contact: Prof. H. Irwin
Web: www.une.edu.au

Austria

Institut fur Grenzgebiete der Wissenschaft
Universitaets Strasse 7, A-1010 Vienna, Austria
Web: parapsychologie.ac.at
Contact: Prof. Peter Mulacz

Brazil

Instituto De Investigações Cientificas em Parapsicologia
Rua Visconde De Nova Granada, 2 Paraiso, CEP: 01323080 Saõ Paulo/SP
Publishes *Revista Brasileira de Parapsicologia*

Centro Latino-American de Parapsicologia (CLAP)
Avenida Leonardo da Vinci, No. 2123, 0 4313-002 São Paulo
Publishes *Revista Portuguesa de Parapsicologia*

France

Institut Métapsychique International
51 Rue de L'Aqueduc, – 75010
Paris
Web: imi-paris.org
Publishes *Revue Metapsychique*

L'Organisation pour la recherche en Parapsychologie
Departement de Mathematiques,
University de Toulouse le Mirail,
31058 Toulouse, Cedex
Web: www.multimania.com
Publishes *Revue Française de Parapsychologie*

Germany

Institut fur Grenzgebiete der Psychologie und *Psychohygiene (IGPP)*
Wilhelmstrasse 3a, D-79098
Freiburg i. Br.
Web: www.igpp.de
Contact: Eberhard Bauer
Publishes *Zeitschrift fur Parapsychologie und Grenzgebiete*

Italy

Archivo di Documentazione Storca
Via Marconi. 8, I-40122 Bologna
Web: www2.comune.bologna.it
Publishes *Luce e Ombra*

Japan

Japan Psychic Science Association
1-12-22 Kamoichaiai Shinjuku-ku,
Tokyo 161-0034
Publishes *Psychical Research and Spiritualism*

International Society of Life Information Science (ISLIS)
c/o Division of Radiation Research,
National Institute of Radiological
Sciences, 9-1, Anagawa – 4,
Chiba-shi 263-8555
E-mail: islis@nirs.go.jp
Web: wwwsoc.nii.ac.jp/islis
Publishes *Journal of Islis*

Mexico

Institute Latino Americano de Parapsicologia
Apartado de Correos 156, San Juan
de Rio, 76800 Queretaro
E-mail: 74174,
1323@compuserv.com
Publishes *Revista Mexicana de Psicologica*

Netherlands

University of Amsterdam Anomalous Cognition Group
Roetersstraat 15, 1018 WB,
Amsterdam
Web: www.psy.uva.nl/resedu/pn/res/
ANOMALOUSCOGNITION/
anomal.shtml
Contact: Prof. Dick Bierman
Offers online experiments. Good
links to literature

Nederlands Vereniging voor Parapsychologie
Postbus 271-3720 AG Bilthoven
Publishes *Spiegel der Paraspsychologie*

Parapsychologist Instituut
Springweg, 3511-VH Utrecht
Publishes *Parapsychogische Niewsbrief*

Norway

Norsk Parapsykologisk Selskap
Postboks 629, Sentrum, 0106 Oslo
Web: home/c2i.net/parapsykologi
Publishes *Parapsykologiske Notiser*

Portugal

CLAP-Portugal
Rua Prof. Machado-Vilela, 191 -3° Dto, 4710 Braga
Director: Maria Luisa Albuquerque
Web: estudar-na.net
Publishes *Revista Portuguesa de Parapsicologia*

Sweden

Department of Psychology
University of Göteborg, Box 500, SE 405 30 Göteborg
Contact: Nina Johansson, Dr Adrian Parker
Web: www.psy.gu.se
Publishes *European Journal of Parapsychology*

United Kingdom

Anomalistic Psychology Research Unit
Department of Psychology, Goldsmiths College, University of London, New Cross, London SE14 6NW
Web: www.goldsmiths.ac.uk/apru
E-mail list on the psychology of the paranormal
Contact: Prof. Christopher French
Research into paranormal belief

Association for Skeptical Enquiry
Contact: Tony Youens
Web: www.aske.org.uk/
Publishes *The Skeptical Intelligencer* magazine, organises conferences and meetings on sceptical issues

The British Alliance of Healing Associations
26 Highfield Avenue, Herne Bay CT6 6LM,
Tel: 44 (0)1227 373804
Contact organisation for healers

British Psychological Society Consciousness and Experiential Psychology Section
BPS, St Andrews Ho, 48 Princess Rd East, Leicester LE1 7DR
Web: www.bps.org.uk
Contact: Jane Henry
Studies include exceptional experience
Publishes *Consciousness & Experiential Psychology*

The Centre for the Study of Anomalous Psychological Processes (CSAPP)
University College Northampton Psychology Department, Boughton Green Road, Northampton NN2 7AL
Web: http://www.northampton.ac.uk
Contact: Prof. Deborah Delanoy
E-mail: deborah.delanoy@northampton.ac.uk
Parapsychological courses research and PhD students

The Churches' Fellowship for Psychical and Spiritual Studies
The Rural Workshop, South Road,

North Somercotes, Louth, Lincs. LN11 7PT
Publishes *The Christian Parapsychologist*

Consciousness and Transpersonal Psychology Research Unit
Centre for Applied Psychology, Liverpool John Moores University, Henry Cotton Campus, Liverpool L3 2ET
Web: www.livjm.ac.uk/hum/ctp
www.mdani.demon.co.uk/para/parapsy.htm
Second site offers information on parapsychology and many links to other parapsychology websites
Contacts: Prof Les Lancaster and Dr Mike Daniels
Parapsychological research and psychological aspects of spiritual development

Experiential Research Group
Open University, Michael Young Building, Milton Keynes MK7 6AA
Contact: Jane Henry
E-mail: j.a.henry@open.ac.uk
Psychology of experience, exceptional experience

Koestler Parapsychology Unit
Psychology Dept, Edinburgh University, 7 George Square, Edinburgh EH8 9JZ
Contact: Prof. Robert Morris
Web: moebius.psy.ed.ac.uk
Parapsychology research
Takes Ph.D. students in parapsychology

National Federation of Spiritual Healers
Old Manor Farm Studio, Church Street, Sunbury-on-Thames, Middlesex TW16 6RG
Tel: 44 (0)1932 783164/5
Can put UK readers in touch with healers

Perrott-Warrick Research Unit
Department of Psychology, University of Hertfordshire, Hatfield Campus, College Lane, Hatfield, Herts AL10 9AB
Web: phoenix.herts.ac.uk/pwru
Studies cognitive aspects of parapsychological experience

Religious Experience Research Centre
University of Wales, Lampeter, Ceredigion SA48 7ED
Studies religious experience
Publishes *De Numine*

The Scientific and Medical Network
Web: www.scimednet.org
E-mail: info@scimednet.org

Rupert Sheldrake
Web: www.sheldrake.org
Offers papers, experiments, links and information including animal psi, telepathy and staring

The Society for Psychical Research
49 Marloes Road, Kensington, London W8 6LA
Web: www.spr.ac.uk
Publishes *Journal of the SPR*, *Proceedings*, and *Paranormal Review*
Good library. Rare books held at the University of Cambridge. Website has research directory. Annual conference

UK Skeptics
Website: www.skeptic.org.uk
Address as APRU above
Contact: Prof. Chris French
Publishes *The Skeptic*

University of Coventry
Parapsychology Studies Group, School of Health and Social Studies, Coventry University, Priory Street, Coventry CV1 5FB
Contact: Tony Lawrence

United States

Academy of Religion and Psychical Research
PO Box 614, Bloomfield, CT 06002
Web: www.lightlink.com/arpr
Publishes the *Journal of Religion and Psychical Research*

The Association for Research and Enlightenment
215 67th Street, Virginia Beach, VA 23451-2061, USA
Web: www.are-cayce.com

American Society for Psychical Research
5 West 73rd Street, New York, NY 10023
Web: www.aspr.com
Publishes *Journal of the ASPR* and *Newsletter*

Committee for the Scientific Investigation of Claims against the Paranormal (CSICOP)
Box 703, Amherst, NY 14226
Web: www.csicop.org
Publishes *Skeptical Inquirer*

Consciousness Research Laboratory
Web: www.psiresearch.org/
Contact: Dean Radin

Division of Personality Studies
University of Virginia Health Systems, Box 8000152, Charlottesville, VA 22908
Director: Prof. Bruce Greyson
Web: www.healthsystem.virginia.edu/DOPS/
Studies evidence for reincarnation and other paranormal phenomena

Exceptional Human Experiences Network
2 Plane Trees Lane, Dix Hills, New York, NY 11746
Web: www.ehe.org
Contact: Rhea White

Institute of Noetic Sciences (IONS)
101 San Antonio Rd, Petaluma, California 94952-9524
Web: www.noetic.org/
Contacts: Drs Marilyn Schlitz and Dean Radin
Conducts parapsychological research amongst other activities. Website offers online psi tests

Institute of Transpersonal Psychology
744 San Antonio Road, Palo Alto, CA 94303-4613
Director: Dr William Braud
Consciousness research

International Association of Near-Death Studies
PO Box 7767, Philadelphia, PA 190101
Web: www.iands.org

The Mutual UFO Network (MUFON)
Web: www.rutgers.edu/~mcgre/MUFON
Extensive informative site

Parapsychological Association
2474-342 Walnut St, Cary, NC 27511
Web: www.parapsych.org
Publishes *Research in Parapsychology*

Parapsychology Foundation
PO Box 1562, New York, NY 10021
Web: parapsychology.org
Publishes *Parapsychological Monographs and International Journal of Parapsychology*

Princeton Engineering Anomalies Research
C-131 Engineering Quadrangle, Princeton University, Princeton, NJ 08544
Web: www.princeton.edu/~pear
Contact: Prof. Robert Jahn, Dr Brenda Dunne
Psychokinesis research

Rhine Research Center
2741 Campus Walk Avenue, Durham, NC 27705
Web: www.rhine.org
Publishes *Journal of Parapsychology*
Parapsychological Research

Saybrook Graduate School and Research Center
3rd Floor, 747 Front Street, San Francisco, CA 94111
Web: www.saybrook.edu
Contact: Prof. Stanley Krippner
Postgraduate qualifications in parapsychology

The Skeptics Society
PO Box 338, Altedena, CA 91001
Contact: Michael Shermer
Web: www.skeptic.com
Publishes *Skeptic*

Society for Scientific Exploration
ERL 306 Stanford University, Stanford, CA 94305-4055
Web: www.scientificexploration.org
Publishes *Journal of Scientific Exploration*

Wholistic Healing Research
Web: wholistichealingresearch.com
Extensive healing research references

Index